# Contents

W9-BFA-421

# Introduction

"Savour St. Louis" offers a widely variegated selection of recipes always reflecting the intriguing mingling of cultures and traditions in the great Gateway City.

A Culinary and Pictorial Journey through St. Louis.

Menus for Everyday Fare, delicious and nutritious: and for Special Occasions, elegant and memorable.

Comfort Food, basic, time-honored recipes.

Epicurean Delights, glamorous gourmet dishes.

Soups from Duck Gumbo to Avocado Senegalese.

Entrees from Chicken Breasts Stuffed With Morels and Wild Rice to Oven Steamed Halibut In A Ginger Tomato Broth.

Desserts from Peach Bread Pudding to Chocolate Raspberry Cheesecake.   Unique sauces, stuffings, relishes and breads.

Proceeds from the sale of this book benefit the many projects of the Barnes Hospital Auxiliary.

# Cookbook Committee

| | |
|---|---|
| Mary Ann Fritschle | Chairman |
| Darlene B. Roland | Co-Chairman |
| Timmie Cullen | Editor |
| William Keeline | Treasurer |
| Norma Stern | Marketing Chairman |
| Dolores Shepard | Testing Chairman |
| Elizabeth Herring | Writer |
| Martha Eyermann | Proof-Reader |
| Nina Hutchinson | Proof-Reader |

## Section Leaders

| | |
|---|---|
| Margaret Case | Vicki Primrose |
| Gloria Elliott | Ginny Ruzicka |
| Patty Finan | Joan Teaford |
| Marge Gable | Christopher Wolf |
| Margaret Kinnaman | |

## Artwork by Create Studio at Washington University

| | |
|---|---|
| Kristin Anderson | Graphic Design & Project Co-ordinator |
| Patricia Ferrer | Cover Design |

## Illustrators

| | |
|---|---|
| Kristin Anderson | Lara Harris |
| Patricia Ferrer | Melissa Nichols |

## Photography by Jack Zehrt

## Wine Selections by Parker Almond Wines & Food

| | |
|---|---|
| Lynne Piening | Auxiliary President 1993-95 |
| Jeanne Shirley | Auxiliary President 1995-97 |

# Barnes Hospital History

Little did Robert Barnes, St. Louis merchant and banker know that the $940,000 bequest he left in 1892 to build and endow a hospital would result in a medical institution recognized as a leader in healthcare.

Robert Barnes' vision of "a hospital for sick and injured persons without distinction of creed" became a reality when Barnes Hospital opened its doors on December 7, 1914.

Barnes' affiliation with the Washington University School of Medicine ensures that the hospital will be staffed by School of Medicine faculty and serve as a home for medical education and research.

Barnes is one of the few American institutions that performs bone marrow, heart, heart-lung, lung, liver, cornea and kidney transplants.

In the early 1990s Barnes joined with several other hospitals to form the BJC Health System and in January of 1996 Barnes and Jewish Hospitals merged to form Barnes-Jewish Hospital.

Since Robert Barnes' dream became reality Barnes Hospital's reputation for excellence in healthcare has been widely recognized. Through our commitment to excellence and cost-effective care Barnes-Jewish Hospital will continue to meet the medical challenges of the 21st century.

# Auxiliary History

The Barnes Hospital Auxiliary was founded in 1959 following many years of dedicated service by members of several preceding organizations.

Our archives report some rather unique earlier volunteer activities such as preparation of the heart-lung machine and manning a food cart which went to doctors and nurses in the surgical area.  As the Barnes complex has grown, volunteer duties have increased and diversified.

While not all volunteers are auxilians, all auxiliary board members are active volunteers. Many of our volunteer hours of service go hand-in-glove with our fund-raising activities as our members staff the Plaza Gift and Flower Shop and the Nearly New resale shop. Other programs, which include the Auxiliary Tribute Fund, the annual Tree of Life, and baby photos have enabled the Auxiliary to donate in excess of $11,000,000 to the hospital.

Over the years, Auxiliary funds have provided such diverse gifts as $75 for radios in the hospital nurseries in 1964 to the recently completed $2,000,000 Neurology/Neurosurgical Intensive Care Unit.

Other major contributions include the pedestrian bridge from the underground garage, the Barnes Lodge (a home away from home for patients and their families), and its current pledge of $2,000,000 for the Surgical Intensive Care Unit and an additional $200,000 for renovation of the Chapel.

A $50,000 endowment provides for the Robert E. Frank Scholarship in Hospital Administration at Washington University, and the Auxiliary yearly donates additional funds for scholarships at the Barnes College of Nursing at the University of Missouri, St. Louis.

Since the first group of volunteers organized early in this century, the purpose of our organization has been and continues to be service to the hospital and its patients in promoting the health and welfare of the community.

Through the years, our organization has had the advice, guidance and encouragement of three very special people — Barnes Hospital Presidents Robert E. Frank, Max Poll, and John J. Finan, Jr. It is with love and gratitude that we recognize them.

# Corporate Sponsors

J. S. Alberici Construction Co., Inc.

Barnes Hospital Society

Blue Cross Blue Shield of Missouri

Boatmen's Bank

Coca-Cola Bottling Co.

The Daniele Hotel

Dietary Products

Emerson Electric

Jay and Carolyn Henges

The Hermann Foundation

Jones Vending and OCS Distributing

Laclede Gas

G. T. Lawlor Construction Co., Inc.

Mackey Mitchell Associates

Mosby Year Book, Inc.

North Star Ice Cream Specialties

Pepsi Cola Co.

Renard Paper Co., Inc.

Compliments of a Friend

Our heartfelt thanks to our Corporate Sponsors, Patrons and Sponsors for their generous contributions to this project.

# Patrons

Harriett K. Anderson

Lynn E. Bachmann

Robbie and Ted Beaty

Linda Billington and Darrel Wunderlich

Patricia L. Daniels

Elizabeth Fritschle Duffy

Helen M. Elam

Martha Eyermann

Pansy Fell

Mr. and Mrs. John J. Finan, Jr.

Mr. and Mrs. Robert E. Frank

Mary Ann and Parker Fritschle

Robert F. Fritschle

Marge and Ken Gable

Susan and Clifford Graham

Marlene A. Hartmann

Mrs. Florence Weld Hawes

Rita and Harry Houghasian

Dr. and Mrs. Michael M. Karl

Gisela and Max Kasselt

Anita LaTurno

Nancy J. Lich

Mrs. Charles C. Long (Joan)

Marilyn MacDonald

Ingla Maul

Marion M. Mills

Susan C. Phelan

Lynne and Bob Piening

Mr. and Mrs. Max Poll

Eleanor D. Potter

Darlene and Chuck Roland

Dolores and John Shepard

Jeanne Shirley

Norma Stern

Ruth D. Todd

Betty and Robert Tucker

Johnnie Waldman

Janet M. Weakley

Edith Wolff

Jacquelyn Zeitinger

# Sponsors

Marilynn Anderson

Aleene C. Atwater

Joann and Marshall Conrad

Beth A. Cooper

Sara W. Davidson

Linda C. Dill

John E. Hanna

Mr. and Mrs. R. S. Hawes III

Fern Bridgeforth Heider

Fannie M. Henry

Margaret and Walter Kinneman

Mary K. Kennedy

Mary M. Leyhe

Elly Painter

Vicki Primrose

Mr. and Mrs. Raymond A. Ruzicka

Barbara Schneider

Jane Schraudenbach

Catherine Vivrett

Jean G. Whipple

# Confluence of Rivers and Convergence of Cultures

Like a shimmering steel rainbow, the Gateway Arch graces the banks of the mighty Mississippi. With monumental simplicity it reaches from the bedrock of history to the sky-reaching vision of the future, proclaiming its site, the gateway to the west, as the beginning of the fullness of an entire nation. A few miles upstream and several miles downstream, the Missouri River from the west, the Illinois River from the north, and the Ohio River from the east join the Mississippi in its endless coursing. This confluence of great rivers is reflected in the convergence of diverse ethnic cultures which continue to flourish in the city of St. Louis.

Founded in 1763 by Pierre Laclede, with the assistance of young Auguste Chouteau, as a fur trading outpost, the small French village was soon thriving. Strategically located on river and overland trade routes, it became a leading market for furs, leather, mules, horses, and farm produce. It was also the main outfitter for the wagon trains on their arduous journey to settle the west. From 1770 to 1800 when France ceded all its colony west of the Mississippi and the City of New Orleans to Spain, it became the Spanish capital.

Laclede's village was by then named St. Louis in honor of the French king's patron saint and was secretly transferred back to French ownership in 1800.

Here at the site of the Gateway Arch, this frontier village witnessed Thomas Jefferson's Louisiana Purchase in 1804. Here the formal transfer of the vast western territory then known as Upper Louisiana, took place between France and the United States. That same year another historic celebration took place at this site as Lewis and Clark began their expedition to explore this new territory. German immigrants arrived in the early 1800's bringing their brewing and culinary arts as well as sponsoring one of the country's first and finest symphony orchestras.

"Yankees" arrived to settle the nearby farmlands along with Irish, Italian, Polish, and other nationalities. All joined with the French and Spanish in making their own cultural contributions to the prospering frontier town.

Now, in the shadow of the Gateway Arch, a graceful
cathedral, consecrated in 1832, rises from the site of the first
log church in Laclede's village. Nearby is the handsome
courthouse in which the historic Dred Scott trial was held.
From the stone auction block at its east door slaves were
sold before the Civil War. A spacious park stretches from
the Arch and Old Courthouse to the new courthouse. In
this area Clark Milles' fountain sculpture "The Meeting of
the Rivers" expresses the spirit of the city geographically
and culturally.

Photo courtesy of Missouri Historical Society, St. Louis.

To the southwest lies 1400 acre Forest Park, site of the 1904 World's Fair of "Meet Me in St. Louie, Louie" fame. Within this park is the St. Louis Zoo, one of the first cageless zoos; the Muny Opera, a 12,000 seat open air theater; a renowned Art Museum; an innovative Science Center; and the Jefferson Memorial. This latter building houses the original documents of the Louisiana Purchase, papers from the Lewis and Clark expedition, and trophies from Lindbergh's historic flight across the Atlantic in the "Spirit of St. Louis." The Missouri Botanical Garden, or Shaw's Garden, lies to the southeast adjoining Tower Grove Park. A newly renovated theater district to the northeast houses offices for the St. Louis Symphony, the State Ballet of Missouri, several theater companies, and the city's own resident "Circus Flora." The internationally acclaimed Opera Theatre of St. Louis is located at one of the city's leading universities.

Within sight of the Arch, festivals proclaiming ongoing pride in heritage and tradition fill the streets of ethnic neighborhoods throughout the year. The St. Louis Fair is a unique annual celebration including the Veiled Prophet Parade and a ball during which a mysterious "prophet" chooses a queen to rule over his Court of Love and Beauty. Italian festivals take place on "The Hill" to the south; the German sector celebrates with a yearly "Strassenfest." The French recall their heritage in a "Valley of the Flowers" fete; the Irish revive traditions in the St. Patrick's Day Parade; and African-Americans commemorate their culture in the Annie Malone Parade.

St. Louis cuisine ranges from a delectable repast served in one of the city's fine French, Spanish, Italian, Greek, German restaurants or in a private mansion, to a delightful tailgate picnic served at the Cardinal ballpark, a charity polo match, or the National Horse Show. Each reflects the city's cultural heritage. Laclede and Madame Chouteau discussed the Enlightenment and fur trading over a table graced with airy soufflés and delicate sauces.

Creole cooks prepared gumbos, spit-roasted turkeys and quail. Spanish women pounded their tortillas and added robust spices to their stews. The Germans concocted wondrous wines, brews, sausages, and pastries. The Italians created their delicious pastas and sauces. Steamboat chefs combined Southern cuisine of fried chicken, catfish, hams with fresh fruits and vegetables purchased along the river routes. Trappers and frontiersmen cooked fat pork, hominy, and game over their campfires.

The hot dog, ice cream cone and toasted ravioli originated in St. Louis as did the culinary "bible" for many, Mrs. Rombauer's "Joy of Cooking." The true essence of St. Louis cuisine, however, lies in the fact that divergent cultural groups integrated indigenous foods—the remarkable bounty of the land—while retaining and nurturing their own individual ethnic heritages. The formula is simple and unpretentious. Grains, vegetables, fruits, game, corn-fed poultry, cattle and pigs form the basis for seasonal cooking from the land. The mode in which they are prepared and any embellishments may reflect ethnic tradition.

As the great rivers join together on their journey, so the joining of these cuisines holds people and their traditions together in its flow.

Our treasured recipes tell us
about our families and the past.
They reach back through
centuries of memory and
bonding. So—reminisce,
ruminate, and rejoice!

# Christmas Open House

*Brie Cheese Puffs with Parmesan Garlic Aïoli*
*Crab Cakettes with Mango Chutney or Red Pepper Coulis*
*Three Layer Cheese Wheel with Apple and Pear Slices*
*Sun-dried Tomato & Pesto Torte*
*Gingered Chicken Saté with Peanut Sauce*
*Sliced Smoked Salmon on Herb-buttered Pumpernickel*
*Sliced Beef Tenderloin on Herb-buttered Baguettes of French Bread*
*with Horseradish Cream*
*Large Iced Bowl of Jumbo Shrimp with Pink Mayonnaise*
*Cold Mussels Vinaigrette*
*Ham with Cider Raisin Sauce, Assorted Breads, and a Variety of Mustards*

*Racquet Club Egg Nog*

*Trénel Mâcon-Villages*
*Chateau Bellegrave*
*Lagaria Pinot Grigio*
*Mosaico Montepulciano d'Abruzzo*

# New Year's Eve Champagne Toast
# After The Symphony

*Pastry Barquettes lined with Sour Cream, filled with Salmon Roe, Golden*
*and Black Caviar, and garnished with Chopped Chives*

*Chicken Curry with Coconut & Mint on Endive Barquettes*

*Oysters Bienville*

*Orange Cocktail Triangles*

*Billecarte Salmon Brut*
*L'Ermitage Brut Tête de Cuvee*

# Sliced Beef Tenderloin on Herb-buttered Baguettes of French Bread with Horseradish Cream

*...the only way this superb cut of meat can be ruined is by overcooking it!*

Rub a 3-4 pound beef tenderloin with salt, pepper and rosemary. Bake at 450° for 20 minutes. Remove from the oven, wrap in foil and let stand 20 minutes before slicing. Process 2 sticks unsalted butter with ¼ cup minced parsley and 2 tablespoons minced fresh tarragon. Spread butter on slices of French bread. Top with a slice of beef and a sprig of watercress. Serve with horseradish cream.

# Sliced Smoked Salmon on Herb-buttered Pumpernickel

Make herb butter using dill or chervil instead of tarragon. Spread butter on cocktail pumpernickel. Top with smoked salmon, black pepper and a sprig of fresh dill. Serve with lemon wedges and chopped onion.

# Pink Mayonnaise

Combine chili sauce with mayonnaise.

It was from "The Millionaire's Table" at Tony Faust's restaurant that the Westward Expansion was planned and financed.

# Three Layer Cheese Wheel

*...serves 40, generously - with crackers and sliced pears and apples*

## cheese wheel

- 6 (8-ounce) packages cream cheese, softened, divided
- ½ cup chopped scallions
- 1 clove garlic, minced
- 2 cups grated sharp cheddar cheese
- 8 ounces Roquefort cheese, softened

## toppings

- 2 tablespoons red caviar, drained
- 2 tablespoons chopped black olives, drained
- 2 tablespoons minced fresh parsley
- 2 tablespoons chopped pimiento, drained
- 2 tablespoons diced and cooked bacon
- 2 tablespoons chopped stuffed Spanish olives
- 2 tablespoons black caviar, drained
- 2 tablespoons chopped capers, drained

**Yield: 40 servings**

Combine 2 packages of cream cheese with scallions and garlic. Mix 2 packages of cream cheese with cheddar cheese. Mix remaining 2 packages of cream cheese with Roquefort cheese. Line bottom of a well-oiled 8 to 10-inch springform pan with wax paper. Oil paper. Carefully layer cheese mixtures in pan in order prepared. Chill. To serve, loosen cheese from side of pan with a moistened knife. Invert onto a serving dish. Remove paper. Using kitchen string, mark 8 sections on top of cheese wheel. Cover each section with one topping, moving around wheel in order toppings are listed. Refrigerate until ready to serve.

The more precise the division between toppings, the more attractive the wheel will be. Substitute blue cheese for Roquefort, if desired.

# Gingered Chicken Saté With Peanut Sauce

*...meaning "skewered and grilled", saté can be the center of a great family dinner - serve the peanut sauce in peach halves*

To prepare peanut sauce, blend all ingredients. Store at room temperature for at least 24 hours. To make saté, combine chicken with remaining ingredients in a nonmetal bowl and marinate at least 2 hours or overnight. Remove meat, reserving marinade. Skewer meat on 6-inch bamboo skewers. Place in a shallow pan and pour marinade over top until ready to cook. Broil or grill 4 to 5 minutes, turning once. Serve with peanut sauce.

*Substitute pork or steak for chicken.*

**peanut sauce**
- ⅓ cup crunchy peanut butter
- 3 tablespoons packed brown sugar
- ½ teaspoon crushed red pepper flakes
- ¼ cup lemon juice
- 2 tablespoons chili sauce or ketchup
- ½ teaspoon soy sauce

**saté**
- 3 pounds boneless, skinless chicken breasts, cubed
- 1 (3 to 4-inch) hot chili pepper, chopped
- 1 medium onion, minced
- 1 tablespoon minced fresh ginger root
- 3 tablespoons fresh lime juice
- 2 tablespoons soy sauce
- 2 tablespoons vegetable oil

**Yield: 6 to 8 entree servings, 20 buffet servings**

# Crab Cakettes

*...Bob Frank, much loved president of Barnes Hospital for 20 years, created and named his crab cakes*

1 cup cracker or bread crumbs, divided
1 (6-ounce) can crabmeat, drained
1 egg, beaten
1/4 cup minced onion
1 1/2 tablespoons mayonnaise
1/4 teaspoon dry mustard
1/4 teaspoon cayenne pepper
1/2 tablespoon Cajun or Creole seasoning
vegetable oil

Mix together 1/2 cup crumbs, crabmeat, egg, onion, mayonnaise, mustard, pepper, and Cajun seasoning. Shape into patties. Dredge in remaining 1/2 cup crumbs. Chill 60 minutes. Brown patties on both sides in a lightly oiled 375° electric skillet.

Serve with hot mango chutney, rémoulade sauce, or red pepper coulis.

**Yield: 10 cakettes**

# Orange Cocktail Triangles

*...reminiscent of grandmother's kitchen*

1 (8-ounce) package cream cheese
2 cups all-purpose flour
2 sticks margarine, softened
orange marmalade

Blend cream cheese, flour, and margarine until a soft dough forms. Chill overnight. Roll dough into a thin layer. Cut into 2-inch squares. Place a small amount of marmalade in center of each square. Wet edges of dough with water and fold dough over to make triangles. Crimp edges with a fork. Pierce top and place on a buttered baking sheet. Bake at 350° for 15 to 20 minutes. Watch carefully while baking to prevent burning.

# Oysters Bienville

*...the Greeks used the oyster shell as ballot paper, the voter scratching his choice on it with a sharp instrument*

Fill bottom of 3 pie pans with rock salt and place in oven while preheating. Sauté shallot in butter for 5 minutes. Blend in flour and cook slowly for 5 minutes. Remove from heat and add broth, sherry, salt, and cayenne pepper. Blend in egg yolk. Return to heat and add shrimp, mushrooms, Worcestershire sauce, and parsley. Simmer 15 minutes. Place oysters in half shells on rock salt. Top each oyster with sauce. Sprinkle with breadcrumbs, cheese, and paprika. Bake at 350° for 10 to 15 minutes.

To open oysters, wedge the pointed tip of a church-key between the shells of an oyster at the hinged end and give it a quick twist of the wrist. Pry the shells open and slide the can opener between the shells to pull them apart.

rock salt
½ cup minced shallot
1 stick butter
¼ cup all-purpose flour
1 cup fish or chicken broth
3-4 tablespoons sherry
salt to taste
cayenne pepper to taste
1 egg yolk, beaten
1 cup chopped cooked shrimp
½ cup finely chopped mushrooms
1 tablespoon Worcestershire sauce
2 teaspoons chopped fresh parsley
12 oysters on the half shell
buttered breadcrumbs
Parmesan cheese
paprika

**Yield: 12 servings**

# Brie Cheese Puffs with Parmesan Garlic Aïoli

*...aïoli can embellish many dishes, such as Grilled Shrimp Wrapped In Prosciutto or Grilled Scallops Wrapped In Bacon*

## parmesan garlic aïoli

- 2 egg yolks
- 1 tablespoon Dijon mustard
- 1 teaspoon salt
- 1 tablespoon minced garlic
- 1 teaspoon Worcestershire sauce
- ½ teaspoon black pepper
- ½ cup Parmesan cheese
- ¼ cup tarragon vinegar
- 1 cup olive oil

## brie cheese puffs

- 1 (17¼-ounce) box frozen puff pastry
- 1 (4½ ounce) Brie cheese wheel
- 2-4 eggs, beaten

**Yield: 24 servings**

Whip egg yolks in a food processor. Add mustard, salt, garlic, Worcestershire sauce, pepper, and cheese. Blend well. With machine running, add in an alternating manner, vinegar and 1 tablespoon at a time of oil. Chill at least 2 hours. To prepare puffs, use a biscuit cutter to cut pastry into about 24 pieces. Cut cheese into about 24 pieces. Place one piece of cheese in middle of each piece of pastry. Brush edges with egg. Fold over pastry and crimp edges. Brush outside of pastry with egg. Bake at 425° for 8 to 10 minutes. Serve with aïoli.

# Blue Cheese Twists

*...great to serve with soup*

In a small bowl, combine cheese, butter, and sugar. On a lightly floured surface, roll pastry into a 12-inch square. Spread cheese mixture on upper two-thirds of square. Sprinkle pecans over cheese mixture. Fold bottom third of pastry over and fold top third over bottom. Lightly roll into a 12X5 inch rectangle. Cut into twenty-four (5X½ inch) strips. Beat together egg and water. Brush egg mixture over strips. Twist each strip 3 or 4 times and place about 1 inch apart on an ungreased baking sheet lined with parchment paper. Bake at 400° for 12 to 15 minutes or until lightly browned.

2 ounces blue cheese
2 tablespoons butter, softened
⅛ teaspoon sugar
1 sheet frozen puff pastry, thawed
3 tablespoons finely chopped pecans
1 egg
1 tablespoon water

**Yield: 24 twists**

# Garlic Cheesecake

*...ancient Sicily, in its day, was renowned for its cheesecake*

Combine breadcrumbs, pecans, and butter in a small bowl. Pat into bottom of an 8-inch springform pan. In a large bowl, blend cream cheese and sour cream until smooth. Beat in egg. Stir in garlic. Pour mixture carefully over crust. Bake at 350° for 25 to 30 minutes or until set. Cool and serve at room temperature.

Herbed Cream Cheese: Combine 8 ounces cream cheese, 1 teaspoon garlic and 1 teaspoon Italian seasoning.

¼ cup seasoned breadcrumbs
¼ cup chopped pecans
1 tablespoon butter, melted
8 ounces herbed cream cheese, softened
½ cup sour cream
1 egg, lightly beaten
3 cloves garlic, minced

**Yield: 8 to 10 servings**

# Cheese Fondue

*...the perfect companion to a warm fire on a snowy, winter night. It can be prepared on the stove in the fondue pot or chafing dish - or in a saucepan and transferred to the fondue pot*

1 clove garlic, peeled
1 cup dry white Rhine wine
4 cups grated Jarlsberg cheese
2 tablespoons cornstarch
salt and pepper to taste
nutmeg to taste
cayenne pepper to taste
1 tablespoon lemon juice
2 tablespoons kirsch
1 small loaf French bread, cubed

**Yield: 6 servings**

Use the back of a wooden spoon to rub garlic clove over inside of a chafing dish or a fondue pot. Pour in wine and heat but do not boil. Toss cheese with cornstarch to coat well. Stir into wine until smooth and creamy. Continue to stir until mixture simmers. Blend in salt, pepper, nutmeg, cayenne pepper, lemon juice, and kirsch until smooth. Keep warm, or cool and reheat when ready to use. Allow bread cubes to sit out and dry slightly. Serve fondue with bread cubes and wooden skewers or fondue forks.

If desired, substitute 2 cups grated Emmentaler cheese and 2 cups grated Gruyère cheese for Jarlsberg cheese.

# Con Queso

Blend equal amounts of cream cheese and salsa in a bowl and microwave at high until melted. Stir in grated Monterey Jack cheese and return to microwave to melt cheese. Stir and serve with tortilla chips.

# Roquefort And Walnut Gougère

*...serve as an hors d'oeuvre or with a salad*

Heat water, butter, and salt in a saucepan until butter melts and water boils. Remove from heat. Add flour all at once and stir with a wooden spoon until a dough forms and leaves the sides of the pan in a ball. Return to heat and cook, stirring 1 minute or until the dough begins to form a film on bottom of saucepan. Process dough and walnuts briefly in a food processor. With machine running, add eggs one at a time. Process 30 seconds after each addition. Add cheese and blend until combined. Drop rounded tablespoonfuls of dough on a buttered baking sheet. Bake at 425° for 10 minutes. Reduce temperature to 375° and bake 45 minutes or until lightly browned and puffy. Cool slightly and serve warm.

1 cup water
1 stick unsalted butter, cut in small pieces
½ teaspoon salt
1 cup all-purpose flour
½ cup shelled walnuts, ground
4 eggs
6 ounces Roquefort cheese, crumbled

**Yield: 6 to 8 servings**

# Pear With Mascarpone And Prosciutto

Quarter and seed pear. Halve again each pear wedge, top with a spoonful of mascarpone and wrap each wedge in a slice of prosciutto.

# Salmon Mousse

*...if you have or can borrow a fish mold, line it with plastic wrap, pour in mousse and unmold when ready to serve; garnish with cucumber slices, hard-cooked egg, and capers*

2 (¼-ounce) packages unflavored gelatin
½ cup cold water
1 cup boiling water
1 tablespoon vinegar
3 tablespoons lemon juice
1 (16-ounce) can red salmon, drained and flaked
1 cup mayonnaise, plus extra for garnish
1 cup heavy cream, whipped
½ teaspoon salt
1 tablespoon Worcestershire sauce
1 medium onion, grated
2 cups diced celery or cucumber
minced fresh dill for garnish

**Yield: 6 to 8 servings**

Soak gelatin in cold water. Add boiling water and stir to dissolve. Add vinegar and lemon juice and chill until thickened to the consistency of egg whites. Combine salmon and mayonnaise in a bowl. Fold in cream. Add thickened gelatin mixture, salt, Worcestershire sauce, onion, and celery. Pour into an oiled 2-quart mold and chill until set. Unmold and garnish.

The flavor is best if dish is prepared a day in advance. Serve with crackers.

# Grilled Shrimp, Papaya, And Pepper On A Skewer

*...serve on a large silver tray with a tropical flower*

Whisk together oil, lime juice, sherry, garlic, bourbon, and soy sauce. Add shrimp and refrigerate 60 minutes. Add papaya and peppers to marinade. Soak 10 wooden skewers in water to prevent burning. Thread skewers in order listed: papaya, peppers, shrimp, peppers, and papaya. Grill or broil 3 minutes on each side or until shrimp are done.

½ cup olive oil
3 tablespoons fresh lime juice
¼ cup sherry
2 cloves garlic, finely minced
2 tablespoons bourbon
½ cup soy sauce
10 large shrimp, peeled and deveined
2 firm papayas, cut in 1-inch cubes
2 green bell peppers, cut in 1-inch cubes
2 red bell peppers, cut in 1-inch cubes

**Yield: 10 servings**

# Shrimp Canapé

*...for a true canapé, serve on toasted, sliced baguette bread*

Combine all ingredients in a food processor and mix well. Chill to blend flavors.

Serve on crackers or toast rounds.

*Substitute one (16-ounce) can, drained or 2 cups poached salmon plus 1 teaspoon horseradish for the shrimp.*

4 ounces cooked fresh or frozen shrimp
1 stick butter, softened
1 (8-ounce) package cream cheese, softened
¼ cup mayonnaise
2 tablespoons lemon juice
1 tablespoon minced onion
½ teaspoon salt

**Yield: 12 to 14 servings**

# Smoked Oyster Canapé

*...as oysters were considered brain food, Louis XI invited the Sorbonne professors to an oyster feast once a year lest their scholarship should become deficient*

1 (3¾-ounce) can smoked oysters, chopped
1 (8-ounce) package cream cheese
¼ cup milk
¼ cup grated onion
¼ teaspoon Worcestershire sauce
pinch of garlic salt
toast rounds or squares

**Yield: 24 servings**

Blend oysters, cream cheese, milk, onion, Worcestershire sauce, and garlic salt together. Arrange toast rounds on a baking sheet and cover with oyster mixture. Broil until brown.

# Smoked Whitefish Pâté

*...trout may be substituted for the Michigan whitefish*

1 cup boned and crumbled smoked whitefish
1 (8-ounce) package cream cheese, softened
½ cup minced celery
¼ cup minced scallions
¼ cup minced fresh parsley
¼ teaspoon powdered thyme

**Yield: 2½ cups**

Combine all ingredients in a bowl. Let stand at least 30 minutes to allow flavors to blend. If mixture is too thick, add a dollop of sour cream and blend. Serve at room temperature.

Serve with slices of toasted French bread or plain crackers.

# Seviche With Avocado

*...a cold fish salad, best served as a first course*

Place fish and enough lime juice to cover in a glass bowl. Refrigerate overnight. Drain fish and add remaining ingredients. Chill.

Use fish such as haddock, swordfish, or halibut. Serve in butter or boston lettuce "cups".

*You can "overcook" fish by marinating it in lime juice too long; the acid breaks down the fish until it falls apart and takes on a grainy texture.*

2 pounds raw firm whitefish, julienned
lime juice
¾ cup olive oil
1 (4-ounce) can green chili peppers, drained and chopped
2 avocados, peeled and cubed
2 tablespoons chopped fresh lemon balm or lemon grass
2 tomatoes, diced
2 shallots, minced
2 tablespoons capers
dash of Tabasco sauce, or to taste
salt to taste (optional)

**Yield: 6 to 8 servings**

# Summer Starter

*...or summer has started!*

Arrange tomatoes on an oven-proof plate or platter. Drizzle with oil and sprinkle with salt and pepper. Place cheese slices over tomatoes. Drizzle with more oil and sprinkle with salt and pepper. Bake at a low temperature or broil until cheese melts. Garnish with basil sprigs.

Serve with sliced sourdough or French bread.

home-grown tomatoes, sliced
extra virgin olive oil
salt and pepper to taste
mozzarella cheese, thinly sliced
fresh basil sprigs for garnish

# California Sushi Roll

*...this is the Sushi with no raw fish—also known as Maki Nori*

1 cup short grain rice
1 cup + 2 tablespoons
   cold water
¼ cup rice vinegar
¼ cup sugar
2 teaspoons salt
2 tablespoons sesame
   seeds, dry roasted
1 teaspoon wasabi
   powder
several drops water
3 sheets nori (dried
   laver seaweed)
1½ cups crabmeat
3 tablespoons golden
   or salmon caviar
1 avocado, julienned
4 ounces smoked
   salmon, julienned

**Yield: 18 to 24 slices**

Wash rice several times in cold water until water runs clear. Let drain 30 minutes. Place in pot with water. Bring to a boil, tightly covered. Lower heat to a simmer and cook 10 minutes, without peeking! Turn off heat and let sit for 10 to 15 minutes. Combine vinegar, sugar and salt in a saucepan. Bring to to boil, stirring until dissolved. Remove from heat and stir into rice. Add sesame seeds. Combine wasabi powder and water to make a paste. Let stand 5 to 6 minutes. Toast nori by drawing it over a gas flame or above an electric element set on medium, being careful not to burn it. Place a sheet of nori on a bamboo mat or heavy cloth napkin. Spread 1 cup rice over two-thirds of nori, leaving a 2-inch edge at the top of nori exposed. Combine wasabi paste, crabmeat, and caviar. Spread ⅓ of mixture in a line across middle of rice and lay ⅓ avocado and ⅓ smoked salmon on top. Starting from the bottom, roll nori and rice around mixture, pressing firmly to form a neat cylinder. Let stand about 5 minutes. Remove mat and cut roll crosswise in 6 to 8 pieces. Repeat with remaining nori.

# Baked Mushroom Rolls

*...another "toast" for a luncheon soup*

Sauté onion in butter until tender. Add mushrooms and cook until tender. Remove from heat. Mix in cream cheese. Season with salt, pepper, and garlic. Trim bread crusts and roll out to flatten. Spoon mushroom mixture onto bread. Roll and cut into bite-size pieces. Chill until ready to serve. To serve, place on a buttered baking sheet. Brush tops with butter. Bake at 350° for 15 to 20 minutes or until golden brown.

1 medium onion, chopped
1 stick butter
8 ounces fresh mushrooms, chopped
1 (8-ounce) package cream cheese
salt and pepper to taste
garlic powder to taste
1 loaf thin sandwich bread
melted butter for topping

**Yield: 48 pieces**

# Bruschetta With Tomatoes

*...in Umbria, bruschetta is a thick slice of country bread, toasted over a wood fire and anointed with a good virgin olive oil, served as an appetizer or with a luncheon salad*

Place bread on a foil-lined baking sheet. Bake at 375° for 10 minutes on each side. Remove from oven and rub both sides of each slice with garlic halves. Arrange slices of bread on a platter and place one basil leaf on top of each slice. Warm oil in a small saucepan over low heat for 5 minutes. Pour oil over bread. Sprinkle with salt and pepper. Place a tomato slice on each piece of bread and serve immediately.

18 (1-inch thick) slices crusty Italian bread
2 cloves garlic, halved
18 fresh basil or arugula leaves
½ cup olive oil
salt and pepper to taste
2 large ripe tomatoes, halved and sliced 1-inch thick

**Yield: 6 servings**

# Roasted Yellow Pepper Cheese Spread

*...David was delivering cheese when he had his famous battle with Goliath*

1 medium onion, sliced
3 large cloves garlic, halved
1 tablespoon olive oil
2 yellow bell peppers
1½ cups grated cheddar cheese
dash of cayenne pepper
salt and pepper to taste
⅓ cup chopped fresh chives

**Yield: 8 to 10 servings**

Place onion and garlic in a small baking dish. Pour oil over top. Bake at 375° for 60 minutes or until soft. Cool. Char whole peppers until blackened on all sides. Cool. Peel, seed, and chop peppers. Pat dry. Purée onion mixture, chopped pepper, cheese, and cayenne pepper in a blender or food processor. Transfer to a serving bowl. Season with salt and pepper. Mix in chives. Refrigerate at least 3 hours to allow flavors to blend.

Serve with party rye bread or crackers. For variety, serve in a hollowed out bell pepper.

# Crabmeat Dip

*...bake in bite-size tartlet shells or a ramekin, serve surrounded by crackers*

1 (8-ounce) package cream cheese
1 egg, lightly beaten
2 tablespoons minced onion
1 tablespoon milk
juice of ½ lemon
½ teaspoon horseradish
¼ teaspoon salt
¼ teaspoon white pepper
1 (6½-ounce) can crabmeat, drained
½ cup slivered almonds (optional)

**Yield: 1½ cups**

Combine all ingredients except almonds in a food processor. Blend until smooth. Place in a ramekin, cover, and chill until ready to use. Bake at 350° for 20 minutes. Top with almonds.

# Smoked Salmon Pizza

*...Puttin' on The Ritz!*

Process cream cheese, mayonnaise, parsley, dill, chives, salt, lemon juice, and pepper in a blender or food processor until well blended. Within an hour of serving, spread mixture over crust, leaving a 1-inch border. Arrange salmon over mixture. Spoon caviar in center and slice into wedges.

*Use two (8 to 10-inch) flour tortillas instead of pizza crust. Bake, on a baking sheet, at 425° until lightly browned. If tortillas puff while baking, pierce with a sharp knife. Cool.*

1 (8-ounce) package cream cheese
½ cup mayonnaise
1 tablespoon chopped fresh parsley
2 tablespoons chopped fresh dill
2 teaspoons chopped fresh chives
½ teaspoon seasoned salt
2 teaspoons fresh lemon juice
¼ teaspoon black pepper
1 (12-inch) pizza crust, baked
4-6 ounces smoked salmon, thinly sliced
2-3 teaspoons black caviar

**Yield: 8 to 10 servings**

# Roasted Red Pepper With Capers Pizza

*...charring red peppers over a flame loosens their tough skin and gives them their roasted flavor*

1 (12-inch) pizza crust, partially baked
4 teaspoons olive oil
½ cup grated mozzarella cheese
½ cup grated Fontina cheese
2-3 red bell peppers, roasted and chopped
1 tablespoon capers

**Yield: one (12-inch) pizza**

Brush pizza crust with olive oil. Cover with cheeses. Arrange pepper over cheeses. Sprinkle with capers. Bake at 425° for 10 minutes or until cheese melts.

# Chicken Curry With Coconut And Mint On Endive Barquettes

*...curry, coconut, and mint give this hors d'oeuvre an Indian flavor*

1 cup heavy cream
½ tablespoon Madras curry powder
cayenne pepper to taste
black pepper to taste
½ banana, diced
½ green apple, diced
1 cup diced cooked chicken
4-5 large endive
freshly grated coconut
fresh mint sprigs for garnish

**Yield: 20 to 25 servings**

Combine cream, curry powder, and peppers in a saucepan. Stir constantly over low heat until reduced by half. Add banana and apple. Cook 1 minute. Add chicken and cook 1 minute or until mixture thickens. Separate endive into barquettes. Spoon 1 teaspoon chicken mixture into each barquette. Sprinkle with coconut and garnish. Serve warm.

# Black Bean Hummus

*...just a bit spicier than Hummus Bi Tahina*

Purée black beans in a food processor. Add remaining ingredients except for garnish and pita. Pulse to blend well. Garnish and serve with warmed pita.

*Variation:*

*For a traditional Hummus Bi Tahina, combine 2 (15-ounce) cans garbanzo beans, tahini, garlic, olive oil, lemon juice, cumin and cilantro. Season with salt and pepper to taste. Thin to desired consistency adding warm water.*

1 (8-ounce) can black beans, drained
½ cup tahini
1 (15-ounce) can garbanzo beans, drained
2 ears fresh corn, roasted and kernels cut from core
1 red bell pepper, roasted, peeled, and seeded
1 jalapeño pepper, seeded and chopped
3 cloves garlic, minced
⅓ cup olive oil
⅓ cup lemon or lime juice
2 teaspoons ground cumin
½ cup chopped fresh cilantro
fresh cilantro sprigs and lemon wedges for garnish
pita, torn into bite-size pieces

**Yield: 4 cups**

# Meatballs In A Creamy Dill Sauce

*...serve with Warm Potato Salad, egg noodles, or rice for a Scandinavian smorgasbord*

**meatballs**
1½ pounds ground chuck
 1 pound ground veal
 1 (4½-ounce) can
    deviled ham
 1 (6-ounce) can
    evaporated milk
 2 eggs
 1 tablespoon grated
    onion
 1 cup soft whole wheat
    breadcrumbs
 ½ teaspoon salt
 ½ teaspoon allspice
 ¼ teaspoon black
    pepper
 ¼ cup shortening or oil
 ¼ cup water

**creamy dill sauce**
 2 tablespoons butter
 2 tablespoons all-
    purpose flour
 ½ teaspoon salt
 1 cup water
 1 cup sour cream
 1 tablespoon ketchup
 1 tablespoon dried dill
chopped fresh dill

**Yield: 72 meatballs**

Combine chuck, veal, ham, milk, eggs, onion, breadcrumbs, salt, allspice, and pepper in a large bowl. Mix lightly with a fork. Shape into balls. Brown, a few at a time, in shortening in a large skillet. Drain fat. If making ahead, chill meatballs until ready to proceed. Return all meatballs to skillet and add water. Cover and simmer 20 minutes. To prepare dill sauce, melt butter in a small saucepan. Blend in flour and salt and stir until mixture bubbles. Add water slowly, stirring until sauce thickens. Bring to a boil for 1 minute. Stir in sour cream, ketchup, and dill. Heat to a boil. Serve with meatballs and garnish with fresh dill.

If serving for dinner, double Creamy Dill Sauce recipe.

# Sun-dried Tomato And Pesto Torte

*...line a small bread loaf tin with plastic wrap and layer torte, unmold and garnish as described*

Combine butter, cream cheese, and garlic and blend well. Spread one-fourth of butter mixture in a small bread tin lined with plastic wrap. Add a thin layer of tomato. Spread another fourth of butter mixture over top. Add a thin layer of pesto. Repeat layers. If desired, freeze and defrost when ready to serve. Unmold onto a serving dish, garnish and serve with crackers.

1 stick butter, softened
1½ (8-ounce) packages cream cheese, softened
1 teaspoon minced garlic, or to taste
oil-packed sun-dried tomatoes, drained and chopped
pesto to taste
fresh basil sprigs for garnish

**Yield: 8 to 10 servings**

# St. Louis' Toasted Ravioli

*...Charlie Gitto's restaurant in St. Louis' Hill Neighborhood makes toasted ravioli using homemade pasta, but shares his eatery's fabled recipe*

Beat together milk and egg. Dip ravioli in egg mixture, then coat with breadcrumbs. Deep-fry ravioli, a few at a time, in 2 inches of 350° shortening. Fry 1 minute per side or until golden. Drain on paper towels. Keep fried ravioli warm in a 300° oven while remainder of ravioli cook. Sprinkle with cheese and serve with warmed sauce for dipping.

2 tablespoons milk
1 egg
1 (1-pound) package frozen ravioli, thawed
⅔-1 cup fine dry breadcrumbs
shortening or oil for deep-frying
Parmesan cheese
1 cup spaghetti or pizza sauce

**Yield: 12 to 14 servings**

# Goat Cheese Ravioli With Garlic Tomato Sauce

*...could also be a pasta course for a more formal dinner*

12 ounces Montrachet
   cheese, or other mild
   creamy goat cheese
salt and pepper to taste
  3 tablespoons ricotta
   cheese
⅓ cup finely chopped
   prosciutto
¼ cup minced fresh basil
½ teaspoon lemon zest
  1 egg, lightly beaten
  3 large cloves garlic,
   thinly sliced
¼ cup olive oil
  1 (28-ounce) can plum
   tomatoes, drained and
   finely chopped
1½ teaspoons fresh thyme
60 won ton skins
  6 sprigs fresh basil for
   garnish (optional)

**Yield: 6 servings**

Combine Montrachet cheese, salt, pepper, ricotta cheese, prosciutto, basil, zest, and egg in a bowl. Mix well. Cover and chill 60 minutes or until cold. In a skillet, sauté garlic in oil over medium-low heat until golden. Remove garlic with a slotted spoon and discard. Add tomatoes to skillet and bring to a boil. Cook and stir over medium-high heat for 10 minutes or until thick. Stir in thyme and season with salt and pepper. Reduce heat and cover, keeping sauce warm while preparing ravioli. Place a won ton skin on a lightly floured surface. Mound 1 tablespoon of cheese mixture in the center. Place a second wrapper over the top. Press down around the filling to force out air. Seal edges well and trim excess dough around the filling with a sharp knife or decorative cutter. Repeat with remainder of won ton skins. As ravioli are made, place on a dry kitchen towel, turning occasionally to allow them to dry slightly. Cook ravioli in batches in gently boiling salted water for 2 minutes or until they rise to the surface and are tender. Remove cooked ravioli with a slotted spoon and place on a dry kitchen towel to drain. Keep warm and heat 6 individual serving plates. Arrange 5 ravioli on each plate. Spoon sauce over the top and garnish with basil.

# Chicken Liver Pâté

*...for a richer taste, add brandy*

Melt butter in a 10-inch skillet over medium heat for 2 minutes. Add livers, onion, and garlic. Cook 5 minutes, stirring occasionally. Add remaining ingredients. Bring to a boil. Reduce heat and cover. Simmer 5 minutes or until livers are done. Pour mixture into a blender and purée until smooth. Place in a serving dish. Cover and chill at least 24 hours to allow flavors to blend.

Serve with a variety of crackers or with sliced apples.

1 stick unsalted butter
1 pound chicken livers
¼ cup chopped onion
1 clove minced garlic
½ teaspoon salt
¼ teaspoon black pepper
¼ teaspoon dried thyme
1 teaspoon Worcestershire sauce
⅛ teaspoon Tabasco sauce
⅓ cup dry white wine

**Yield: 2 cups**

# Bacon-wrapped Water Chestnuts

*...the taste of caramelized bacon with a water chestnut*

Cut bacon slices in half crosswise and then lengthwise. Marinate water chestnuts in soy sauce for 30 minutes. Roll chestnuts in sugar and then wrap in a bacon strip. Secure with a toothpick. Arrange on a cooling rack in a shallow, foil-lined pan. Bake at 400° for 20 minutes. Drain on paper towels. Just prior to serving, reheat in a 350° oven for 5 minutes.

4 slices bacon
1 (8-ounce) can water chestnuts, drained
¼ cup soy sauce
¼ cup sugar

**Yield: 16 servings**

# Super Nacho

*...there are no secrets to this "casserole" hors d'oeuvre - it's always gone!*

8 ounces ground beef
8 ounces chorizo
1 large onion, chopped
Tabasco sauce to taste
salt to taste
1-2 (16-ounce) cans
   refried beans
1 (4-ounce) can green
   chili peppers,
   chopped
2-3 cups grated Monterey
   Jack cheese
¾ cup taco sauce
¼ cup chopped scallions
1 cup sliced black olives
1 avocado, mashed
1 cup sour cream
tortilla chips

**Yield: 8 to 10 servings**

Brown beef, chorizo, and onion in a skillet over high heat. Drain fat. Season with pepper sauce and salt. Spread beans in a shallow 10X15 inch casserole dish. Top with meat mixture, chili peppers, cheese, and taco sauce. Bake, uncovered, at 400° for 20 to 25 minutes. Top with scallions, olives, avocado, and sour cream. Serve with chips.

If chorizo is not available, use a hot Italian sausage and refried beans with sausage.

# Bodacious Bean Dip

*...served in a bright blue pottery bowl with a basket of tortilla chips and healthy appetites waiting for the Sunday Night Barbecue*

1 (16-ounce) can
   refried beans with
   cheese or sausage
1 cup sour cream
1 cup medium or hot
   salsa

**Yield: 8 servings**

Combine all ingredients. Chill at least 4 hours.

# Tostada Dip

*...with salsa and guacamole - "Mas cervezas!" on Cinco de Mayo*

Cook and stir beef and onion until meat is browned. Drain well. Add tomato sauce, picante sauce, taco sauce, chili peppers, and chili powder. Reduce heat and cover. Simmer 60 minutes, stirring occasionally. Season with salt and pepper. Transfer mixture to a chafing dish. Sprinkle with cheese.

Serve with tortilla chips. Reheat leftovers and serve as chili.

*For variety, stir in a can of refried beans with sausage when adding salt and pepper.*

2 pounds ground beef
1 large onion, chopped
2 (15-ounce) cans tomato sauce with tomato pieces
1 (12-ounce) jar mild picante sauce
1 (8-ounce) jar hot taco sauce
2 (4-ounce) cans green chili peppers, undrained and chopped
2 tablespoons chili powder
salt and pepper to taste
2 cups grated sharp cheddar cheese

**Yield: 6 cups**

# BLT Dip

*...everything but the lettuce*

Combine mayonnaise and sour cream. Add bacon and tomato to mixture. Serve immediately on melba toast.

*For a spicier dip, use salsa instead of tomatoes.*

1 cup mayonnaise
1 cup sour cream
1 pound bacon, cooked and crumbled
2 large tomatoes, chopped
melba toast

**Yield: about 4 cups**

# Quesadillas

*...a simple, quick appetizer for good friends and family*

1 stick butter, softened
6 flour tortillas
1 pound Monterey Jack
  cheese, grated
8 scallions, chopped
½ cup chopped
  pimientos, drained
4 jalapeño peppers,
  seeded and minced
2 tablespoons chopped
  fresh cilantro
1 teaspoon ground
  cumin

**Yield: 10 servings**

Butter both sides of tortillas. Combine remaining ingredients and spread on 3 tortillas. Top with remaining tortillas and press together. Bake at 400° for 5 to 8 minutes. Cool slightly and cut into wedges.

Serve with guacamole, sour cream, and Bonnie's Salsa.

# Bonnie's Salsa

*...there are lots of very good salsas in the market, but this is a great one!*

1 (6-pound, 6-ounce)
  can whole tomatoes,
  drained and chopped
2 medium onions, diced
2 bunches scallions,
  finely chopped
1 tablespoon finely
  chopped fresh
  cilantro, or more to
  taste
⅓ cup taco seasoning
1 tablespoon minced
  garlic
⅓ cup seeded and diced
  jalapeño pepper
1 (4-ounce) can chili
  peppers, diced
salt and pepper to taste

Combine all ingredients and serve.

# New Year's Day Brunch

*Don's Best Breakfast Drink     Mimosas*
*Smoked Salmon Pizza     Black Eyed Peas*

*Bourbon Orange Glazed Ham*
*Buttermilk Biscuits     Butter & Jams*
*Tomato Bread Pudding     Garlic Cheddar Grits*
*Swedish Roesti Potatoes     Warm Green Bean & Walnut Salad*
*Creamed Oysters & Ham over Buckwheat Cakes*
*Eggs Chevrolet*

*Palm Beach Brownies     Apple Crisp     Praline Cookies*

# Scallion Pancakes With Parsley Lemon Butter

*...a thin pancake creating a scrambled egg and bacon "sandwich" with a parsley lemon butter*

To make lemon butter, melt butter in a saucepan over low heat. Add parsley and lemon juice and heat without boiling. Prepare pancakes by combining flour, baking powder, and salt in a large bowl. In a small bowl, lightly beat 2 eggs. Whisk in milk and butter. Add egg mixture and scallions to dry ingredients. Stir gently until smooth. Cook 12 pancakes in a skillet in butter and keep warm. Scramble remaining 12 eggs and cook in a skillet until done. To assemble, place 1 pancake on a heated individual serving plate. Top with scrambled egg, 2 strips of bacon, and another pancake. Drizzle lemon butter over each portion. Serve immediately with sautéed spinach.

**parsley lemon butter**
- 2 sticks butter
- ¼ cup minced fresh parsley
- 2 tablespoons lemon juice

**pancakes**
- 1 cup all-purpose flour
- 2½ teaspoons baking powder
- ½ teaspoon salt
- 14 eggs, divided
- 1¼ cups milk
- 3 tablespoons butter, melted, plus extra to cook pancakes
- ½ cup minced scallions
- 12 strips bacon, cooked
- sautéed spinach

**Yield: 6 servings**

# Creamed Oysters And Ham Over Buckwheat Cakes

*...a hearty winter brunch, serve with a spinach salad*

## creamed oysters and ham

16-20  large oysters, shucked, liquid reserved
 1  cup heavy cream
 ⅛  teaspoon cayenne pepper
 ¾  cup slivered cured ham

## buckwheat cakes

 1  cup buckwheat flour
 1  cup all-purpose flour
 1  tablespoon sugar
 2  teaspoons baking powder
 1  teaspoon baking soda
 ½  teaspoon salt
 2  eggs
 2  cups buttermilk
 4  tablespoons clarified butter, plus extra for topping

**Yield: 8 servings**

Reduce 1 cup of reserved oyster liquid by half over medium heat. In a separate saucepan, reduce cream by half over medium heat. Add cayenne pepper to cream. Strain reduced oyster liquid into cream. Fold oysters into cream sauce and cook over medium heat until edge of oysters begin to curl. Stir in ham and keep warm. To prepare buckwheat cakes, sift together flours, sugar, baking powder, baking soda, and salt. In a separate bowl, beat eggs. Mix in buttermilk. Stir in butter. Fold egg mixture into dry ingredients. Blend well. Cook cakes in a skillet. Pour a small amount of butter over each cake. Stack cakes in individual portions. Spoon creamed oyster sauce over each serving.

Batter thickens as it stands. Add buttermilk as needed to thin batter.

# Oatmeal Pancakes

*...whipping the egg whites and folding them into the mixture is the secret behind the lightness of this pancake!*

Mix oats and buttermilk and refrigerate overnight. Cool melted butter slightly. Add butter and egg yolks to oatmeal mixture. Combine flours, sugar, baking powder, baking soda, and salt. Stir into oatmeal mixture. Whip egg whites and fold into batter. Add extra buttermilk if batter is too thick. Cook pancakes on a hot griddle until golden brown on both sides.

2 cups oats
2 cups buttermilk
2 tablespoons butter, melted
2 eggs, separated
½ cup unbleached flour
½ cup whole wheat flour
2 teaspoons sugar
1½ teaspoons baking powder
1½ teaspoons baking soda
1 teaspoon salt

**Yield: 12 to 15 pancakes**

# Super Pancakes

*...don't use a mixer - do it all by hand and don't over mix!*

Combine flour, sugar, salt, baking powder and baking soda in a bowl. In a separate bowl, beat together remaining ingredients. Stir egg mixture into dry ingredients by hand. Batter will be very thick, but will spread when poured on a warm skillet. Cook pancakes until golden brown on both sides.

To make half of recipe, use 2 eggs and cut all other ingredients in half.

2 cups all-purpose flour
2 teaspoons sugar
1 teaspoon salt
1½ teaspoons baking powder
1 teaspoon baking soda
3 eggs, beaten
1 cup buttermilk
1 cup sour cream
2 tablespoons butter, melted

**Yield: 16 to 18 pancakes**

# Gingerbread Pancakes

*...fills the house with the smells of Christmas*

1 cup all-purpose flour
1 tablespoon sugar
1 teaspoon baking powder
½ teaspoon baking soda
½ teaspoon salt
¾ teaspoon cinnamon
1 teaspoon ginger
dash of ground cloves
2 tablespoons molasses or honey
1 tablespoon vegetable oil
1 cup buttermilk
1 egg, lightly beaten

**Yield: 10 to 12 pancakes**

Combine flour, sugar, baking powder, baking soda, salt, cinnamon, ginger, and cloves. Whisk together molasses and remaining ingredients. Slowly stir molasses mixture into dry ingredients until smooth. Cook pancakes on a warm, lightly buttered griddle until golden brown on both sides.

# Eggs Chevrolet

*...scooped out baked potato, filled with creamed spinach, topped with a poached egg and hollandaise sauce!*

1 large baked potato, halved
sautéed or creamed spinach
2 eggs, poached
Hollandaise Sauce

**Yield: 1 serving**

Scoop out pulp of baked potato. Reheat potato shells. Fill each shell with spinach. Top each half with an egg and hollandaise sauce.

Hollandaise Sauce, page 179

# Corned Beef Hash

*...a natural for leftovers, corned beef or roast beef flavored with a touch of Worcestershire sauce and topped with a poached egg*

Toss chunked vegetables with 1 tablespoon oil in a roasting pan. In a separate pan, toss potatoes with remaining 1 tablespoon oil. Season both pans of vegetables with salt and pepper and bake at 350° for 60 minutes or until softened. Cut potatoes into chunks. Allow vegetables to cool. Combine beef and all vegetables except potatoes in a food processor. Pulse to coarsely blend. Do not purée. In a large mixing bowl, combine beef mixture and potato. Form into large patties. Fry in butter until brown on both sides. Top each serving with a poached egg.

If desired, freeze patties before frying. Thaw when ready to use.

2 carrots, cut into chunks
2 purple-topped turnips, cut into chunks
1 medium or large celery root, cut into chunks
1 large Spanish onion, cut into chunks
1 green bell pepper, cut into chunks
2 tablespoons oil, divided
9 small red potatoes
salt and pepper to taste
3 pounds cooked corned beef, shredded
butter for frying
10 poached eggs

**Yield: 10 servings**

# John Wayne's Favorite

*...hop off your horse, drop your six shooter, and dig in!*

1 (18-ounce) loaf
   sandwich bread, crust
   trimmed
butter
3 large canned chili
   peppers, chopped
8 ounces cheddar
   cheese, grated,
   divided
8 ounces Monterey
   Jack cheese, grated,
   divided
5 eggs
3 cups milk
¼ cup chopped fresh
   parsley or cilantro

**Yield: 10 servings**

Butter one side of each slice of bread. Place a single layer of bread, buttered-side down, in a buttered 9X13 inch baking dish. Top with chilies. Sprinkle with half of each cheese. Top with another layer of bread, buttered-side up. Beat together eggs and milk. Pour over bread. Sprinkle with remaining half of each cheese. Scatter parsley over top. Cover and refrigerate overnight. Bake at 350° for 45 minutes or until a knife inserted in the center comes out clean.

Save time and effort by substituting 8 ounces jalapeño pepper jack cheese for the Monterey Jack cheese and the chili peppers.

# French Toast Casserole

*...serve with your favorite syrup or honey*

1 (8-ounce) French
   bread, sliced 1-inch
   thick
8 eggs
3 cups milk
4 teaspoons sugar
¾ teaspoon salt
1 tablespoon vanilla
2 tablespoons butter

**Yield: 6 to 8 servings**

Arrange bread in a single layer on the bottom of a buttered 9X13 inch baking dish. Beat together eggs, milk, sugar, salt, and vanilla. Pour over bread. Cover and refrigerate overnight. When ready to bake, dot with butter. Bake, uncovered, at 350° for 45 to 50 minutes or until puffy and lightly browned.

# Baked Omelet

*...a classic brunch dish*

In a 10-inch ovenproof skillet, sauté onion, pepper, and potatoes in butter until vegetables start to soften. Add zucchini and cook and stir 2 minutes. Beat eggs and milk together. Add egg mixture, thyme, cilantro, salt, and pepper to vegetables. Bake at 400° for 20 minutes. Sprinkle cheese over top. Bake 5 minutes longer.

½ cup chopped onion
½ red bell pepper, chopped
8-10 new potatoes, sliced
2 tablespoons butter
½ cup grated zucchini
4 eggs
2 tablespoons milk
¼-½ teaspoon thyme
½ teaspoon cilantro
salt and pepper to taste
1 cup grated cheddar cheese, or cheese of choice

**Yield: 4 servings**

# Mexican Cornbread Casserole

*...for a spicier dish, add a few drops of Tabasco sauce to drained ground beef*

Combine cornmeal, milk, salt, eggs, baking soda, and corn. Cover bottom of a buttered 2½ to 3-quart casserole dish with half of the cornmeal mixture. Cook beef and drain. Spread beef over cornmeal mixture. Layer onion on beef. Add chili peppers and sprinkle with cheese. Top with remaining cornmeal mixture. Bake at 350° for 45 minutes or until a toothpick inserted in the center comes out clean.

1 cup yellow cornmeal
1 cup milk
¾ teaspoon salt
2 eggs, well beaten
½ teaspoon baking soda
1 (16-ounce) can cream-style corn
1 pound ground beef
1 onion, finely chopped
2 (4-ounce) cans chili peppers, chopped
8 ounces longhorn cheese, grated

**Yield: 6 servings**

# Baked Hash Browns

*...experiment with more flavorful hard cheeses that can be easily grated*

4-5 slices bacon
  1 (10-ounce) package
    frozen hash browns,
    thawed
¾-1 cup grated Swiss,
    Gruyère, or cheddar
    cheese, divided
  5 eggs, lightly beaten
  1 cup half-and-half
  ¼ teaspoon white
    pepper
  ½ teaspoon salt
4-5 drops Tabasco sauce

**Yield: 4 servings**

Cook bacon until crisp, reserving fat. Drain bacon on paper towels and crumble. Use some of reserved bacon fat to coat the bottom of a square pan or a shallow casserole dish. Brown hash browns slightly in bacon fat in a skillet. Spread hash browns evenly over bottom of pan. Sprinkle with half of cheese and half of bacon. Beat together eggs and remaining ingredients. Pour egg mixture over top. Sprinkle with remaining cheese and bacon. Bake at 450° for 10 minutes. Reduce heat to 350° and bake 10 to 15 minutes longer or until eggs set, top browns, and edges pull away from sides of pan. Cut into squares and serve hot.

# Sausage Apple Ring

*...garnish with fresh fruit and serve with Baked Omelet*

  2 pounds pork sausage
1½ cups cracker crumbs
  2 eggs, beaten
  ½ cup milk
  ¼ cup chopped onion
  2 apples, peeled and
    grated

**Yield: 8 servings**

Combine all ingredients. Press into a buttered ring mold. Bake at 350° for 30 minutes. Drain fat and unmold onto a rimmed baking sheet. Bake 30 to 40 minutes longer.

# Brunch Quesadillas

*...serve with wedges of cantaloupe and honeydew*

Scramble eggs and cook until soft curds form. Mix together cheeses. Place a tortilla in a greased skillet over medium heat. As tortilla begins to brown, sprinkle with ¼ cup of cheese mixture. Spread a fourth of egg over cheese. Top with another ¼ cup of cheeses. Place a second tortilla on top. When bottom tortilla is golden and bottom layer of cheese has melted, turn quesadilla. Continue to cook until second tortilla is golden, egg is cooked through and cheese is melted. Transfer to a warm serving platter and hold in a warm oven. Repeat above assembly and cooking procedure with remaining ingredients. Spoon salsa over top of each serving. Sprinkle with remaining cheese mixture. Serve with extra salsa on the side.

12 eggs
2 cups grated cheddar cheese
2 cups grated Monterey Jack cheese
8 flour tortillas
salsa

**Yield: 4 servings**

# Torta Milanese

*...a blend of ham, spinach, and cheese "sandwiched" with an herbed omelet and topped with a flaky puff pastry - served at St. Peter's Christmas Bazaar*

2 large red bell peppers, chopped
2 cloves garlic, minced
1 tablespoon vegetable oil
3 tablespoons plus 2 teaspoons butter, divided
1 pound fresh spinach, stems removed
½ teaspoon nutmeg
salt and pepper to taste
1 (16-ounce) package puff pastry, thawed
10 eggs, divided
1 tablespoon chopped fresh chives
1 tablespoon chopped fresh parsley
¾ teaspoon tarragon
¼ teaspoon salt
12 ounces ham, thinly sliced
3 cups grated Swiss cheese
fresh spinach, fresh parsley, and pimiento cutouts for garnish

**Yield: 8 servings**

Sauté bell peppers and garlic in oil and 1 tablespoon butter in a skillet. Remove with a slotted spoon, reserving liquid in skillet. Add spinach to skillet. Season with nutmeg, salt, and pepper. Stir gently. Cover and cook over high heat for 3 to 5 minutes. Chop and drain well. Line a buttered 8 to 10-inch springform pan with 1 pastry sheet, allowing ½ inch to hang over sides. Cover with a damp cloth and set aside. Beat together 9 eggs, chives, parsley, tarragon, and salt. Melt 2 teaspoons butter in a hot 8-inch omelet pan, rotating pan to coat surface. Using a fourth of the egg mixture at a time, prepare 4 omelets in heated pan. Add 2 teaspoons butter to pan before making each omelet. Place one omelet in the pastry-lined springform pan. Set the other 3 omelets on wax paper until needed. Layer a third of spinach mixture, ½ cup cheese, a third of ham, ½ cup cheese, and a third of bell pepper mixture in order listed in pan. Top with another omelet. Repeat layers 2 more times. Place another pastry sheet over top. Seal by rolling over edges of bottom pastry and crimping. Cut slits in top pastry to allow steam to escape. Beat remaining egg and brush over

## Torta Milanese (continued)

top pastry. Place in a shallow pan in the lower third of the oven. Bake at 350° for 60 minutes. Remove from oven and let stand for 5 minutes before removing sides of pan. Place on a spinach-lined serving plate. Decorate with parsley and pimiento.

If desired, substitute 2 (10-ounce) packages frozen spinach for fresh. Drain and press between paper towels before adding to skillet. Cook for about 1 minute rather than 3 to 5 minutes.

Prepare omelets the night before, if desired, and stack between layers of wax paper.

# Herb Tomato Cheese Pie

*...when tomatoes are at their peak, serve poolside with grilled chicken*

Dip tomatoes in boiling water for 30 seconds. Discard skins and chop coarsely. Pierce pie crust several times with a fork. Bake at 425° for 5 minutes. Place tomato in pie crust. Sprinkle with pepper, garlic powder, basil, oregano, and chives. Combine mayonnaise and cheeses. Spread mayonnaise mixture over top, extending to all edges. Bake at 400° for 20 to 25 minutes or until crust is lightly browned.

4 medium tomatoes
1 (9-inch) pie crust, unbaked
coarsely ground black pepper to taste
garlic powder to taste
1 teaspoon fresh basil leaves
1 teaspoon fresh oregano leaves
¼ cup chopped fresh chives
1 cup mayonnaise
¾ cup grated mozzarella cheese
¾ cup grated cheddar cheese

**Yield: 4 to 6 servings**

# Salmon Cakes

*...use leftover grilled or poached salmon and serve with dill hollandaise for an elegant brunch*

1½ cups minced onion
2 stalks celery, minced
4 tablespoons butter, divided
2 pounds poached salmon, flaked
2 baked potatoes, chilled, peeled, and grated
3 tablespoons mayonnaise
1 egg, beaten
1 tablespoon Worcestershire sauce
1 teaspoon minced fresh dill
2 tablespoons capers, drained and minced
all-purpose flour for dredging

**Yield: 6 servings**

Sauté onion and celery in 2 tablespoons butter until softened. Cool and combine with salmon and potato in a large bowl. Add mayonnaise, egg, Worcestershire sauce, dill, and capers. Blend well and shape into 12 patties. Dredge in flour. Sauté in remaining 2 tablespoons butter for 2 to 3 minutes per side or until golden brown. Serve hot.

Serve with Dill Hollandaise (page 180), a Béarnaise Sauce using dill instead of tarragon.

# Anadama Bread

*...a Cape Ann tradition that began with a Rockport fisherman...the legend goes, that after many months at sea, he'd come home to his wife Anna, who was not a cook, forcing him to fend for himself in the kitchen - therefore his bread, "Anna, damn her"*

1¼ cups milk, scalded, divided
½ cup yellow cornmeal
2 tablespoons shortening
2½ teaspoons salt
¼ cup molasses
1 (.06-ounce) yeast cake
3½-4 cups white bread flour

**Yield: 1 loaf**

Combine 1 cup milk and cornmeal in a large mixing bowl. Add shortening, salt, and molasses. Cool remaining ¼ cup milk to about 85°. Dissolve yeast cake in cooled milk for 10 minutes. Combine cornmeal mixture and yeast mixture. Stir in enough flour for dough to knead easily. Knead 10 minutes. Place in an oiled bowl, cover, and set in a warm place. Allow to rise 60 minutes or until doubled in bulk. Punch down and shape into a buttered loaf pan. Allow to rise until almost doubled. Bake at 375° for 40 minutes.

*To make in a bread machine, add to machine in the following order: 2½ teaspoons active dry yeast, 2½ teaspoons salt, 3½ cups bread flour, ½ cup cornmeal, ¼ cup molasses, 2 tablespoons shortening, and 1¼ cups milk. Start machine. If dough seems too wet at start of the knead cycle, add up to ½ cup extra flour.*

# Garlic Olive Bread Wreath

*...there's nothing more comforting than the aroma of baking bread, especially when spiced with a hint of Provence*

½ cup chopped black olives

2 tablespoons capers

1 frozen bread dough, thawed

1 cup grated Swiss cheese, divided

2 tablespoons minced garlic

½ cup chopped walnuts

½ teaspoon dried oregano

½ teaspoon dried basil

**Yield: 2 rings, 6 to 8 servings each**

Press moisture out of olives and capers with paper towels. Cut dough in half. Roll each half into a 10X14 inch rectangle on an unfloured board. Press edges of dough to board to hold its shape while working. Combine ¾ cup cheese and remaining ingredients. Sprinkle mixture evenly over 2 rectangles, leaving a 1-inch border around each. Top with olives and capers. Roll up rectangles, starting with the long ends. Form into 2 rings. Place seam-side down on a lightly buttered baking pan. Cut 10 slashes into each ring, slicing through the layers almost to the base. Loosely cover and allow to rise in a warm place for 60 minutes. Sprinkle remaining ¼ cup cheese on top of rings. Bake at 350° for 35 minutes. Cool on a rack.

*For variety, use any combination of cheeses, roasted peppers, sun-dried tomatoes, scallions, or fresh herbs.*

# French Bread

*...baguettes, wreaths, Eloise even wore them as shoes - most versatile of all breads*

Place flour, salt, and 2 teaspoons sugar in a large mixing bowl. Combine milk and boiling water. Allow to cool. Mix yeast and warm water. Let stand 10 minutes. Combine milk and yeast mixtures. Add shortening and remaining 1 tablespoon sugar. Pour liquid mixture into dry ingredients. Stir thoroughly without kneading. Cover with a damp cloth and let rise for 2 hours. Punch down and place on a floured board. Divide into 2 balls. Shape each into French loaves and place on a buttered baking sheet. Cut slashes in top and allow to rise. Place in oven along with a pan of water and bake at 400° for 15 minutes. Reduce heat to 350° and bake 30 minutes longer.

*To prepare a holiday wreath, divide dough into 4 balls. Roll 3 of the balls into long strands. Braid strands together and form into a ring. Form fourth ball into a bow for bottom of wreath. Use bow to connect ends of wreath. Fill center of wreath with Baked Brie. By measuring size of Brie cheese, and placing a same sized baking dish in center of wreath while baking, wreath will hold its shape so Baked Brie will fit inside.*

4 cups all-purpose flour
2 teaspoons salt
1 tablespoon plus 2 teaspoons sugar, divided
½ cup milk
1 cup boiling water
1 (¼-ounce) package active dry yeast
¼ cup warm water
1½ tablespoons shortening, melted

**Yield: 2 loaves**

# Focaccia

*...serve warm with olive oil and freshly grated Parmesan*

### sponge
- 1 teaspoon active dry yeast
- ½ cup warm water
- ¾ cup unbleached all-purpose flour

### dough
- 1 teaspoon active dry yeast
- 1 cup warm water
- 3 tablespoons extra-virgin olive oil
- Sponge
- 3¼ cups unbleached all-purpose flour
- 2 teaspoons sea salt

### topping
- 2 tablespoons extra-virgin olive oil
- 1 teaspoon coarse sea salt

To make sponge, sprinkle yeast over water in a large mixing bowl. Whisk together and let stand 10 minutes or until frothy. Stir in flour. Cover tightly with plastic wrap and let rise 45 minutes or until very bubbly and doubled in bulk. To make dough, sprinkle yeast over water in a small bowl. Whisk together and let stand 5 to 10 minutes or until frothy. Using a wooden spoon, stir yeast mixture and oil into sponge and mix well. Transfer to an electric mixer bowl. Mix with a paddle attachment until well blended. Add flour and salt and stir 1 to 2 minutes or until thoroughly mixed. Change to dough hook attachment and knead at medium speed for 3 to 4 minutes or until dough is soft, velvety, and slightly sticky. Dough should form peaks when pulled up with fingers. Knead dough briefly on a floured surface until it comes together nicely. Place dough in a lightly oiled container. Cover tightly with plastic wrap and let rise 1 hour, 15 minutes or until doubled in bulk. Flatten dough onto an oiled 11X17 inch baking pan and press out with oiled or wet hands. Because dough will be sticky and may not cover the bottom of the pan, cover it with a towel and let it relax for 10 minutes. Stretch dough again until it reaches the edges,

## Focaccia (continued)

or shape into six 5-inch disks. Cover with a towel and let rise for 45 to 60 minutes or until dough is full of air bubbles. Just before baking, dimple dough vigorously with knuckles or fingertips, leaving visible indentations. Drizzle oil topping over dough, leaving oil pools in the indentations. Sprinkle with coarse salt. Preheat oven, and a baking stone if available, to 425° at least 30 minutes before baking. Place baking pan on stone. Spray oven walls and floor with cold water 3 times during first 10 minutes of baking. Bake 20 to 25 minutes or until crust is crisp and top is golden. If desired, remove focaccia from pan and bake directly on stone during last 10 minutes of baking. When done, remove from pan immediately and cool on a rack.

*For whole wheat focaccia, use 2½ cups unbleached all-purpose flour and ¾ cup whole wheat flour.*

*Try topping focaccia with a combination of 2 teaspoons chopped fresh sage, 4 ounces coarsely grated Gorgonzola cheese, and 2 tablespoons olive oil. Sprinkle on dough after "dimpled" and let rest 15 minutes. Bake as directed.*

Decorate top of focaccia with caramelized onions, peppers and cheese or sliced cherry tomatoes, slivers of goat cheese, cheddar, Roquefort, etc. and herbs, such as basil leaves, rosemary, sage; chunks of sausage or ham and eat like a pizza or for sandwiches, split it open and fill with grilled or roasted vegetables, herbs, and goat cheese. To caramelize onions, cook sliced onions over low heat in a covered pan with 2 tablespoons olive oil, ¼ teaspoon salt, and a big pinch of sugar for 8 to 10 minutes or until tender and translucent. Uncover pan, increase heat to medium, and brown - a drop or two of wine vinegar added near the end will give it some bite.

# Honey Wheat Bread

*...when you make a loaf of bread, pick a day when your schedule is relaxed*

¼ cup shortening
4-5 cups bread flour,
   divided
 2 teaspoons salt
 2 (¼-ounce) packages
   active dry yeast
 I cup water
½ cup honey
 4 tablespoons butter
 I cup creamed cottage
   cheese
 2 eggs
 I cup whole wheat
   flour
½ cup rolled oats
 I cup chopped pecans
   or walnuts
melted butter (optional)

**Yield: 16 servings**

Use shortening to generously grease two 8X4 or 9X5 inch loaf pans, or two 8 to 9-inch round cake pans. In a large mixing bowl, combine 2 cups bread flour, salt, and yeast. In a saucepan, heat water, honey, butter, and cottage cheese to 120° to 130°. Add hot mixture and eggs to flour mixture. Blend with an electric mixer on low until moistened. Increase to medium speed and beat 3 minutes. By hand, stir in whole wheat flour, oats, and pecans. Mix in enough of remaining bread flour to form a soft dough. Knead on a floured surface for 10 minutes or until dough is smooth and elastic. Place in an oiled bowl and cover loosely with plastic wrap or a cloth. Let rise in a warm place for 60 minutes or until doubled in size. Punch down. Divide dough into 2 equal parts and form into balls. Place on counter and cover with bowls. Let sit 15 minutes. Shape into 2 loaves and place in prepared pans. Cover and let rise in a warm place for 60 minutes or until doubled in size. Bake at 375° for 35 to 40 minutes or until loaves sound hollow when lightly tapped. Remove from pans immediately and cool on a rack. For soft crusts, brush top with melted butter.

# Irish Wheat Bread

*...letting dough proof at room temperature develops a more complex flavor and interesting texture*

Soak cracked wheat in enough warm water to cover for 60 minutes. Combine flour, wheat germ, and salt in a large mixing bowl. Mix molasses and 2½ cups warm water in another bowl. Stir in yeast and let stand in a warm place for 10 minutes or until frothy. Add yeast mixture to dry ingredients. Mix in cracked wheat. Stir until dough forms a ball and comes clean from edges of bowl. Divide dough into well-oiled loaf pans. Cover and let stand in a warm place for 20 minutes or until dough rises to top of pans. Bake in center of oven at 350° for 35 minutes or until a knife inserted comes out clean and bread sounds hollow when tapped. Remove from pans and cool on a wire rack.

1 cup cracked wheat
8 cups whole wheat flour
1 cup wheat germ
1 teaspoon salt
2 tablespoons blackstrap molasses
2½ cups warm water
½ tablespoon active dry yeast

**Yield: 2 loaves**

# Irish Whole Wheat Soda Bread

*...traditionally, soda bread was baked over a peat fire in a 3-legged iron pot that could be raised or lowered over the fire in the old-fashioned way. Soda bread is round, with a cross cut in the top and has a velvety texture, quite unlike yeast breads.*

3 cups whole wheat flour
1 cup all-purpose flour
1 tablespoon salt
1 teaspoon baking soda
¾ teaspoon baking powder
1½-2  cups buttermilk

**Yield: 1 loaf**

Mix together flours, salt, baking soda, and baking powder. Add enough buttermilk to make a soft dough, similar in quality to a biscuit dough but firm enough to hold its shape. Knead on a lightly floured board for 2 to 3 minutes or until smooth and velvety. Form into a round loaf and place in a well-buttered 8-inch cake pan or on a well-buttered baking sheet. Cut a cross on top with a sharp, floured knife. Bake at 375° for 35 to 40 minutes or until loaf is nicely browned and sounds hollow when tapped. Cool and slice very thin.

*For white soda bread, use 4 cups all-purpose flour, omit whole wheat flour, and decrease baking soda to ¾ teaspoon.*

# Portuguese Bread

*...sweet, but not too sweet; a great sandwich, breakfast toast, or tea bread*

Sprinkle yeast over warm water in a glass or ceramic bowl. Let stand 12 to 15 minutes or until bubbly. Scald milk and pour into a large mixing bowl. Add sugar, salt, and butter. Let cool for about 10 minutes. Add eggs, one at a time, beating after each addition. Stir in yeast mixture. Add zest. Slowly mix in flour, adding enough for dough to pull away easily from sides of bowl. Knead dough 10 minutes. Cover with a damp cloth. Allow to rise in a warm place for 1 hour, 15 minutes to 1 hour, 30 minutes or until doubled in bulk. Knead 1 minute. Shape into a loaf and place in a buttered 9X3X1½ inch baking pan. Bake at 350° for 60 minutes.

1 (¼-ounce) package active dry yeast
¼ cup warm water
½ cup milk
⅔ cup sugar
¼ teaspoon salt
4 tablespoons butter, melted
3 eggs, at room temperature
1 teaspoon lemon zest
3½-4 cups unsifted flour

**Yield: 1 loaf**

# Whole Wheat Bread

*...for rising, choose a draft-free corner of your kitchen, or you can place the dough under a lamp if the kitchen is very cool*

1 (¼-ounce) package active dry yeast
2¾ cups warm water, divided
½ cup packed brown sugar
1 tablespoon salt
¼ cup shortening
3½ cups whole wheat flour
4 cups all-purpose flour, divided

**Yield: 2 loaves**

Dissolve yeast in ¼ cup warm water. Dissolve sugar and salt in remaining 2½ cups warm water. Add shortening, whole wheat flour, and 1 cup all-purpose flour to sugar mixture. Add yeast mixture and beat thoroughly. Stir in enough of remaining flour to form a dough that leaves sides of bowl. Turn out onto a floured board. Cover and let rest 10 to 15 minutes. Knead 10 minutes or until smooth and elastic. Place in an oiled bowl and turn to grease top. Cover and let rise in a warm place for 1 hour, 30 minutes or until doubled. Punch down and turn onto a board. Divide in half and form into balls. Cover and let rest 10 minutes. Shape into loaves and place in buttered loaf pans. Allow to rise 1 hour, 15 minutes. Bake at 375° for 15 minutes. Cover with foil and bake 15 to 30 minutes longer. Do not brown.

# Apple Bread

*...can be baked in small loaf pans, sliced, and served for a luncheon or at tea time - baking time will be reduced*

Combine oil and sugar. Stir in flour and baking soda. Mix in eggs, vanilla, and apple. Pour batter into a buttered 8X4X2½ inch loaf pan. To prepare topping, combine sugar, flour, and cinnamon. Cut in butter until a coarse crumb mixture forms. Sprinkle topping over batter. Bake at 350° for 60 minutes.

**bread**
- ¾ cup vegetable oil
- 1 cup sugar
- 1½ cups all-purpose flour
- 1 teaspoon baking soda
- 2 eggs, beaten
- 1 teaspoon vanilla
- 1 cup peeled and chopped apple

**topping**
- 2 tablespoons sugar
- 2 tablespoons all-purpose flour
- ½ teaspoon cinnamon
- 1 tablespoon butter

**Yield: 1 loaf**

# Banana Bread

*...an ideal use for those bananas that have passed their prime*

Cream sugar and oil together. Sour milk by mixing milk and vinegar together. Add milk and eggs to creamed mixture. Combine flour, baking soda, and salt. Add dry ingredients and banana to creamed mixture. Mix until blended. Pour batter into 2 buttered 9X5X2 inch loaf pans. Bake at 350° for 60 minutes or until a toothpick inserted in the center comes out clean.

- 1½ cups sugar
- ½ cup corn oil
- ½ cup milk
- 1 teaspoon vinegar
- 3 eggs, beaten
- 2 cups all-purpose flour
- 1 teaspoon baking soda
- dash of salt
- 1 cup mashed ripe banana

**Yield: 2 loaves**

# Blueberry Streusel Muffins

*...tested, tasted, and smiled over by many Auxiliary volunteers*

## muffins

2 cups all-purpose flour
½ cup sugar
2¼ teaspoons baking powder
1 teaspoon salt
¼ teaspoon baking soda
1 egg, lightly beaten
1 cup buttermilk
4 tablespoons butter, melted
1 teaspoon vanilla
1½ cups blueberries

## streusel topping

½ cup sugar
½ cup all-purpose flour
½ teaspoon cinnamon
4 tablespoons butter, softened

**Yield: about 14 muffins**

Combine flour, sugar, baking powder, salt, and baking soda in a large mixing bowl. In a separate bowl, mix egg, buttermilk, butter, and vanilla. Make a well in the center of the dry ingredients. Pour in liquid ingredients. Stir until just moistened. Fold in blueberries. Spoon batter into buttered muffin cups, filling two-thirds full. To prepare topping, combine sugar, flour, and cinnamon. Cut in butter until crumbly. Sprinkle over muffins. Bake at 375° for 25 to 30 minutes.

# Bran Muffins

*...muffins were sold in the streets of England by the muffin man carrying his tray and bell*

Cream egg and butter together. Soak bran in buttermilk. Add to creamed mixture. Add bran cereal, sugar, flour, salt, and baking soda. Beat until mixed. Stir in dates. Refrigerate at least 12 hours, or for up to 2 weeks. Do not stir again. Pour batter into buttered muffin cups. Bake at 375° for 25 minutes.

1 egg
1 stick butter, softened
1 cup bran
2 cups buttermilk
1 cup bran cereal
½ cup packed brown sugar
1 cup all-purpose flour
½ teaspoon salt
2 teaspoons baking soda
½-1 cup chopped dates

**Yield: 12 muffins**

# English Muffin Loaves

*...this bread makes a wonderful house-warming, hostess, or even Christmas present when accompanied with jellies, jams, and specialty coffees or teas*

Combine 3 cups flour, yeast, sugar, salt, and baking soda. Heat milk and water together to 120° to 130°. Pour into dry ingredients and beat well. Stir in remaining 3 cups flour. Grease two 8½X4½ inch pans and sprinkle with cornmeal. Spoon batter into pans. Cover and let rise in a warm place for 45 minutes. Bake at 400° for 25 minutes. Remove from pans immediately and cool.

6 cups all-purpose flour, divided
2 (¼-ounce) packages active dry yeast
1 tablespoon sugar
2 teaspoons salt
1 teaspoon baking soda
2 cups milk
½ cup water
cornmeal

**Yield: 2 loaves**

# Sweet Potato Muffins

*...turn out as soon as they are baked and serve piping hot*

¾ cup all-purpose flour
2 teaspoons baking powder
½ teaspoon salt
½ teaspoon cinnamon
½ teaspoon nutmeg
4 tablespoons butter
½ cup sugar
⅔ cup puréed cooked or canned sweet potatoes
1 egg
½ cup milk
¼ cup chopped pecans or walnuts
¼ cup chopped raisins
cinnamon sugar for topping (optional)

**Yield: 30 muffins**

Sift together flour, baking powder, salt, cinnamon, and nutmeg. Cream butter and sugar together. Beat in sweet potatoes and egg. Alternately, mixing by hand, add dry ingredients with the milk and the nuts and raisins. Mix just until blended. Spoon into buttered muffin cups, filling each completely full. Sprinkle with cinnamon sugar. Bake at 400° for 25 minutes.

# Zucchini Bread Or Muffins

*...serve a variety of muffins with crocks of sweet butter in an antique basket lined with a red and white-checked cloth*

Beat together eggs, sugar, vanilla, and oil. Add zucchini. Sift together flour, cinnamon, baking powder, and baking soda. Stir dry ingredients into zucchini mixture. Mix until well blended. Add walnuts and dates. Pour into a buttered 9X5X3 inch loaf pan or buttered muffin cups. Bake loaf at 350° for 30 minutes. Bake muffins at 350° for a shorter length of time.

2 eggs
1 cup sugar
1 teaspoon vanilla
½ cup vegetable oil
1½ cups grated zucchini
1½ cups all-purpose flour
1 teaspoon cinnamon
½ teaspoon baking powder
½ teaspoon baking soda
½ cup chopped walnuts
½ cup chopped dates

**Yield: 1 loaf or 10 muffins**

# Popovers

*...Bob Green's blender popover makes a great Yorkshire Pudding - substitute 3 tablespoons of roast beef pan drippings for the butter and pour into a 10-inch pie pan or a 9X13 inch baking dish. Bake at 425° for 20 to 25 minutes or until puffed and golden brown*

Beat eggs lightly in a blender. Add butter and milk. With machine running, slowly add flour and salt. Pour batter into 5 buttered glass cups, filling each about half full. Bake at 400° for 60 minutes. *or 'til brown on top*

3 eggs
3 tablespoons butter, melted
1 cup milk
1 cup all-purpose flour
½ teaspoon salt

**Yield: 5 servings**

# Oma's Dinner Rolls

*...a recipe adaptable to all sorts of variations, such as dried herbs, wheat germ, oat bran, or cinnamon*

1 (.06-ounce) yeast
   cake
2 tablespoons plus 1
   teaspoon sugar,
   divided
¼ cup warm water
1 cup milk
2 tablespoons butter
½ teaspoon salt
4 cups all-purpose flour
2 eggs, lightly beaten
melted butter
egg white, lightly beaten,
   salt, and caraway
   seed for topping

**Yield: 32 rolls**

Dissolve yeast cake and 1 teaspoon sugar in warm water. Cover and set aside. Warm milk until bubbles form. Add butter and salt. In a large bowl, combine flour and remaining 2 tablespoons sugar. Stir in egg and yeast mixture. Add milk, a little at a time, mixing well with each addition. Knead 10 minutes or until dough no longer clings to hands. Grease surface of dough and place in a bowl. Cover and let rise until doubled in bulk. Punch down and divide dough into 4 equal portions. Flatten each section into a 12-inch circle. Cut each circle into 8 wedges. Brush with melted butter. Starting with the wide end, roll each wedge toward the point. Place on a buttered baking sheet, point-side down, 2 to 3 inches apart. Brush with egg white and sprinkle with salt or caraway seed or both. Place in a 400° oven. Immediately reduce heat to 325° and bake 12 to 15 minutes or until golden brown.

# Cinnamon Crunch Coffeecake

*...what a wonderful way to start your day*

Combine flour, sugar, baking powder, and salt in a large mixing bowl. Add oil and milk and beat 1½ minutes. Add eggs and beat another 1½ minutes. Pour batter into a buttered 9X13 inch baking dish. To prepare topping, mix together ingredients. Sprinkle two-thirds of mixture over batter. Push the back of a spoon into batter at 12 to 15 places. Sprinkle with remaining topping. Bake at 375° for 30 to 40 minutes.

**batter**
2 cups all-purpose flour
¾ cup sugar
1 tablespoon baking powder
½ teaspoon salt
½ cup vegetable oil
1 cup milk
2 eggs

**topping**
⅔ cup packed brown sugar
2 teaspoons vegetable oil
1 teaspoon cinnamon
1 cup chopped nuts
2 teaspoons all-purpose flour

**Yield: 10 to 12 servings**

# Hot Spiced Tea

*...there is no better accompaniment to relaxation and reminiscence on a cold winter afternoon*

12 cups water
1 teaspoon whole cloves
1 cinnamon stick
1½ cups orange juice
⅓ cup lemon juice
1 cup sugar
2 bags tea *( lge bags)*
1 orange, sliced
1 lemon, sliced

**Yield: 3½ quarts**

Combine water, cloves, cinnamon, juices, and sugar in a large pot. Bring to a boil. Add tea bags and simmer 3 minutes. Remove cloves, cinnamon stick, and tea bags. Float orange and lemon slices on top. Serve hot or cold.

# Hot Mulled Punch

*...a percolator punch*

8 cups unsweetened pineapple juice
8 cups cranberry juice cocktail
3¾ cups water
½-1 cup packed brown sugar
6 cinnamon sticks, broken
3 tablespoons orange-flavored tea, or 3 bags
3-4 teaspoons whole cloves
¾ teaspoon salt

**Yield: 5 quarts**

Place pineapple juice, cranberry juice cocktail, water, and sugar in the bottom of a 30-cup percolator. Combine cinnamon sticks and remaining ingredients in the percolator's basket. Brew and serve hot.

*For a different flavor, substitute 4 cups of apricot juice for 4 cups of cranberry juice cocktail.*

# Hot Buttered Rum

*...great on hot cereal, without the rum!*

Combine butter, sugar, cinnamon, ginger, nutmeg, and cloves in a saucepan. Heat and stir until melted. Transfer to a storage container and chill. When ready to use, place a heaping tablespoon of mixture and a jigger of rum in a mug. Fill mug with boiling water and serve.

4 sticks butter
1 (16-ounce) package brown sugar
1½ teaspoons cinnamon
½ teaspoon ground ginger
dash of nutmeg
dash of ground cloves
rum

**Yield: about 1½ cups**

# Don's Best Morning Drink

*...better than a Bloody Mary and it improves with age*

Mix all ingredients in a plastic jug. Refrigerate until ready to serve.

9 cups tomato juice (not V-8)
1 scant cup ketchup
4 cups vodka
1¼ cups lemon juice
1¼ cups Worcestershire sauce
splash of Tabasco sauce

**Yield: 1 gallon....after tasting!**

"First in booze, first in shoes and last in the American league" ...The St. Louis Browns

# Ramos Gin Fizz

*...with a delicate hint of orange, it's a great brunch drink*

¾ cup gin
ice cubes
  6 tablespoons fresh
    lemon juice
  4 teaspoons powdered
    sugar
  4 teaspoons granulated
    sugar
  2 egg whites
  1 cup half-and-half
  1 tablespoon orange-
    flower water or
    orange juice
    concentrate

**Yield: 4 servings**

Combine gin and ice cubes in a blender. Process briefly on high. Add remaining ingredients and blend.

Serve in wine glasses with an orange twist.

# Whiskey Smash

*...long white dresses, parasols, and croquet on the lawn*

  1 (12-ounce) can
    frozen lemonade
    concentrate
  1 (6-ounce) can frozen
    orange juice
    concentrate
  6 cups water
  2 cups brewed tea
  1 cup sugar
1½ cups bourbon
club soda or lemon-lime
    carbonated drink

**Yield: 3 quarts**

Combine lemonade, juice, water, tea, sugar, and bourbon in order listed. Freeze. To serve, add a scoop of slush to a glass. Fill glass with club soda and mix.

# Southside

*...a minty Tom Collins*

Combine sugar syrup, lemon juice, gin, and mint in a tall ice-filled glass. Fill glass with club soda. Stir and serve immediately.

1 tablespoon sugar syrup
juice of 1 medium lemon
2 jiggers gin, vodka, or rum
1 tablespoon chopped fresh mint
club soda or lemon-lime carbonated drink

**Yield: 1 serving**

# Champagne Sangría

*...bubbles and some fruit are great for the summer, especially when they're together*

Combine Triple Sec, Calvados, and sugar in a large pitcher. Stir until sugar dissolves. Add fruit and let stand 5 minutes. Mix in champagne. Add ice cubes and serve.

*If desired, use blueberries or raspberries in place of strawberries.*

2 tablespoons Triple Sec
3 tablespoons Calvados
¼ cup sugar
1 cup seedless white grapes
4 slices orange
1 small green apple, peeled and cut in wedges
8 strawberries
1 (25-ounce) bottle dry champagne, chilled

**Yield: 1 quart**

The Tyrolean Alps, operated by Tony Faust and August Luchow served an 1893 vintage Louis Roederer Brut Champagne at $6 a quart.

# Margarita

*...3-2-1, the bartender's secret to a great margarita*

3 parts
limeade/lemonade
mix
2 parts tequila
1 part Triple Sec
margarita salt (optional)
lime slices for garnish

Combine limeade/lemonade mix, tequila, and Triple Sec. Chill. Dip moistened rim of margarita glasses in salt. Serve mixture in glasses straight up or on the rocks. Garnish.

# Bernie's Rum Punch

*...originated in Captiva and perfected in Boca Grande*

4 cups fresh orange
juice
3 (6-ounce) cans frozen
pineapple juice
concentrate, thawed
1 (46-ounce) can fruit
punch
2 cups dark rum
2 cups light rum
¾ cup coconut rum
liqueur
1 tablespoon nutmeg
1 (12-ounce) can
lemon-lime
carbonated drink

Mix all ingredients in a large plastic container and chill.

Serve over ice cubes with an orange slice or wedge for garnish.

**Yield: 2½ quarts**

# Mai Tai

*...simply wonderful*

Combine, garnish, and serve!

2 cups light rum
2 cups dark rum
1 cup curaçao
1 cup orgeat syrup
juice of 8 lemons
juice of 4 limes
1 cup sugar syrup
    (optional)
sprigs of mint and spears
    of fresh pineapple for
    garnish

**Yield: 6 servings**

# Christmas Nog

*...apricot brandy makes this the quintessential holiday treat*

Mix all ingredients in a blender and serve.

4 eggs
¼ cup heavy cream
2 cups milk
¼ cup sugar
¼ teaspoon vanilla
¼ cup apricot brandy
1¼ cups rum

**Yield: 4 servings**

# Racquet Club Eggnog

*...a holiday tradition at The Racquet Club, eggnog is available for harried shoppers seeking holiday cheer and a respite from the bustling crowd*

12 egg yolks
2 cups powdered sugar
2 quarts milk
2 cups cream
½ cup Jamaican rum
4 cups bourbon

**Yield: 1 gallon**

Beat egg yolks and sugar together thoroughly. Blend in remaining ingredients separately, beating well after each addition.

*For extra flavor and richness, add 1 cup brandy and ½ gallon eggnog-flavored ice cream.*

# Iced Mint Tea

*...mint, from the Latin "mentha" - however, Greek mythology has it that Mintha was rather unkindly turned into a mint plant by the jealous goddess, Prosperina*

4 cups boiling water
6 tea bags
½ cup sugar
6 sprigs mint, plus
   extra for garnish
zest of 2 lemons
juice of 2 lemons
lemon wedges or slices
   for garnish

**Yield: 4 cups**

Combine boiling water, tea bags, sugar, mint, and zest. Remove from heat and allow to steep. Strain liquid. Add lemon juice to liquid and chill. When ready to serve, add cold water to taste. Garnish.

# Italian Summer Dinner

*Prosciutto with Melon   Volpi's Salami      Blue Cheese Twists*
*Black Olives              Bruschetta with Tomatoes*

*Risotto with Lobster & Shrimp with Freshly Grated Parmesan*
*Avignonesi Chardonnay*

*Charbroiled Steak with Grilled Vegetables*
*Garlic Olive Bread Wreath*
*Fontodi Chianti Classico Riserva*

*Cantaloupe Sherbet with Fresh Blueberries*

*\*for a winter Italian dinner serve Minestrone instead of risotto and Tiramisu for the sherbet*

# Whole-wheat Spaghetti With Goat Cheese And Arugula

*...a subtle blend of colors and tastes with the arugula giving the pasta a nice "bite"*

In a large skillet, sauté onions, garlic, salt, and pepper in oil over moderate heat, stirring until onions are golden. Remove from heat and keep warm. In boiling salted water, cook spaghetti al dente. Drain well, reserving ¼ cup of liquid. In a serving bowl, whisk together Montrachet cheese and reserved liquid until cheese melts and mixture is smooth. Add spaghetti, onion mixture, arugula, walnuts, Parmesan cheese, and basil. Season with salt and pepper to taste and garnish.

3 red onions, thinly sliced
6 cloves garlic, slivered
salt and pepper
3 tablespoons olive oil
8 ounces whole wheat spaghetti
6 ounces Montrachet cheese, or other soft, mild goat cheese
1 pound arugula, stems discarded and leaves chopped
½ cup chopped walnuts, lightly toasted
⅓ cup Parmesan cheese
½ cup finely shredded fresh basil
diced red onion for garnish

**Yield: 4 servings**

# Pasta With Roasted Tomato, Asparagus, and Shrimp

*...legend has it that Marco Polo brought pasta to Italy from China*

12 plum tomatoes, quartered lengthwise
4 teaspoons olive oil, divided
black pepper to taste
1 small head garlic
1 pound asparagus, cut in 2-inch lengths
1 pound large shrimp, peeled and deveined
12 ounces fusille, cooked al dente
salt to taste
2 tablespoons lemon juice
1 tablespoon fresh oregano, or 1 teaspoon dried
1 tablespoon fresh thyme, or 1 teaspoon dried

**Yield: 2 to 4 servings**

In a large roasting pan, toss tomatoes with 2 teaspoons oil and pepper. Slice top ½-inch off garlic head and discard loose papery skin. Wrap bottom of garlic head in aluminum foil. Place garlic and roasting pan in lower third of a 450° oven. Bake, without stirring, 20 minutes or until tomatoes are wrinkled and beginning to brown. Scatter asparagus and shrimp over tomatoes and roast 10 minutes or until shrimp are curled. Remove roasting pan from oven and cover. Remove garlic from oven, separate cloves, and squeeze out pulp. Mash garlic to a paste. Drain pasta and return to pot. Add remaining 2 teaspoons oil, garlic, pepper, salt, lemon juice, oregano, and thyme. Toss to coat. Transfer pasta mixture to roasting pan and toss.

# Spaghetti Alla Puttanesca

*...popular as a way to attract their clients with the enticing aroma of this flavorful and gutsy dish or as a quickly prepared dish between clients!*

Heat oil in a large skillet. Quickly add capers, parsley, red pepper flakes, garlic, and oregano. Sauté over low heat about 1 minute without browning. Add anchovies and olives and continue to sauté. Add tomatoes and cook and stir over medium heat until sauce thickens. Season with salt and pepper. Toss with hot, drained spaghetti.

3 tablespoons olive oil
2 teaspoons small capers, rinsed
1 tablespoon chopped Italian parsley
1 teaspoon crushed red pepper flakes, or to taste
2 cloves garlic, minced
½ teaspoon dried oregano
1 (2-ounce) can flat anchovies, drained and diced
¼ cup chopped salt-cured black olives
1 (28-ounce) can Italian-style tomatoes, undrained
salt and pepper to taste
1 pound spaghetti, cooked al dente

**Yield: 4 servings**

# Linguine With Scallops

*...an intense, but delicate seafood flavor*

1 teaspoon butter
1 teaspoon olive oil
1 pound fresh or
   frozen scallops
1½ cups chicken broth
¾ cup dry vermouth
3 tablespoons lemon
   juice
¾ cup sliced scallions
¾ cup chopped fresh
   parsley
2 tablespoons capers,
   drained
1 tablespoon chopped
   fresh dill, or 1
   teaspoon dried
¼ teaspoon black
   pepper
12 ounces linguine,
   cooked al dente

**Yield: 6 servings**

Heat butter and oil in a skillet. Add scallops and sauté 3 to 5 minutes or until opaque. Remove from skillet. Add broth, vermouth, and lemon juice to skillet. Bring to a boil and cook 10 to 12 minutes or until reduced to about 1 cup. Stir in scallions, parsley, capers, dill, and pepper. Reduce heat and simmer about 1 minute. Add scallops and cook until heated through. Toss in linguine and serve.

# Pasta With Sun-dried Tomato Pesto

*...consider using this sun-dried tomato pesto on other dishes calling for traditional pesto*

Place tomatoes in a deep bowl. Cover with boiling water and let stand 10 minutes. Drain, reserving liquid. Place tomatoes, ¼ cup of reserved liquid, olives, pine nuts, oil, garlic, lemon juice, and cilantro in a blender or food processor. Blend on low speed until coarsely ground. Add extra lemon juice or tomato liquid if pesto is too thick. Place hot, drained fusille in a warm serving dish. Add pesto and toss. Serve immediately.

Optional garnishes for this dish include sliced black olives, Parmesan cheese, chopped red or yellow bell peppers, and crumbled feta cheese.

If using oil-packed sun-dried tomatoes, let drain, but do not reserve ¼ cup oil.

- 1½ cups sun-dried tomatoes
- ½ cup pitted black olives, preferably kalamata olives
- 1 cup pine nuts, toasted
- ¾ cup extra virgin olive oil
- 2 cloves garlic
- 2 tablespoons fresh lemon juice
- 2 bunches cilantro, stems removed
- 1 pound fusille, cooked al dente

**Yield: 4 or 5 servings**

# Conchiglie Al Forno With Mushrooms And Radicchio

*...so named for its conch-shaped pasta*

6 ounces shiitake
    mushrooms, stems
    removed
1 stick unsalted butter,
    divided
1 pound imported
    conchiglie rigate
    (ridged pasta shells)
1 tablespoon olive oil
    (optional)
2½ cups heavy cream
2 small heads radicchio,
    finely shredded
½ cup freshly grated
    Parmesan cheese
½ cup grated Bel Paese
    cheese
½ cup crumbled
    Gorgonzola cheese
coarse salt to taste
6 fresh sage leaves,
    chopped (optional)

**Yield: 6 entrée
    servings, or 10
    appetizer servings**

Slice mushroom caps ¼-inch thick. Heat 6 tablespoons butter in a skillet over medium heat. Add mushrooms and cook, stirring frequently, 3 to 4 minutes or until softened. Add pasta and oil to a large pot of boiling salted water. Cook 5 minutes. Drain, cool under running cold water, and drain again. Combine mushrooms, cream, radicchio, and cheeses in a large bowl. Add pasta and toss. Stir in salt and sage. Place mixture in a buttered 9X13-inch baking dish. Dot with remaining 2 tablespoons butter. Bake at 450° for 30 to 35 minutes or until bubbly and crusty brown on top. Remove from oven and let stand 5 minutes before serving.

# Pasta With Tomatoes, Brie, And Basil

*...a raw tomato sauce using the summer's best, combined with Brie or mozza-rella cheese and fresh basil*

Combine tomatoes, ½ cup oil, Brie cheese, basil, and garlic in a large serving bowl. Season with salt and pepper. Let stand at room temperature for at least 2 hours. Cook pasta in water with remaining 1 tablespoon oil for 8 to 10 minutes or until tender but firm. Drain and immediately toss with tomato sauce. Serve with Parmesan cheese and a pepper mill.

*In a pinch, substitute pesto sauce for fresh basil.*

4 large ripe tomatoes, cut into ½-inch cubes
½ cup plus 1 tablespoon olive oil, divided
1 pound Brie cheese, rind removed and cut in irregular pieces
1 cup julienned fresh basil
3 cloves garlic, minced
salt and pepper to taste
1½ pounds linguine, spaghetti, or other pasta
Parmesan cheese

**Yield: 4 to 6 servings**

# Penne Smoked Salmon

*...wonderful first course for a beef tenderloin dinner*

4 tablespoons butter
1 teaspoon dried dill
1 teaspoon powdered chicken base
dash of black pepper
2 teaspoons chopped onion
2 tablespoons vodka
¼ cup julienned smoked salmon
2 tablespoons green peas
6 tablespoons cream
2 tablespoons tomato sauce
2 tablespoons Parmesan cheese
8 ounces penne, cooked al dente

**Yield: 2 servings**

Combine butter, dill, chicken base, pepper, and onion in a skillet. Cook 2 to 3 minutes or until onion caramelizes. Stir in vodka, salmon, peas, cream, and tomato sauce. Bring to a boil. Remove from heat and add cheese. Toss with hot, drained pasta. Serve immediately.

# Clam Lasagna

*...seaside twist on the regular lasagna*

Sauté clams and garlic in butter and oil until browned. Stir in tomatoes. Add basil, oregano, salt, and pepper. Heat to a simmer. In a separate bowl, combine eggs, Parmesan cheese, ricotta cheese, and parsley. Season to taste. Assemble lasagna in a buttered 9X13 inch baking dish. Layer ½ of noodles, ½ of clam mixture, all of ricotta mixture, and ½ of mozzarella. Repeat layers (except for ricotta mixture). Bake at 350° for 45 to 60 minutes or until mozzarella is golden brown and lasagna is heated through. Remove from oven and let stand 10 to 15 minutes before serving.

4 (10-ounce) cans clams, drained
4 cloves garlic, minced
4 tablespoons butter
¼ cup olive oil
48 ounces canned tomatoes, drained
1 teaspoon dried basil
1 teaspoon dried oregano
salt and pepper to taste
2 eggs, lightly beaten
¾ cup Parmesan cheese
2 cups ricotta cheese
½ cup chopped fresh parsley
10 lasagna noodles, cooked al dente
1 pound mozzarella, sliced

**Yield: 8 to 10 servings**

# Risotto Milanese

*...from the Biffi Scala restaurant in Milan, is bright yellow with an abundance of cheese and butter*

5 cups chicken or beef broth
4½ tablespoons butter, divided
½ medium onion, finely chopped
1 cup Arborio rice
1 teaspoon powdered saffron
½ cup white wine
3 tablespoons heavy cream
½ cup freshly grated Parmesan cheese, or to taste

**Yield: 2 to 4 servings**

Bring broth to a steady simmer in a saucepan. Heat 3 tablespoons butter in a heavy 4-quart saucepan over medium heat. Add onion and sauté 1 to 2 minutes or until softened, but not brown. Mix in rice and saffron, stirring with a wooden spoon for 1 minute to coat all grains well. Add wine and stir until absorbed. Add broth, ½ cup at a time, allowing each addition to be completely absorbed before adding more broth. Reserve ¼ cup of broth to add at the end. Stir frequently to prevent sticking. Keep the risotto at an even boil to ensure proper rate of evaporation of the broth. After about 18 minutes, when rice is tender but still firm, add the reserved broth, remaining 1½ tablespoons butter, cream, and cheese. Stir vigorously and serve immediately on preheated plates.

*Fold in cooked chicken livers just before serving.*

# Risotto With Lobster And Shrimp

*...picture a cafe overlooking The Grand Canal with Peggy Guggenheim wearing her pigeon-shaped, diamond-covered sunglasses - a sight few Venetians can forget!*

Sauté shrimp and lobster in 1 tablespoon oil and 3 tablespoons butter for 2 minutes. Add wine and cook 2 minutes. Coarsely chop tomatoes in a food processor, season with salt and pepper, and simmer 3 minutes in a small saucepan. Bring broth to a steady simmer in a saucepan. Heat remaining 1 tablespoon oil and 3 tablespoons butter in a heavy 4-quart saucepan over medium heat. Mix in rice, stirring with a wooden spoon for 1 minute to coat all grains well. Add broth, ½ cup at a time, allowing each addition to be completely absorbed before adding more broth. After the first cup of broth has been incorporated, add ¾ cup of tomato mixture. Reserve ¼ cup of broth to add at the end. Stir frequently to prevent sticking. Keep the risotto at an even boil to ensure proper rate of evaporation of the broth. After about 18 minutes, when rice is tender but still firm, add the reserved broth. Season and place rice in a buttered ring mold. Let sit for 2 minutes. Meanwhile, reheat shrimp and lobster. Unmold rice onto a large, preheated serving platter. Pour ¾ cup of tomato mixture over top and fill center with seafood. Serve immediately.

2 pounds medium shrimp, peeled and deveined
¼ pound cooked lobster meat
2 tablespoons olive oil, divided
6 tablespoons butter. divided
½ cup dry white wine
1 pound fresh tomatoes, or 1 (16-ounce) can plum tomatoes, drained
salt and pepper to taste
4 cups chicken broth, or more if needed
2 cups Arborio rice

**Yield: 6 servings**

# Risotto With Fresh Peas

*...one of Venice's signature dishes, "Risi e bisi" vegetable stock is made from simmering the pea pods*

2 pounds fresh peas

7 tablespoons butter, divided

2 tablespoons olive oil

4 ounces pancetta or smoked ham, diced

1 stalk celery, finely chopped

10 sprigs Italian parsley, finely chopped

½ cup dry white wine

salt and pepper to taste

3 cups beef broth

3 cups vegetable or chicken broth

2 cups Arborio rice

¼ cup freshly grated Parmesan cheese

**Yield: 4 servings**

Shell peas. Heat 4 tablespoons butter and oil in a saucepan. Add pancetta and sauté 5 minutes. Add celery and parsley and sauté 5 minutes longer. Add peas and cook 5 minutes. Stir in wine, salt, and pepper. Cover and cook over low heat for 20 minutes. Remove from heat and set aside. Combine broths in a saucepan and bring to a steady simmer. Heat 2 tablespoons butter in a heavy 4-quart saucepan over medium heat. Mix in rice, stirring with a wooden spoon for 1 minute to coat all grains well. Add broth, ½ cup at a time, allowing each addition to be completely absorbed before adding more broth. Reserve ¼ cup of broth to add at the end. Stir frequently to prevent sticking. Keep the risotto at an even boil to ensure proper rate of evaporation of the broth. After about 18 minutes, when rice is tender but still firm, add the reserved broth and pea mixture. Remove from heat when broth is absorbed. Add remaining 1 tablespoon butter and cheese and serve immediately.

To make a vegetable broth, simmer empty pea pods in 4 cups salted water.

# Black Beans And Rice

*...beans eaten with rice form a complete protein equal to meat - and obviously lower in fat!*

Soak beans in 4 cups of water overnight, or boil 2 minutes and let soak 1 to 2 hours. Drain beans, rinse, and drain. Place in a Dutch oven and add remaining 3 cups water. Bring to a boil. Reduce heat and simmer 2 to 3 hours or until beans are falling apart. Remove half of the beans, mash, and return to Dutch oven. Sauté onion and pepper in oil. Add to beans. Brown sausage, drain, and add with tomatoes and seasonings and stir. Serve over hot rice with Tabasco sauce.

*This dish is equally good without sausage.*

½ pound dry black beans, rinsed and drained
7 cups water, divided
1 medium onion, chopped
1 medium green bell pepper, chopped
olive oil for sautéing
½ pound hot sausage
1 (28-ounce) can tomatoes, drained and chopped
½ teaspoon salt
½ teaspoon black pepper
6-8 cups cooked rice

**Yield: 6 to 8 servings**

# Basmati Rice With Cilantro And Mint

*...one of the most interesting tastes, combining the aromatic mint with the sharp flavor of the coriander*

½ pound basmati rice, washed

½ teaspoon saffron threads

4 ounces ghee (clarified butter) or 2 tablespoon oil

1 (2-inch) cinnamon stick

4 whole cloves

1 (3-inch) piece fresh ginger, peeled and finely chopped

1 cup yogurt

1 medium onion, chopped

2 tablespoons chopped fresh cilantro

2 tablespoons chopped fresh mint

2 teaspoons salt

2 teaspoons black pepper

**Yield: 4 servings**

Place rice in a heavy saucepan and cover with water. Bring to a boil and add saffron. Boil rapidly for 10 minutes. Remove from heat and drain. Heat ghee in a large saucepan until it begins to smoke. Reduce heat and add cinnamon and cloves. Cook about 1 minute. Stir in ginger. Add rice and stir well to coat. Mix in yogurt. Add onion, cilantro, mint, salt, and pepper and cover tightly. Increase heat, shaking pan constantly. Serve when all liquid is absorbed and rice is tender.

# Green and Red Rice

*...in Java, no girl would be considered for marriage unless she could cook a good bowl of rice*

Melt butter in a saucepan. Add rice and sage. Cook until golden brown, stirring occasionally. Add broth and water. Bring to a boil and cover. Reduce heat and simmer 15 minutes. Add peas and simmer 10 minutes. Stir in pimiento.

4 tablespoons butter
1 cup uncooked rice
¼ teaspoon sage
2 (10¾-ounce) cans chicken broth
1 cup water
1 (10-ounce) package frozen peas
¼ cup diced pimiento

**Yield: 6 servings**

# White And Wild Rice Casserole

*...at least one Native American tribe got their tribal name - Menominee - from the Indian word for wild rice, Menomin*

Place wild rice in a saucepan and cover with 2 inches of water. Bring to a boil. Reduce heat and simmer 20 minutes. Drain and set aside. In a large skillet, melt butter. Add onion and celery and sauté until translucent but not brown. Add white rice and sauté 2 to 3 minutes. Stir in wild rice. Transfer to a 2½-quart casserole dish and cover. If desired, refrigerate several hours or overnight. When ready to bake, combine broth, soy sauce, and wine in a saucepan. Bring to a boil. Pour over rice. Bake, covered, at 350° for 60 minutes or until liquid is absorbed.

1 cup wild rice
2 tablespoons butter
1 large onion, chopped
1 large stalk celery, chopped
1 cup long-grain white rice
2 (14-ounce) cans chicken broth
2 tablespoons soy sauce
¼ cup dry white wine

**Yield: 8 servings**

# Wild Rice Pancakes

*...particularly good with any meat or poultry that has a fruit sauce, such as Fruit-Stuffed Pork Loin*

1 cup water
½ cup wild rice
2 cloves garlic, minced, divided
2 tablespoons grated onion
1 cup chopped mushrooms
¼ cup chopped fresh parsley
oil for sautéing
1 cup all-purpose flour
2 teaspoons baking powder
1 teaspoon salt
½ teaspoon white pepper
¼ teaspoon dry mustard
1¼ cup milk
3 eggs, lightly beaten
4 tablespoons butter

**Yield: twenty (3-inch) pancakes**

Bring water to a boil. Add rice, reduce heat to a simmer, cover, and cook 30 to 45 minutes. Drain. Sauté 1 clove garlic, onion, mushrooms, and parsley in oil. In a separate bowl, combine flour, baking powder, salt, pepper, and mustard. Blend in sautéed vegetables, remaining 1 clove garlic, milk, and eggs. Mixture should be a little thicker than a crêpe batter. Stir in rice. Use butter to cook pancakes in a hot skillet.

Serve pancakes topped with honey mustard sauce, applesauce, or sour cream.

# Rice Pilaf

*...serve with Lamb With Dill - it's the best!*

Melt butter over medium-low heat in a heavy pot with a tight-fitting lid. Add noodles and sauté 4 minutes or until lightly browned, being careful not to burn them. Stir in rice and cook until grains lose their translucent quality. Add salt and broth, being careful of steam. Mix well and bring to a boil. Reduce heat to low and cover. Cook 20 minutes.

4 tablespoons butter
½ cup fine egg noodles
1½ cups long-grain rice
2 teaspoons salt
3 cups chicken broth

**Yield: 6 servings**

# Gorgonzola And Pear Millet Pilaf

*...serve with Jerk Chicken*

In a heavy saucepan, melt butter over medium-high heat. Add millet and sauté until golden brown. Stir in water, salt, and paprika. Simmer, covered, 18 to 20 minutes or until millet is tender and water is absorbed. Transfer to a bowl and fluff with a fork. In a separate bowl, combine pear and lemon juice. When millet has cooled slightly, add pear, cheese, almonds, and pepper. Toss gently.

1 tablespoon butter
1 cup millet
2 cups water
1 teaspoon salt
½ teaspoon paprika
2 (6-ounce) pears, diced
1 tablespoon fresh lemon juice
½ cup crumbled Gorgonzola cheese
½ cup sliced almonds, toasted
black pepper to taste

**Yield: 8 servings**

# Basil Couscous With Summer Squash

*...a soft, subtle alternative to potatoes, rice, or pasta*

¾ cup water
1 tablespoon olive oil
¾ teaspoon salt
1 cup julienned fresh basil
½ cup couscous
1 cup diced zucchini
1 cup diced yellow squash

**Yield: 4 servings**

In a small saucepan, bring water and oil to a boil. Add salt and basil. Simmer 30 seconds or until basil wilts. Stir in couscous. Cover, remove from heat, and let stand 5 minutes. Steam zucchini and squash for 3 minutes or until tender. Transfer to a bowl and stir in couscous.

# Herbed Couscous With Lemon

*...couscous is known as "Moroccan pasta" and is as versatile*

1½ cups water
½ teaspoon lemon zest
¾ teaspoon dried thyme
1 cup couscous
salt and pepper to taste
½ cup minced fresh parsley
2 tablespoons olive oil
fresh lemon juice to taste

**Yield: 4 servings**

Bring water to a boil. Stir in zest, thyme, and couscous. Cover, remove from heat, and let stand 5 minutes. Fluff couscous and stir in salt, pepper, parsley, oil, and lemon juice.

# Garbanzo Croquettes

*...croquettes are traditionally cone-shaped forms of ground meat - this is the vegetarian alternative*

Soak wheat in water for 20 minutes. Drain and press out excess moisture. Purée garbanzo beans in a food processor. Transfer to a mixing bowl and stir in lemon juice, cilantro, pepper flakes, cumin, and salt. Melt butter in a saucepan. Stir in cinnamon, garlic, and flour until smooth. Add broth and stir. Add broth mixture and wheat to beans. Mix in 1 cup breadcrumbs. Stir and adjust seasoning as needed. Chill 2 hours. Form into 1½ to 2-inch round balls. Dredge balls in flour, then dip in egg and remaining breadcrumbs. Deep-fry in 350° oil until crisp and brown. Serve on a bed of sautéed spinach with salsa and sour cream.

⅓ cup dried bulghur wheat
⅔ cup water
2 cups cooked garbanzo beans
¼ cup fresh lemon juice
3 tablespoons chopped fresh cilantro or parsley
½ teaspoon crushed red pepper flakes
½ teaspoon ground cumin
1 teaspoon salt
3 tablespoons butter
⅛ teaspoon cinnamon
1½ teaspoons minced fresh garlic
3 tablespoons all-purpose flour, plus extra for dredging
¾ cup hot vegetable broth
2 cups dry breadcrumbs, divided
2 eggs, lightly beaten
vegetable oil for frying

**Yield: 16 croquettes, 4 servings**

# Creamy Polenta With Grilled Vegetables

*...served on its own plate and topped with grilled vegetables and Tomato Coulis*

4 cups chicken broth
2 cups polenta
2 cups water
1½ teaspoons salt
½ cup Parmesan cheese
2 tablespoons unsalted butter
salt and pepper to taste
12 baby carrots, blanched 2 minutes, drained, and patted dry
18 scallions, trimmed
12 baby eggplants, halved lengthwise
olive oil and fresh herbs for grilling vegetables: rosemary, chervil, thyme, etc.

**Yield: 6 servings**

Bring broth to a rapid boil over high heat. Combine polenta, water, and salt and stir until smooth. Slowly add to boiling broth, stirring constantly. Cook and stir until polenta is still thin and will fall from a spoon in a continuous stream. Stir in cheese, butter, salt, and pepper. Remove from heat, cover surface with wax paper, and keep warm. Brush carrots, scallions, and eggplant with oil and herbs. Season with salt and pepper. Grill vegetables in batches over medium-high heat on a well-oiled grill or in a hot, oiled heavy skillet for 5 to 7 minutes or until crisp-tender. Transfer vegetables to a plate when done. Divide polenta among 6 warm plates and arrange vegetables in a fan design on top.

If using large eggplants, slice and salt them. Let them sit 20 to 30 minutes, drain and pat dry.

# Sissy's Tomato Coulis

*...when the tomato season hits, a good, simple tomato sauce recipe is invaluable*

Melt 2 tablespoons butter in a skillet over low heat. Add onion, mushrooms, shallots, leek, and salt. Sauté 7 minutes or until vegetables soften. Add brandy and 4 tablespoons Madeira. Increase heat to high and light alcohol with a match. Cook until liquid reduces by half. Add broth, tomatoes, thyme, and bay leaf. Reduce heat to low and simmer, uncovered, 20 minutes. Purée mixture and strain. Return puréed mixture to pan over medium heat. Break remaining tablespoon of butter into small pieces. Whip butter and remaining tablespoon of Madeira into puréed mixture. Season with salt and pepper.

Serve with grilled polenta or as a pasta sauce. Store sauce up to 1 week in the refrigerator.

3 tablespoons unsalted butter, divided
½ small onion, thinly sliced
3 mushrooms, thinly sliced
2 shallots, thinly sliced
1 small leek, white part only, thinly sliced
¼ teaspoon salt
1 tablespoon brandy
5 tablespoons Madeira, divided
1 cup chicken broth
3 ripe tomatoes, chopped with skins
2 sprigs fresh thyme
1 bay leaf
black pepper to taste

**Yield: 2 cups**

# Creamy Morel Sauce For Polenta Terrines

*...cook the polenta until firm and "mold" in buttered ovenproof ramekins - the sauce alone can enhance any meal either over wild rice or veal scallops*

8 ounces fresh morel mushrooms, or reconstituted dried
1 tablespoon butter
2 tablespoons minced shallots
1 cup sherry or Madeira
freshly squeezed lemon juice
1½ cups chicken broth
1 cup crème fraîche
salt and pepper to taste
12 green peppercorns
4 tablespoons chopped chervil leaves
2 tablespoons snipped fresh chives
6 (6-ounce) terrines of firm cooled polenta, heated

**Yield: 6 servings**

Cut large morels into smaller pieces. Melt butter in a saucepan and gently sauté morels 3 minutes or until soft, but not brown. Add shallots and cook another minute. Add sherry and a few drops of lemon juice. Cook over high heat until liquid is reduced by half. Add broth and reduce by half. Add crème fraîche and reduce until sauce coats the back of a spoon. Season with salt, pepper, and peppercorns. Stir in chervil and chives. Correct seasoning as needed. Unmold polenta terrines on plates and top with sauce. Garnish with chervil leaves and chives.

# Crème Fraîche

Whisk ½ cup heavy cream with ½ cup sour cream. Cover loosely with plastic wrap and let stand overnight in a reasonably warm spot - pilot light, under a lamp - until thickened. Cover and refrigerate, at least 4 hours, until thick.

# Tailgate Picnic

*Black Bean Hummus with Warm Pita Wedges*
*Hot Bloody Mary    Minted Iced Tea*

*New England Corn Chowder*
*Grilled Lamb in Pita Pockets with Yogurt Sauce*
*Veal & Ham Pie    Three Bean Salad*
*French Bread with Wedges of Cheese and Fresh Fruit*

*Palm Beach Brownies*

*Côtes de Sonoma Sauvignon Blanc*
*Shooting Star Cabernet Franc*

# Apple And Squash Soup

*...a winter staple, the secret is in the green apples which give the soup an unusual flavor*

Combine squash, apples, onion, rosemary, marjoram, broth, water, bread, salt, and pepper in a saucepan. Bring to a boil. Reduce heat and simmer, uncovered, for 45 minutes. Purée in a blender in batches. Return to saucepan and bring to a boil. Remove from heat and stir in cream. Cook over low heat, stirring constantly. Do not boil. When warm, garnish and serve.

1 (1-pound) butternut squash, halved, peeled and cubed
3 tart green apples, peeled and chopped
1 medium onion, coarsely chopped
1/4 teaspoon dried rosemary
1/4 teaspoon dried marjoram
3 (14½-ounce) cans chicken broth
3½ cups water
2 slices white bread
1 teaspoon salt
1/4 teaspoon black pepper
1/4 cup heavy cream
chopped fresh parsley for garnish

**Yield: 6 servings**

# Black Bean And Steak Soup

*...thanks to The Racquet Club*

## southwest seasoning

- 1 tablespoon chili powder
- 1 tablespoon paprika
- 1 teaspoon cumin seed
- 1 teaspoon ground coriander
- 1 teaspoon sugar
- 1 teaspoon salt
- ½ teaspoon black pepper
- ½ teaspoon cayenne pepper

## soup

- 8 ounces beef sirloin, cut in ½-inch cubes
- 1 tablespoon olive oil
- 1½ cups diced onion
- ½ cup diced celery
- ½ cup diced green bell pepper
- 1 jalapeño pepper, seeded and diced
- minced fresh garlic to taste (optional)
- 5 cups beef broth
- 1½ tablespoons Southwest Seasoning
- 2 (15-ounce) cans black beans, drained
- ½ tablespoon chopped fresh cilantro

**Yield: 8 servings**

Combine all seasoning ingredients and store in a glass jar for up to 1 month. To prepare soup, brown beef in oil in a pot. Add onion, celery, bell pepper, jalapeño pepper, and garlic and cook until tender. Add broth and southwest seasoning and simmer 15 minutes. Mix in beans and cilantro.

If consistency of soup is too thin, thicken with a mixture of 4 tablespoons melted butter and ¼ cup flour. Blend into soup and simmer 15 minutes.

# Cream Of Cauliflower Soup

*...best served in a colorful bowl*

Melt butter over medium heat in a 3 or 4-quart saucepan. Add onion and sauté 5 minutes or until softened. Pour in broth and bring to a boil. Add carrots and cauliflower. Reduce heat, cover, and simmer 7 minutes or until vegetables are tender. Purée in batches in a blender until smooth. Return to saucepan. Stir in salt, pepper, half-and-half, nutmeg, and sherry. Heat to a simmer. Sprinkle with parsley to garnish.

2 tablespoons butter
1 large onion, chopped
2 (14½-ounce) cans chicken broth
2 medium carrots, sliced ¼-inch thick
1 medium head cauliflower, cut into small flowerets
salt and pepper to taste
1 cup half-and-half or light cream
⅛ teaspoon nutmeg
1 tablespoon dry sherry (optional)
1 tablespoon chopped fresh parsley for garnish

**Yield: 4 to 6 servings**

# Cheese Chowder

*...it is critical to use a white Vermont cheddar, not the bag of orange grated stuff*

4 tablespoons butter, melted
¼ cup all-purpose flour
3 potatoes, peeled and diced
1 leek, sliced
1 bunch scallions, minced
4 teaspoons salt
2 teaspoons black pepper
2 (12-ounce) bottles beer
2 quarts milk
7 ounces cream cheese, cut in small pieces
1¾ cups grated Vermont cheddar cheese

**Yield: 8 servings**

Prepare a roux by blending butter and flour together. Bake at 350° for 20 minutes. Meanwhile, combine potatoes, leek, scallions, salt, pepper, and beer in a saucepan. Cook until potatoes are tender. Heat milk to just scalding. Stir roux into milk until smooth. Add milk mixture to vegetable mixture. Stir in cheeses and cook until blended. Serve immediately.

Serve with focaccia strips and a salad.

# Consommé Bellevue

*...the perfect preface to a very elegant dinner*

4 cups clam broth, strained
5 cups homemade or canned chicken consommé
½ cup heavy cream, whipped

**Yield: 10 to 12 servings**

Combine clam broth and consommé in a saucepan. Heat over low heat. Top each serving with a dollop of whipped cream.

# Consommé With Caviar

Gently warm 1 can of beef consommé per person. Add Tabasco sauce to taste. Pour into individual soup cups or bowls until half full. Chill until set. Spread a layer of caviar on top. Fill each cup with remaining consommé. Chill. Top each serving with a dollop of sour cream.

canned beef consommé
Tabasco sauce
red caviar
sour cream

**Yield: I serving**

# Hot Consommé Madrilène

*...superb beginning for a game dinner*

Peel and seed tomato halves, adding peels and seeds to a saucepan. Coarsely chop tomatoes. Add ½ cup chopped tomato to saucepan. Reserve remainder of tomato for later use. Add consommé and bring to a boil. Simmer 5 minutes. Strain consommé through a fine sieve and return to saucepan. Place over low heat and add reserved tomato. Simmer 5 minutes. Stir in port and herbs. Season with salt and pepper.

4 large tomatoes, halved
8 cups beef consommé
I cup port
½ cup minced fresh herbs: parsley, chives, and thyme
salt and pepper to taste

**Yield: 8 servings**

# New England Corn Chowder

*...hearty enough when all that's needed to round out the meal are interesting breads and a fabulous dessert.*

8 ounces bacon, diced
salt and pepper to taste
1 large green bell
   pepper, minced
1 large onion, minced
½ leek, minced
4 stalks celery, minced
½ teaspoon dried thyme
½ teaspoon sage
1 (2-pound) package
   corn
4 cups chicken broth
2 quarts milk
4 tablespoons butter,
   melted
¼ cup all-purpose flour

**Yield: 8 servings**

Cook bacon in a large pot. Remove from pot and set aside. Remove all but 2 tablespoons bacon fat from pot. Add salt, pepper, bell pepper, onion, leek, celery, thyme, and sage to pot and sauté. Add corn and toss until well mixed. Pour in broth and simmer 15 minutes or until vegetables are tender. In a separate pot, heat milk. Mix butter and flour together until smooth. Blend into hot milk and stir until smooth. Stir milk mixture into vegetable mixture. Cook, stirring constantly, until thoroughly heated and smooth.

# Corn And Potato Chowder

*...the name chowder comes from the French "chaudière", a large, heavy pot used by the farmer and fisherman to cook their local soups and stews*

Cut kernels from ears of corn. Place half of corn in a food processor or blender and purée. Combine puréed corn and remaining corn in a bowl. Place salt pork in a small saucepan. Cover with water and bring to a boil over high heat. Cook 5 minutes and drain. Combine salt pork and oil in a large pot. Cook until browned. Add leek and onion. Sauté 15 minutes or until golden. Blend in flour. Cook and stir about 2 minutes. Add broth, potatoes, thyme, and bay leaves. Bring to a boil over medium-high heat. Reduce to low heat and partially cover. Simmer 30 minutes or until potatoes are tender. Stir in corn mixture and simmer 3 minutes. Add cream and simmer 5 minutes or until thoroughly heated. Season with salt and peppers. Remove bay leaves. Garnish each serving with a sprig of thyme.

8 medium ears of corn, or 4 cups canned or frozen, thawed kernels

6 ounces salt pork, diced, or 6 slices bacon, cut in 1-inch pieces

2 tablespoons safflower oil, or other vegetable oil

1½ cups finely chopped leek, white and pale green sections

2 cups chopped yellow onion

3 tablespoons all-purpose flour

4 cups chicken broth

4 cups diced or sliced peeled boiling potatoes

1 tablespoon minced fresh thyme, or 1 teaspoon dried, crumbled

2 bay leaves

1 cup heavy cream

salt to taste

black or white pepper to taste

cayenne pepper or Tabasco sauce to taste

fresh thyme sprigs for garnish

**Yield: 8 to 10 side-dish servings, 6 entrée servings**

# Crab Bisque

*...if the hefty Aga Kahn can, if the camels in his caravan can, baby you can can-can too!*

2 (6-ounce) cans
crabmeat, deboned
2 (8-ounce) cans cream
of mushroom soup
1 (8-ounce) can cream
of celery soup
1 (15-ounce) can
cream-style corn
2 cups milk
1 cup half-and-half
1 cup sherry
1 teaspoon
Worcestershire
sauce

**Yield: 10 servings**

Combine all ingredients in the top of a double boiler. Cook over simmering water for 3 hours, stirring occasionally.

*To shorten cooking time, place all ingredients in a slow cooker on high heat. Cook 30 minutes. Reduce to low and heat to desired serving temperature.*

# Zucchini And Leek Soup

*...when soup is served, a mood of easy intimacy prevails*

4 tablespoons butter
2 leeks, cut in 1-inch
pieces
1½ pounds zucchini,
peeled and chopped
1 carrot, chopped
1 large potato, peeled
and chopped
3½ cups chicken broth
salt and pepper to taste
2 tablespoons chopped
fresh parsley
2 cups half-and-half

**Yield: 4 to 6 servings**

Melt butter in a large saucepan. Add leeks, zucchini, carrot, and potato. Stir until vegetables are just coated. Cover and cook over medium heat for 5 minutes. Do not allow vegetables to brown. Add broth, salt, pepper, and parsley. Bring to a boil. Reduce heat and simmer, uncovered, for 15 minutes or until vegetables are tender. Purée mixture in a blender in 1-cup batches. Return to saucepan. Stir in milk and heat until just hot. Do not boil.

# Fish Chowder

*...made a day ahead, the flavor improves overnight*

Skin, bone, and cut halibut into ½-inch chunks. Combine fish, water, and any large bones in a large pot. Bring to a boil. Reduce heat and simmer 15 minutes. Drain fish, reserving 4 cups of broth. Remove large bones and pick over meat for any smaller ones. Place fish in a small bowl, cover, and set aside. Rinse and dry pot. Cook salt pork in pot over medium heat until crisp and golden brown. Remove salt pork with a slotted spoon and drain on paper towels. Add butter, onion, celery, and leek to pork fat in pan. Sauté until vegetables soften but are not browned. Add salt and curry powder. Stir in flour until smooth. Add reserved fish broth and potatoes. Cook and stir over medium heat for 15 minutes or until potatoes are tender. Remove from heat. Add halibut, salt pork, cream, and milk. Cover and chill several hours or overnight. To serve, reheat gently without boiling. Pour into serving dish, add a large dot of butter, and sprinkle with parsley.

1½ pounds halibut or other firm-flesh white fish

6 cups water

2 ounces salt pork, diced

1 stick butter, plus extra for garnish

½ cup chopped onion

½ cup chopped celery

1 small leek, finely chopped

1 teaspoon salt

¼ teaspoon curry powder (optional)

3 tablespoons all-purpose flour

2 cups peeled and diced potatoes

1 cup light cream

½ cup milk

2 tablespoons chopped fresh parsley for garnish

**Yield: 6 to 8 servings**

# Gazpacho With Crabmeat

*...a zesty Spanish soup that reigns as a favorite year round and could be called a "liquid salad"*

3 pounds ripe
  tomatoes, peeled,
  seeded, and chopped
1 cup chopped red
  onion
1 red bell pepper,
  chopped
1 tablespoon minced
  garlic
2 teaspoons seeded
  and chopped jalapeño
  pepper, or to taste
¼ cup coarsely chopped
  fresh cilantro, plus
  extra for garnish
¼ cup olive oil
3 tablespoons red wine
  vinegar
3 tablespoons fresh
  lime or lemon juice
salt and pepper to taste
1½ cups peeled, seeded,
  and diced cucumber
1 pound lump crabmeat
garlic croutons

**Yield: 4 to 6 servings**

Combine tomatoes, onion, bell pepper, garlic, jalapeño pepper, cilantro, oil, vinegar, and lime juice in a food processor. Blend to a coarse consistency. Season with salt and pepper. Cover and chill. Stir in cucumber and crabmeat. Garnish with fresh cilantro and serve with croutons.

If desired, substitute lobster or shrimp for the crabmeat.

# Wild Mushroom And Peppered Bacon Soup

*...again, thanks to The Racquet Club*

In a large pot, sauté bacon until half-cooked. Add onion, celery, and garlic and sauté until onion is transparent. Add mushrooms and cook 2 to 3 minutes. Add chicken broth and cream and simmer 20 minutes. Season with salt and pepper.

For a thicker soup, add a blond roux when done cooking.

*Use any combination of seasonal mushrooms: shiitake, chanterelle, domestic white, or a dry mix of morel, porcini, and woodear. If using dry, soak in a bowl of warm water for 20 minutes before measuring.*

4 ounces peppered bacon, julienned
1 cup diced yellow onion
½ cup diced celery
1 teaspoon minced garlic
4 cups coarsely chopped wild mushrooms
5½ cups chicken broth
2 cups heavy cream
salt and pepper to taste

**Yield: 8 servings**

# Fresh Mushroom Soup

*...reduce soup for an excellent sauce over chicken breasts*

Melt butter in a large saucepan. Add onion and sugar and cook slowly for 25 minutes or until golden but not browned. Slice a third of mushrooms. Finely chop remainder of mushrooms. Add all mushrooms to saucepan and sauté for 5 minutes. Blend in flour until smooth. Cook 2 minutes, stirring constantly. Stir in water until smooth. Add remaining ingredients. Heat to a boil, stirring constantly. Reduce heat and simmer, uncovered, for 10 minutes.

Reheat, covered, over low heat for 10 minutes.

6 tablespoons butter
2 cups minced yellow onion
½ teaspoon sugar
1 pound fresh mushrooms
¼ cup all-purpose flour
1 cup water
1¾ cups chicken broth
1 cup dry white wine or vermouth
1 teaspoon salt
¼ teaspoon black pepper

**Yield: 4 to 6 servings**

# Mussel Bisque

*...a very rich beginning to a game dinner*

2 cups dry white wine
1½ pounds mussels, washed
1½ tablespoons butter, divided
4 mushrooms, thinly sliced
4 shallots, thinly sliced
½ teaspoon salt
½ teaspoon white pepper
½ cup plus 1 tablespoon applejack, divided
3 cups clam juice
3 cups heavy cream
1 tablespoon all-purpose flour
1 small red potato, finely diced
1 small stalk celery, finely diced
½ carrot, finely diced
1 teaspoon fresh lemon juice
dash of Tabasco sauce
salt and pepper to taste

**Yield: 6 servings**

Bring wine to a boil in a large saucepan. Add mussels and cover. Simmer 4 minutes or until shells open. Remove mussels, cover with a wet towel, and set aside to cool. Strain liquid through a cheesecloth and reserve. Melt 1 tablespoon butter in a large pot over low heat. Add mushrooms, shallots, salt, and pepper. Sauté 5 minutes or until softened. Add ½ cup applejack and increase heat to high. Cook until liquid reduces by half. Add clam juice and reserved liquid. Cook until reduced by a fourth. Add cream and bring to a boil. Blend remaining ½ tablespoon butter and flour with fingers to form a smooth paste. Press onto ends of a whisk. Whisk into boiling liquid until dissolved. Simmer liquid 5 minutes. Strain and return to pot. Add potato, celery, and carrot. Season with lemon juice, Tabasco sauce, salt, pepper, and remaining 1 tablespoon applejack. Remove mussels from shells and stir into warm soup.

*Variation: For a smoother bisque, purée before adding mussels.*

# Billi-Bi

*...the most elegant and delicious soup ever created, serve hot or cold and garnish with a mussel*

Combine mussels, salt, pepper, shallots, onions, parsley, wine, butter, bay leaf, and thyme in a large pot. Cover and bring to a boil. Simmer 5 to 10 minutes or until shells open. Discard any unopened shells. Strain through a double-thickness cheesecloth, returning liquid to pot. Reserve mussels for garnish or for some other use. Bring liquid to a boil. Add cream. Bring to a boil and remove from heat. Add egg yolk and cook until soup thickens slightly. Do not boil. Serve hot or cold garnished with a mussel.

**Cold Mussels Vinaigrette:** Place reserved mussels into a wooden salad bowl, lightly toss with a Dijon vinaigrette, garnish with chopped red onions and parsley, and serve as an hors d'oeuvre.

2 pounds mussels, washed
salt and pepper to taste
2 shallots, coarsely chopped
2 small onions, quartered
2 sprigs fresh parsley
1 cup dry white wine
2 tablespoons butter
½ bay leaf
½ teaspoon dried thyme
2 cups heavy cream
1 egg yolk, lightly beaten

**Yield: 4 servings**

# Famous-Barr's French Onion Soup

*...the soup served in Famous-Barr's dining rooms for many years*

1 pound, 6 ounces onions, peeled
6 tablespoons butter
1 teaspoon black pepper
1 tablespoon Spanish paprika
2 bay leaves
½ cup all-purpose flour
6 cups beef broth
1½ teaspoons salt, or to taste

**Yield: 8 servings**

Cut onions in half and slice with the grain about ⅛-inch thick. Sauté over low heat in butter for 20 minutes, stirring frequently. Mix in black pepper, paprika, bay leaves, and flour. Cook and stir for 5 minutes. Slowly stir in broth with a wooden spoon. Cover and simmer for at least 30 minutes. Season with salt and remove bay leaves.

Top individual servings with thin slices of French bread. Sprinkle with grated Swiss cheese and broil until cheese is golden brown.

# Jeanne's Oyster Artichoke Soup

*...it is the rare winter chill that persists in the face of a well-made soup*

1½ cups chopped scallions
1 stick butter
3 tablespoons all-purpose flour
6 cups chicken broth
3 (14-ounce) cans artichoke hearts, drained and chopped
4 cups oysters, halved
¼ teaspoon anise seed
½ teaspoon crushed red pepper flakes
1 teaspoon salt

**Yield: 6 to 12 servings**

Sauté scallions in butter. Blend in flour. Stir in broth. Add artichokes and oysters. Bring to a boil. Remove from heat and refrigerate overnight. When ready to serve, reheat and add anise seed, red pepper flakes, and salt.

# Oyster Stew

*...ancient shell mounds found in America indicate that the Indians ate oysters long before Europeans arrived*

Heat 3 sticks butter and oil until bubbly. Cook 2 minutes and then add scallions, onion, and garlic. Simmer 5 minutes. Stir in salt and cayenne pepper. Add 6 cups half-and-half. Bring to a simmer over low heat. Slowly add frozen butter to stew, stirring constantly. When melted, mix in oysters and remaining 7⅓ cups half-and-half. Simmer 10 minutes over low heat or until oysters are warmed but not thoroughly cooked. Add parsley and simmer 2 minutes.

If preparing ahead of time, cool in an ice bath when done cooking. Reheat in a double boiler. Stew should not boil at any time.

3 sticks butter
¼ cup oil
¼ cup finely chopped scallions
¼ cup finely chopped onion
1 teaspoon minced garlic
2½ teaspoons salt
1 teaspoon cayenne pepper, or to taste
13⅓ cups half-and-half, divided
6 sticks frozen butter, cut in small pieces
6 cups oysters, drained
½ cup chopped fresh parsley

**Yield: 15 servings**

# Chilled Orange Carrot Soup

*...serve in glass cups on the terrace before you call your guests to dinner*

½ teaspoon minced
   fresh ginger
1 (1-pound) package
   fresh carrots, sliced
½ cup sliced leek, white
   only
1 tablespoon butter
3 cups chicken broth
1½ cups orange juice
salt and pepper to taste
orange slices and fresh
   mint sprigs for
   garnish

**Yield: 6 to 8 servings**

Sauté ginger, carrots, leek in butter until vegetables soften. Do not brown. Add broth and simmer 30 minutes. Purée in a blender. Add orange juice and chill. When ready to serve, season with salt and pepper and garnish with mint sprigs.

# Cold Pea Soup

*...cooking peas with lettuce is very French*

7 large leaves iceberg
   lettuce
3 cups fresh or frozen
   peas
3-4 sprigs mint, plus
   extra for garnish
⅓ cup chopped scallions
3 cups chicken broth
1 teaspoon salt
1 teaspoon honey
1 cup cream or half-
   and-half

**Yield: 8 servings**

Line a large saucepan with lettuce. Add peas, mint, scallions, and broth. Bring to a boil. Reduce heat and simmer until peas are cooked. Purée in a blender in 2 batches. Return to saucepan and stir in salt, honey, and cream. Chill and garnish with mint before serving.

# Cream of Roasted Tomato Soup With Parsley Croutons

*...roasting the tomatoes gives this soup a deep, sweet flavor*

Coat tomatoes with olive oil and place cut side down on a foil-lined shallow baking dish. Bake at 400° for 35 to 45 minutes or until tomatoes are soft and skins are dark. Cool and remove skins. Melt butter in a saucepan. Add shallots, carrot, and fennel and sauté 12 minutes or until softened. Add 2 cups of broth, tarragon, and parsley. Simmer over low heat for 30 minutes. Remove herb sprigs and add tomatoes. Purée soup in a blender or food processor. Return to saucepan and add cream. Bring to a simmer. Add remaining broth as needed to reach desired consistency. Season with salt and pepper. Keep warm over low heat until ready to serve. Ladle into warm bowls and float 2 to 3 croutons on top of each serving. To make croutons, brush both sides of bread slices with oil. Rub garlic on tops. Place on a baking sheet and sprinkle with cheese and parsley. Bake at 400° for 5 minutes or until golden brown.

## soup

3 pounds tomatoes, halved crosswise and seeded
olive oil
3 tablespoons unsalted butter
3 small shallots, coarsely chopped
1 small carrot, coarsely chopped
1 small fennel bulb, coarsely chopped
2-3 cups chicken broth, divided
5 sprigs fresh tarragon
5 sprigs fresh parsley
1 cup heavy cream
salt and pepper to taste
Parsley Croutons

## parsley croutons

12 thin slices French bread
olive oil
2 cloves garlic, halved
½ cup grated Teleme or Muenster cheese
¼ cup chopped fresh parsley

**Yield: 6 servings**

# Louisiana Filé Gumbo

*...the word gumbo comes from the African word for okra, now means a dish or soup thickened with okra*

1½ cups diced onion
½ cup diced celery
½ cup diced green bell pepper
1 jalapeño pepper, seeded and diced
¼ cup minced garlic
1 tablespoon olive oil
4 ounces andouille sausage, sliced
4 ounces smoked duck breast, julienned
¼ cup chopped crawfish tail meat or shrimp
5 cups chicken broth
1 cup diced tomatoes
1 tablespoon filé powder
½ teaspoon black pepper
½ teaspoon white pepper
¼ teaspoon cayenne pepper
½ teaspoon dried oregano
¼ teaspoon dried thyme
½ teaspoon dried basil
1½ cups sliced okra
6 tablespoons chopped scallions
steamed clams, shrimp, or crab claws for garnish

**Yield: 8 servings**

Sauté onion, celery, bell pepper, jalapeño pepper, and garlic in oil in a pot until tender. Add sausage, duck, crawfish, broth, and tomatoes. Simmer 20 minutes. Add filé powder, peppers, oregano, thyme, and basil. Simmer 20 minutes. Just before serving, add okra and scallions. Heat and garnish.

For extra thickness and flavor, blend in a dark roux when adding seasonings.

# Senegalese Soup

*...float a sliver of poached chicken in each bowl*

Sauté onions and apple in butter in a skillet. Cook slowly until soft but not browned. Add curry powder, ginger, and mace and simmer 7 minutes. Blend in flour, salt, and peas. Add chicken broth and bring to a boil. Cool. Purée in a blender and chill thoroughly. Stir in cream just before serving.

If desired, freeze soup before cream is added. When ready to serve, thaw in refrigerator and blend again before adding cream.

4 medium onions, diced
1 large apple, peeled and diced
2 sticks butter
1-4 teaspoons curry powder
pinch of ground ginger
pinch of ground mace
3 tablespoons all-purpose flour
1-1½ teaspoons salt
2 (4-ounce) jars strained peas
4 cups chicken broth
3 cups heavy cream

**Yield: 8 servings**

# Avocado Senegalese Soup

*...a delicate taste and equally delicate color*

Sauté onions and celery in butter until softened, but not browned. Add curry, apple, and broth. Simmer 20 minutes. Purée mixture and avocado together until smooth. Add cream and season with salt and pepper. Chill.

4 medium onions, chopped
½ cup chopped celery
2 sticks butter
2 teaspoons curry powder
1 tart green apple, peeled and chopped
4 cups chicken broth
1 avocado, peeled and diced
3 cups heavy cream
salt and pepper to taste

**Yield: 8 servings**

# Spring Soup

*...for a summer dinner on the terrace, followed by Peking Duck, Green Bean Salad, and Corn on the Cob*

**crème fraîche**
⅔ cup heavy cream
1 tablespoon buttermilk

**soup**
6 cups chicken broth, divided
10 ounces fresh spinach, stems removed
4 tablespoons butter
½ cup diced smoked ham
1 cup finely minced scallion
3 tablespoons all-purpose flour
1 cup cooked peas
6 small fresh mushrooms, stems removed, thinly sliced
salt and pepper to taste
½ cup Crème Fraîche
minced fresh parsley and chives for garnish

**Yield: 6 to 8 servings**

Combine cream and buttermilk in a glass jar and whisk until blended. Cover and set in a warm, draft-free place for 8 to 24 hours or until mixture sours and thickens. Store in refrigerator for up to 1 to 2 weeks. To prepare soup, heat 2 cups broth in a large saucepan. Add spinach and cook 3 to 4 minutes or until wilted. Cool. Purée in a blender until smooth. Return to saucepan and add remaining 4 cups broth. Heat over low heat. Melt butter in a 3-quart saucepan. Add ham, cover, and cook 2 to 3 minutes over low heat. Add scallions, cover, and cook 3 to 4 minutes or until scallions are soft but not brown. Stir in flour until smooth. Remove from heat and add spinach mixture all at once. Whisk until smooth. Bring to a boil. Reduce heat and simmer 5 minutes. Add peas, mushrooms, salt, and pepper. Reheat soup without bringing to a boil. Fold in crème fraîche. Adjust seasonings as needed. If soup is too thick, thin by adding more crème fraîche. Garnish and serve hot.

Prepare soup up to 2 days in advance and reheat when ready to serve.

*Variation: Crème Fraîche, page 102.*

# Cold Tomato Cob

*...was originally done in an old-fashioned meat grinder - serve with curried mayonnaise*

Coarsely chop 3 tomatoes. Combine remaining 3 tomatoes and onion in a food processor. Pulse quickly to chop; do not process too fine. Combine coarsely chopped tomato, tomato mixture, salt, and pepper in a glass bowl. Place in freezer for 30 minutes or until thoroughly chilled, but not icy. Serve in bouillon cups with a dollop of Curried Mayonnaise on each serving. To prepare mayonnaise, combine all ingredients well.

To improve flavor, refrigerate overnight instead of chilling in freezer.

**tomato cob**
- 6 large, overripe tomatoes, peeled, divided
- 1 medium onion, minced
- 2 teaspoons salt
- black pepper to taste

**curried mayonnaise**
- 6 tablespoons mayonnaise
- 2 tablespoons minced fresh parsley
- 2 tablespoons curry powder

**Yield: 4 servings**

# Curried Tomato Carrot Soup

*...terrific hot or cold*

Sauté onion in butter in a large pot for 5 minutes. Add carrots and curry powder. Cover and cook 20 minutes. Add tomatoes and broth. Bring to a boil. Reduce heat and simmer 20 minutes. Add 2 tablespoons basil. Season with salt and pepper. Simmer 1 minute. Purée until smooth. Garnish with remaining basil and refrigerate or serve immediately.

If desired, substitute one (28-ounce) can undrained Italian plum tomatoes.

- 1 yellow onion, chopped
- 2 tablespoons butter
- 1½ cups chopped carrots
- 1 teaspoon curry powder
- 7 large plum tomatoes, peeled and chopped
- 3½ cups chicken broth
- 6 tablespoons julienned basil leaves, divided
- salt and pepper to taste

**Yield: 6 to 8 servings**

# The "Dynamite" Vegetable Chowder

*...this hearty winter soup was first served at a Super Bowl party where it was unanimously declared "Dynamite" and has been ever since*

1½ pounds zucchini, halved lengthwise

1 medium onion, chopped

2 tablespoons chopped fresh parsley

1 tablespoon chopped fresh basil, or 1 teaspoon dried

5 tablespoons butter

⅓ cup all-purpose flour

1½ teaspoons salt

¼ teaspoon black pepper

1 tablespoon instant chicken bouillon

1 teaspoon lemon juice

3 cups water

1 (16-ounce) package frozen corn

1 (14-ounce) can evaporated milk

6 medium tomatoes, peeled, seeded, and chopped

1 cup grated fontina cheese

¼ cup grated Romano cheese

**Yield: 12 servings**

Sauté zucchini, onion, parsley, and basil in butter for 8 minutes. Stir in flour, salt, and pepper. Cook over low heat, stirring constantly, until bubbly. Remove from heat and add bouillon, lemon juice, and water. Bring to a boil. Add corn and bring to a boil. Reduce heat and cover. Simmer 8 minutes. Stir in milk and tomato. Bring to a boil. Stir in cheeses and cook until melted. Serve immediately.

Serve with homemade breads, crocks of sweet butter or a platter of assorted sandwiches.

# Cold Yellow Squash Soup

*...a substantial summer soup, which also could be made with zucchini*

Combine squash, onion, and 1 cup broth in a saucepan. Bring to a boil. Simmer 30 minutes or until vegetables soften. Purée in a blender and transfer to a bowl. Stir in sour cream, remaining ½ cup broth, salt, and pepper. Chill. Garnish and serve.

If skin of squash is tough, peel and seed before slicing.

1 pound yellow squash, thinly sliced
1 onion, chopped
1½ cups chicken broth, divided
½ cup sour cream
salt and pepper to taste
fresh dill sprigs for garnish

**Yield: 4 servings**

# Creamed Winter Squash Soup

*...one of the best winter squashes, butternut is so sweet and nutty it can be used in a pie instead of pumpkin - in a soup it's sublime!*

Bake squash at 400° for 45 minutes or until tender. Cool slightly. Cut in half, discard seeds, and scoop out pulp. Purée pulp in a blender or force through a food mill. Combine squash, broth, salt, and pepper in a large kettle. Bring to a simmer over medium heat. Reduce heat to low and slowly whisk in 1 cup cream. Beat until smooth. Heat slowly until very hot. Adjust seasonings as needed. Whip remaining 1 cup cream. Top each serving of soup with a dollop of whipped cream and a sprinkle of nutmeg.

5 pounds butternut squash, or 4 cups cooked
4 (10¾-ounce) cans chicken broth
1 teaspoon salt
white pepper
2 cups heavy cream, divided
nutmeg for garnish

**Yield: 6 servings**

# Wastebasket Soup

*...not because it has everything but the well-known kitchen sink in it, though it has, but because it was found on some crumbled newspaper around an imported wastebasket ordered from somewhere or other in Pennsylvania. It is really a baked minestrone*

1½ pounds lean stew beef, cut in 1-inch cubes
1 cup coarsely chopped onion
1 teaspoon minced fresh garlic
1 teaspoon salt
2 tablespoons olive oil
3 (10½-ounce) cans beef broth
2½ cups water
1½ teaspoons Italian seasoning, or ¾ teaspoon each basil and oregano
1 (14½-ounce) can tomatoes, undrained and chopped
1 (6-ounce) can pitted black olives, undrained
1 (15½-ounce) can great Northern or navy beans, undrained
1½ cups thinly sliced carrots
1 cup dry seashell macaroni
2 cups sliced zucchini
Parmesan cheese

**Yield: 10 to 12 servings**

Combine beef, onion, garlic, salt, and oil in a large, ovenproof pot or Dutch oven. Stir to evenly coat meat. Bake, uncovered, at 400° for about 40 minutes. Stir once or twice while baking. Reduce heat to 350°. Add broth, water, and Italian seasoning. Cover and bake 60 minutes or until meat is almost tender. Stir in tomatoes, olives, beans, and carrots. Bake 20 minutes. Mix in macaroni. Scatter zucchini over the top. Cover and bake 20 minutes longer or until zucchini is crisp-tender and macaroni is tender but not mushy. Serve with Parmesan cheese.

# Minestrone Alla Genovese

*...many Italians believe that a minestrone is successful if it is as good at room temperature as it is hot!*

Combine ¼ cup oil, walnuts, pine nuts, butter, basil, spinach, and garlic in a blender or food processor. Blend to a very fine consistency. Add remaining ½ cup oil and blend until smooth. Transfer to a bowl. Using a wooden spoon, stir in cheese, salt, and pepper. Cover and set aside. To prepare soup, cover beans with running water and soak overnight. Drain and rinse soaked beans. Bring 10 cups cold water to a boil. Add coarse salt and drained beans and partially cover. Simmer, stirring occasionally, for 45 minutes to 1 hour, 30 minutes or until tender but still firm. Cut carrot quarters into ½-inch pieces. Combine carrots, leek, onion, celery, parsley, potato, and oil in a large pot. Sauté 5 minutes, stirring with a wooden spoon. Add tomato and sauté 5 minutes longer. Heat broth and add it to pot. Cook 5 minutes. Season with salt and pepper. Drain beans, reserving liquid. Place beans in a bowl and cover. Add bean liquid to pot and simmer, uncovered, for 30 minutes. Increase heat and bring broth to a boil. Add macaroni and cook 9 to 12 minutes or until macaroni is al dente. Remove from heat and mix in beans. Let stand 2 minutes. Add half of pesto sauce to pot. Stir to mix well and serve. Add some of remaining pesto to each serving.

## pesto sauce
- ¾ cup olive oil, divided
- 6 walnuts
- 1 tablespoon pine nuts
- 1 tablespoon unsalted butter
- 1½ cups loosely packed fresh basil leaves
- 2 heaping tablespoons cooked spinach
- 2 cloves garlic
- ½ cup Parmesan cheese
- salt and pepper to taste

## soup
- ½ cup dried cannellini beans
- 10 cups cold water
- coarse salt to taste
- 3 medium carrots, quartered lengthwise
- 1 leek, coarsely chopped, white only
- 1 medium-size red onion, peeled, coarsely chopped
- 3 medium stalks celery, coarsely chopped
- 15 sprigs Italian parsley, stems removed, coarsely chopped
- 1 (6-ounce) boiling potato, peeled and cut in ½-inch pieces
- ½ cup olive oil
- 1 ripe tomato, peeled, seeded, and coarsely chopped
- 1 cup beef broth
- salt and pepper to taste
- 8 ounces dry macaroni

**Yield: 8 to 10 servings**

# Red Lentil Soup

*...regular lentils will not look, taste, or cook the same*

2 cups chicken broth
¼ teaspoon curry powder
½ bay leaf
2 tablespoons long-grain white rice
¼ cup dried red lentils

Combine broth, curry powder, and bay leaf in a 1-quart saucepan. Bring to a boil. Sprinkle rice and lentils over top. Stir and reduce heat. Cover and simmer for 30 minutes. Remove bay leaf and serve.

**Yield: 2 to 4 servings**


# Hot And Sour Shrimp Soup

*...a subtle blend of hot and sour with lemony overtones, "Tom Yam Goong" is the most famous of all Thai soups*

8 ounces shrimp, peeled and deveined, shells reserved
3 cups water
2 stalks lemon grass
2 cloves garlic, minced
zest of 1 lime
3 thin slices fresh ginger
¼ cup fish sauce
2 shallots, sliced
½ cup sliced straw mushrooms
chili peppers (optional)
¼ cup lime juice
1 teaspoon black chili paste
1 tablespoon chopped fresh cilantro for garnish

Rinse shrimp shells. Combine shells and water in a large pot. Bring to a boil. Strain broth and return to pot. Discard shells. Using only the lower third of stalks, cut lemon grass into 1-inch lengths. Add lemon grass, garlic, zest, ginger, fish sauce, shallots, mushrooms, and chili peppers to broth. Cook gently for 2 minutes. Add shrimp to soup and bring to a boil. Cook until shrimp are done. To serve, place lime juice and chili paste in a large bowl. Add soup to bowl and stir. Garnish and serve.

Fish sauce and black chili paste are available at Oriental grocery stores.

**Yield: 4 servings**

# Lobster And Plum Tomato Soup

*...a Racquet Club favorite*

Boil lobster in salted water until bright red. Cool and split in half. Remove meat from the tail and claws and reserve. Cut lobster shell into 4 or 5 pieces. Sauté carrot, celery, onion, and leek in oil in a saucepan until onion is transparent. Add lobster shell and garlic and sauté 5 minutes longer. Add brandy and ignite. Stir in broth, tomato purée, tarragon, cayenne pepper, peppercorns, and bay leaves. Simmer 20 minutes. Strain and return to pan. Add enough cream to reach desired consistency. Chop reserved lobster meat and add to soup. Season with salt and pepper.

If soup is too thin, thicken with a mixture of 4 tablespoons melted butter and ¼ cup flour. Add to broth just after straining and simmer.

1 whole lobster
1 carrot, chopped
1 large stalk celery, chopped
½ large yellow onion, chopped
1 small leek, chopped
6 tablespoons olive oil
1½ teaspoons minced garlic
½ cup brandy or cognac
4 cups chicken broth
1½ cups tomato purée
1 teaspoon chopped tarragon
cayenne pepper to taste
2 tablespoons black peppercorns
2 bay leaves
2 cups heavy cream, or as desired
salt and pepper to taste

**Yield: 8 to 10 servings**

# Grilled Lamb In Pita Pocket With Yogurt Sauce

*...spicy lamb cubes and mint-flavored yogurt sauce combine in a warm pita pocket or soft flour tortilla for a whole-meal sandwich buffet from the grill*

## sandwich

- ½ cup lemon juice
- ¼ cup olive oil, or other vegetable oil
- 1 teaspoon chopped fresh cilantro
- 1 teaspoon ground cumin
- ½ teaspoon black pepper
- ½ teaspoon ground turmeric
- ½ teaspoon crushed red pepper flakes
- 2 pounds lean, boneless lamb, cut in ¾-inch cubes
- 2 large onions, thinly sliced in rings and separated
- 6 pitas
- 12-24 small leaves romaine lettuce
- 3 medium tomatoes, cut in thin wedges

Yogurt Sauce

## yogurt sauce

- 2 cups plain yogurt
- 1 teaspoon salt
- 1 clove garlic, minced
- 1 tablespoon finely chopped fresh mint

**Yield: 12 servings**

Combine lemon juice, oil, cilantro, cumin, pepper, turmeric, and pepper flakes to make a marinade. Place lamb and onion in separate bowls. Pour half of marinade over each. Cover and chill 2 to 4 hours, stirring occasionally. Drain meat, reserving marinade. Place meat on skewers and place on a lightly oiled grill, 4 to 6 inches from a heat source. Cook, turning and basting frequently with reserved marinade, for 12 to 15 minutes or until lamb is well browned on outside but still pink in the center. As meat cooks, stack pitas on a sheet of foil. Wrap tightly and place near edge of grill, turning often, for 10 minutes or until warm. Drain onion. Cut pitas in half. To assemble, place 1 or 2 lettuce leaves in each pocket. Add about 6 lamb cubes, a spoonful of onion, tomato wedges, and a dollop of Yogurt Sauce. To make sauce, combine all ingredients well.

If desired, use 12 flour tortillas instead of pita halves. When warming, sprinkle each tortilla with a few drops of water before stacking. Roll filling ingredients in warmed tortillas and serve.

*Try adding 1 cup peeled, seeded, and diced cucumber to Yogurt Sauce for a different flavor.*

# Turkey Burgers With Herb Lemon Yogurt Sauce

*...this sure beats the quarter-pounder!*

Combine turkey, onion, parsley, and yogurt. Form into 8 patties. Sprinkle cheese on 4 patties. Cover with remaining 4 patties. Cook for 3 minutes on each side. Serve on rolls with Herbed Lemon Yogurt Sauce on the side. To prepare sauce, combine all ingredients well. Serve with cole slaw.

**sandwich**

- 1 pound ground turkey breast
- ½ cup finely chopped red onion
- ¼ cup finely chopped fresh parsley
- 2 tablespoons fat free plain yogurt
- 2 tablespoons crumbled goat cheese
- 4 sandwich rolls

**herb lemon yogurt sauce**

- 1¾ cups fat free plain yogurt
- 1 tablespoon minced fresh tarragon
- 2 tablespoons minced fresh chives or scallions
- 2 tablespoons chopped fresh basil
- 2 tablespoons lemon juice

**Yield: 4 servings**

# Hot Crab Toasts

*...perfect for an impromptu brunch or lunch*

1 (6-ounce) can white
  crabmeat, drained
1 (5-ounce) jar Old
  English cheese spread
1 stick butter, softened
1 teaspoon garlic
  powder
6 English muffins,
  halved

Combine crabmeat, cheese spread, butter, and garlic powder. Mix well. Spread over English muffin halves. Place on a baking sheet and bake at 450° for 10 to 15 minutes.

**Yield: 12 servings**

# Stuffed Vienna Bread

*...conceived as an appetizer, but so good, it became a meal*

1 pound fresh
  mushrooms, sliced
oil for sautéing
2 small loaves Vienna
  bread
8 ounces Swiss cheese,
  grated
1 stick butter, melted
2 tablespoons finely
  chopped onion
2 tablespoons poppy
  seeds
1 teaspoon seasoned
  salt
½ teaspoon lemon juice
1 tablespoon dry
  mustard

Sauté mushrooms in oil. Cut bread lengthwise without slicing all the way through. Hollow out some of inside of bread. Fill with mushrooms and cheese. Place loaves on heavy foil. Cut bread on the diagonal without slicing through bottom crust. Combine butter and remaining ingredients. Pour over bread. Wrap foil around loaves and bake at 350° for 30 minutes.

**Yield: 4 to 6 servings**

# Bridal Shower Lunch

*Champagne Sangria*

*Cold Billi Bi*

*Gingered Chicken and Cantaloupe Salad*
*Spring Couscous Salad*
*Basket of Warm Breads with Crocks of Sweet Butter*

*Cranberry Raspberry Sorbet*
*Chocolate Cake with Coffee Frosting*

*Veuve Clicquot*

# Three Bean Salad With Cilantro Chili Dressing

*...it is important to soak and cook the black beans and the white beans separately as one can become mushy, while the other is still tender*

Place black beans in one saucepan, white beans in a separate saucepan. Cover each with triple their volume of cold water. Bring each to a boil. Reduce heat and simmer, uncovered, 2 minutes. Remove pans from heat and let soak 60 minutes. Drain beans separately and return to pans. Stir 2½ quarts water into each pan. Cook 15 to 40 minutes or until beans are just tender but still hold their shape. Test for doneness every 5 minutes. Drain beans and let cool to warm. In a blender, purée 1 clove garlic, jalapeño peppers, 1 cup cilantro, ⅓ cup lemon juice, ⅔ cup oil, and salt. Process until smooth. In a large bowl, toss drained beans with dressing. Cover and marinate overnight in a refrigerator, stirring occasionally. Cook green beans in boiling water for 5 minutes or until crisp-tender. Drain and rinse under cold water. Drain again and pat dry. In blender, purée remaining garlic clove, 1 cup cilantro, 2 tablespoons lemon juice, ⅓ cup oil, and salt to taste. Process until smooth. Add green beans and dressing to white and black bean mixture. Toss well. Serve at room temperature. Garnish.

1 pound dried black beans
1 pound dried white beans
2 cloves garlic, divided
2 pickled jalapeño peppers, seeded
2 cups fresh cilantro, rinsed and spun dry, divided
⅓ cup plus 2 tablespoons fresh lemon juice, divided
1 cup vegetable oil, divided
salt to taste
1 pound green beans, trimmed and cut into 1-inch pieces
sprigs of fresh coriander for garnish

**Yield: 10 to 12 servings**

# Black Beans, Corn, And Tomatoes Vinaigrette

*...also good combined with rice or pasta, hot or cold*

1 pound dried black beans
1½ cups cooked fresh corn
1½ cups chopped, seeded tomatoes
¾ cup thinly sliced scallions
⅓ cup minced fresh cilantro
½ cup olive oil
½ cup fresh lemon juice
2 teaspoons salt
fresh cilantro sprigs for garnish

**Yield: 8 servings**

Cover beans with cold water and soak overnight. Drain and place in a large saucepan along with enough cold water to cover 2 inches above beans. Bring to a boil. Reduce heat and simmer 45 to 60 minutes or until tender, but not mushy. Drain. Combine beans, corn, tomatoes, scallions, and cilantro. In a small bowl, whisk together oil, lemon juice, and salt. Pour dressing over bean mixture while beans are still warm. Cool to room temperature, stirring occasionally. Garnish and serve.

# About Poaching Chicken For Salads

*...a great chicken salad does not come from tossing together leftovers and a dressing found in the refrigerator; but a minimum of time and effort, a loaf of bread and a chilled bottle of wine can bring forth memories of lazy summer afternoons*

1 (3-pound) chicken, or 6 chicken breasts
salt and pepper to taste
1 medium onion, halved
1 stalk celery with leaves, cracked
3 whole cloves
4 cups chicken broth
1 carrot, quartered
8 sprigs parsley
1 bay leaf
6 peppercorns

Arrange chicken in a large skillet. Add remaining ingredients. If necessary, add just enough water to cover. Bring to a boil. Reduce heat and simmer 15 minutes. Cool chicken in broth. Remove from broth and discard skin and bones. Cube, shred, or slice chicken according to recipe directions.

Bone-in chicken breasts add extra flavor to the meat during the cooking process.

# Chinese Salad

*...perfect for shredding and eating raw in salads, Chinese cabbage is a common ingredient in stir-fries and soups and is also luscious when slowly braised*

In a small bowl, combine all dressing ingredients. Cover and chill. To prepare salad, combine bean sprouts, lettuce, cabbage, cheese, ham, celery, water chestnuts, scallions, black olives, chicken, bell pepper, and shrimp. Chill. Toss salad with dressing. Top with bacon. Serve with chow mein noodles on the side.

## dressing
1 cup mayonnaise
¼ cup soy sauce
¼ cup vegetable oil
¼ cup lemon juice
Worcestershire sauce to taste

## salad
4 ounces bean sprouts
5 leaves romaine lettuce, julienned
1 head napa cabbage, julienned
4-5 ounces Swiss cheese, julienned
4-5 ounces ham, julienned
1 stalk celery, diced
½ (8-ounce) can water chestnuts, diced
5 scallions, chopped
½ (6-ounce) can black olives, chopped
⅓ pound boneless, skinless chicken breast, cooked and shredded
¼ green bell pepper, diced
1 pound shrimp, cooked and peeled
chopped cooked bacon for garnish
chow mein noodles

**Yield: 10 servings**

# Broiled Chicken Breasts With Mixed Salad

*...an easy meal for summer entertaining*

4 (5-ounce) boneless, skinless chicken breasts
salt and pepper to taste
2 teaspoons chopped fresh rosemary
2 tablespoons ground coriander
6 tablespoons olive oil, divided
2 heads Belgian endive
1 bunch watercress, large stems removed
8 ounces red leaf lettuce
1 medium-size red onion, coarsely chopped
2 tablespoons red wine vinegar
¼ cup coarsely chopped fresh basil
½ cup walnut halves

**Yield: 4 servings**

Sprinkle chicken with salt, pepper, rosemary, coriander, and 1 tablespoon oil. Rub seasoning into chicken. Broil 3 to 4 minutes or until lightly browned. Turn chicken and broil until done. Transfer to a plate and keep warm. Cut endive heads in half crosswise. Reserve lower halves. Arrange leaves from top halves on individual serving plates, radiating leaves out from the center. Chop reserved bottom halves coarsely and place in a salad bowl. Add remaining 5 tablespoons olive oil, watercress, lettuce, onion, vinegar, and basil. Season with salt and pepper. Add any juice that may have accumulated from the cooked chicken. Toss well. Divide salad mixture among serving plates. Thinly slice each chicken breast on the bias. Place slices neatly over the salads. Sprinkle walnuts over top.

# Warm Chicken Salad

*...a delicate year-round salad with a hint of raspberry*

Heat oil in a sauté pan. Lightly coat chicken with flour. Sauté in oil until lightly browned. Remove chicken and discard oil. Deglaze pan with vinegar. Add chicken, scallions, and dill and mix well. Add almonds and butter. Season with salt and pepper. To prepare dressing, blend yolks and mustard in a food processor. With machine running, slowly add oil. Blend in garlic, vinegar, and wine. Season with salt and pepper. Place warm chicken mixture over any combination of salad greens. Serve dressing on the side.

**Salad**
- 2 tablespoons olive oil
- 6 ounces boneless, skinless chicken breast, julienned
- 2 tablespoons all-purpose flour
- 3 tablespoons raspberry vinegar
- 2 tablespoons sliced scallions
- 1 teaspoon chopped dill
- 3 tablespoons almonds, toasted
- 1 tablespoon butter
- salt and pepper to taste

**Dressing**
- 2 egg yolks
- 5 tablespoons whole grain mustard
- 3 cups safflower oil
- ½ teaspoon minced garlic
- ⅔ cup white vinegar
- 2 tablespoons white wine
- salt and pepper to taste

**Yield: 1 salad serving, 4 cups dressing**

# Chutney Chicken Salad

*...for a fuller salad, add fresh pineapple and scallions*

1 cup mayonnaise
¼-½ cup chopped
   chutney
1 teaspoon curry
   powder
2 teaspoons lime zest
¼ cup fresh lime juice
½ teaspoon salt
4-6 boneless, skinless
   chicken breasts,
   poached
8 lettuce leaves
½ cup slivered almonds,
   toasted
red bell pepper strips for
   garnish

Combine mayonnaise, chutney, curry powder, zest, juice, and salt and chill. Slice chicken breasts across the grain. Place lettuce leaves on individual serving plates to make "bowls". Place chicken in lettuce leaves. Drizzle dressing over top and sprinkle with almonds. Garnish.

*Add ½ pineapple, cubed, and ½ cup sliced scallions.*

**Yield: 8 servings**

# Curried Chicken Salad With Peanuts

*...Indians have been using curry for 5000 years*

6 chicken breasts
1 medium cucumber,
   peeled, seeded, and
   diced
1 cup peanuts, roasted
½ cup raisins
salt and pepper to taste
½ cup mayonnaise
½ cup plain yogurt
2 tablespoons curry
   powder
watercress
clumps of seedless green
   grapes for garnish

Poach chicken, cool, and cut into ¾-inch cubes. Combine chicken, cucumber, peanuts, and raisins in a large mixing bowl and toss. In a small bowl, blend salt, pepper, mayonnaise, yogurt, and curry powder. Pour dressing over chicken mixture, mixing gently to coat. Line the rim of individual serving plates with watercress. Mound salad in the middle. Garnish.

**Yield: 6 servings**

# Gingered Chicken And Cantaloupe Salad

*...cantaloupe derives its name from the castle, Cantalupo, near Rome where it was developed in the 17th century*

Poach chicken, cool, and julienne. In a blender or food processor, combine egg, lemon juice, salt, and pepper. Pulse until egg is foamy. With machine running, gradually add oil in a thin stream until mixture thickens. Scrape into a small mixing bowl. Add tarragon and ginger. Fold in whipped cream until well blended. Cover and chill. Peel and seed cantaloupe and tomatoes. Cut each into narrow, short strips. Combine chicken, cantaloupe, tomato, and dressing in a large bowl. Mix until salad is evenly coated. Line individual serving plates with lettuce leaves. Mound salad in center. Garnish with cantaloupe slices.

6 chicken breasts
1 egg
2 tablespoons lemon juice
salt and pepper to taste
1 cup vegetable oil
1 tablespoon finely chopped fresh tarragon
2 tablespoons finely grated fresh ginger
½ cup whipped cream
1 medium cantaloupe
4 ripe tomatoes
leaf lettuce
slices of cantaloupe for garnish

**Yield: 6 to 8 servings**

# Rosemary Vinaigrette

Put ⅔ cup olive oil, ¼ cup balsamic vinegar, 3 tablespoons lemon juice, 1 shallot, 1 tablespoon fresh rosemary, ½ teaspoon brown sugar, salt and pepper in a blender or food processor and blend at high speed until smooth.

# Tropical Chicken Salad In Radicchio Cups

*...ginger, the root of a sweet plant that looks like a tall Iris, is native to the West Indies*

6 chicken breasts
2 mangoes, peeled and cubed
2 cups fresh pineapple, cubed
1 cup seedless green grapes
3 scallions, white only, minced
½ cup coarsely chopped almonds, toasted
1 tablespoon minced ginger
1 tablespoon minced fresh cilantro
1 tablespoon minced fresh mint
salt and pepper to taste
1 large lime, halved
1 cup mayonnaise
½ cup sour cream
6-8 large leaves radicchio or red cabbage
orange slices and strawberries for garnish

**Yield: 6 to 8 servings**

Poach chicken breasts, cool, and cut in ½-inch cubes. Combine chicken, mangoes, pineapple, grapes, scallions, almonds, ginger, cilantro, and mint in a large mixing bowl. Toss lightly. Season with salt and pepper. Squeeze lime halves over top and toss. Refrigerate 60 minutes. In a small bowl, combine mayonnaise and sour cream. Pour dressing over salad and toss gently to coat. Place one radicchio leaf on each plate. Mound salad in each leaf. Garnish each plate with an orange slice topped with a strawberry.

# Chicken, Mein, And Vegetables In Creamy Szechuan Dressing

*...the flavor of the dish improves from an overnight chilling, but wait until the last minute to add the crunchy peas*

Poach chicken, drain, and cool. Cut into bite-size pieces. Blanch snow peas until crisp-tender. Cool in ice water and drain. Cook noodles al dente and drain. Toss hot noodles in a large bowl with ½ cup soy sauce. Mix in peanut oil. Cool to room temperature, occasionally stirring noodles. Combine remaining ¼ cup soy sauce, mayonnaise, mustard, sesame oil, and chili oil. Chill until ready to use. Add chicken, scallions, carrots, bell pepper, bamboo shoots, corn, and cilantro to noodles. Mix gently, but thoroughly with hands. Add mayonnaise mixture and blend well. Cover and refrigerate until ready to serve, preferably overnight. About 30 minutes prior to serving, remove from refrigerator and toss in peas. Add extra soy sauce, peanut oil, or mayonnaise if noodles seem dry. Garnish. Pass extra soy sauce and chili oil when serving.

To toast sesame seeds, place in a small skillet over medium heat. Stir until seeds are golden. Remove from heat and pour onto a plate to cool.

4 chicken breasts, boned and skinned
½ pound fresh snow peas, trimmed and julienned
1 pound Chinese noodles
¾ cup soy sauce, divided
¼ cup peanut oil
2 cups mayonnaise
1 tablespoon Dijon mustard
¼ cup oriental sesame oil
Szechuan chili oil to taste
6 scallions, thinly sliced
2 carrots, coarsely chopped
1 red bell pepper, coarsely chopped
1 (8-ounce) can sliced bamboo shoots, drained
1 (6-ounce) jar baby corn, drained and thickly sliced
½ cup chopped fresh cilantro
fresh cilantro sprigs and lightly toasted sesame seeds for garnish

**Yield: 6 entrée servings, 10 to 12 salad servings**

# Spring Couscous Salad

*...couscous can be used as an alternative to pasta or rice in any salad*

## salad

- 7 cups water, divided
- 1 cup chicken broth
- 1 tablespoon unsalted butter
- 1¾ cups precooked couscous
- 12 ounces fresh asparagus, cut into 1-inch pieces
- 2 slices fresh ginger, minced
- ⅓ cup rice wine or sake
- 1¼ pounds raw medium shrimp in shells
- 1 red bell pepper, diced
- 4 plum tomatoes, seeded and diced
- ⅓ cup finely diced red onion
- 1 cup chickpeas (optional)

## vinaigrette

- ¼ cup balsamic vinegar
- 2 cloves garlic, minced
- ½ teaspoon Dijon mustard
- ½ cup virgin olive oil
- 1 teaspoon salt
- ¼ teaspoon black pepper
- 2 tablespoons chopped fresh cilantro or parsley

**Yield: 6 servings**

Combine 2 cups water, broth, and butter in a saucepan. Bring to a boil. Add couscous, cover, and remove from heat. Let stand 5 minutes. Fluff with a fork and cool completely. Bring remaining 5 cups water to a boil. Add asparagus and partially cover. Cook 5 minutes or until just tender. Remove from water with a slotted spoon and rinse under cold water. Drain. Add ginger and wine to cooking water and cook 10 minutes. Remove from heat and add shrimp. Drain after about 3½ minutes and discard ginger. Peel and devein shrimp. In a large mixing bowl, combine asparagus, shrimp, bell pepper, tomatoes, onion, and chickpeas. To prepare vinaigrette, combine vinegar, garlic, and mustard in a small bowl. Slowly whisk in oil. Season with salt and pepper. Fold in cilantro. Add vinaigrette to salad mixture and adjust seasonings as needed. Spread couscous in a shallow bowl or on a platter and fluff with a fork. Arrange shrimp mixture on top. Serve at room temperature or chill for about 60 minutes before serving.

# Crabmeat And Hearts of Palm Salad

Combine hearts of palm, crabmeat, lime juice, chives, Tabasco sauce, Worcestershire sauce, mustard, and mayonnaise in a large mixing bowl. Toss lightly with a wooden spatula. Line a serving platter with lettuce leaves. Place salad mixture on top. Garnish with tomato.

1 (14-ounce) can hearts of palm, drained and chopped
1 pound cooked crabmeat
juice of 1 lime
1 tablespoon chopped fresh chives
dash of Tabasco sauce
1 teaspoon Worcestershire sauce
1 tablespoon Dijon mustard
1/4 cup mayonnaise
1 head leaf lettuce
1 tomato, peeled, seeded, and thinly sliced for garnish

**Yield: 8 servings**

# Stilton And Pear Salad

In a small bowl, whisk together vinegar, mustard, salt, and pepper. Blend in oil in a stream, whisking until emulsified. Toss lettuce with half the dressing. Divide lettuce among individual serving plates. Cut pears in half, core, and cut into thin, lengthwise slices. Arrange pear slices with Stilton on each plate. Divide pecans among plates. Top with remaining half of dressing.

2 tablespoons white wine vinegar
1/2 teaspoon Dijon mustard
salt and pepper to taste
1/4 cup olive oil
6 cups chopped red and green leaf lettuce
2 large Bartlett pears
8 ounces Stilton cheese, cut in wedges or crumbled
1/2 cup pecans, lightly toasted

**Yield: 4 servings**

# Duck And Pear Salad With Chutney Dressing

*...mixed white and wild rice with chicken is a successful alternative*

**mango chutney dressing**
- 1 egg
- 2 egg yolks
- 1 tablespoon Dijon mustard
- ¼ cup blueberry vinegar
- ⅓ cup mango chutney
- 1 tablespoon soy sauce
- salt and pepper to taste
- 1 cup peanut oil
- 1 cup corn oil

**salad**
- 2 (4½ to 5 pound) ducks
- salt and pepper to taste
- 3 cups cooked wild rice
- 1 cup chopped celery
- 4 scallions, cut diagonally into ½-inch pieces
- zest of 1 orange
- 3 ripe, firm Bartlett pears
- 1 cup lemon juice
- 6 large butter lettuce leaves
- Mango Chutney Dressing

**Yield: 6 servings**

To prepare dressing, combine egg, egg yolks, mustard, vinegar, chutney, and soy sauce in a food processor with a steel blade. Season with salt and pepper and process 1 minute. With machine running, add oils in a slow, steady stream. Correct seasoning as needed. Refrigerate until ready to use. To make salad, roast ducks at 450° for 15 minutes. Reduce heat to 375° and bake another 20 to 30 minutes. Cool and skin ducks. Remove all meat and cut into 1X3-inch slivers. Combine duck, salt, pepper, rice, celery, scallions, and zest in a large mixing bowl. Cut pears in half, core, and cut into thin slices. Arrange lettuce "cups" on individual serving plates. Mound duck salad in center of each plate. Top with dressing and arrange a fan of pear slices across top. Serve immediately.

# Lobster, Corn, Zucchini, And Basil

*...serve with an ocean view in Gloucester, Massachusetts*

Blanch zucchini and corn in boiling water for 1 minute. Drain well, cool, and transfer to a large mixing bowl. Break off claws at body of each lobster. Crack claws and remove meat. Twist tails from lobster bodies, keeping tails intact. Discard bodies. Using a kitchen scissors, remove thin membrane from each lobster tail by cutting just inside outer edge of shell. Remove meat from tail and reserve shell for serving. Cut lobster meat into ½-inch pieces and add to mixing bowl. In a small bowl, whisk together mayonnaise, vinegar, salt, and pepper. Pour over lobster mixture and mix well. Just before serving, stir in basil. Mound equal portions into each reserved lobster tail. Garnish each tail with a sprig of basil.

2 (8-ounce) zucchini, diced
¾ cup fresh corn
6 (1¼ pound) lobsters, cooked
¼ cup mayonnaise
2 tablespoons white wine vinegar or lemon juice
salt and pepper to taste
¼ cup finely shredded fresh basil
6 sprigs of fresh basil for garnish

**Yield: 6 servings**

# Warm Potato Salad

*...beer and brats!*

1½ pounds small, red, waxy potatoes
2 tablespoons white wine vinegar
¼ cup vegetable oil
3 tablespoons finely chopped shallots or scallions
¼ cup finely chopped fresh parsley or tarragon
black pepper to taste

**Yield: 4 servings**

Bring potatoes to a boil in salted water. Reduce heat and simmer 15 minutes or until tender. Do not overcook. Drain and let cool until warm. Peel potatoes and cut into ¼-inch thick slices. Combine potatoes and remaining ingredients in a bowl. Blend well and serve.

# Warm Green Bean And Walnut Salad

*...often the simplest is the best!*

¼ cup chopped walnuts, toasted, divided
4 teaspoons white wine vinegar
¼ cup olive oil
salt and pepper to taste
1½ pounds green beans, trimmed and cut into ¾-inch pieces

**Yield: 4 servings**

In a blender or food processor, blend 2 tablespoons walnuts, vinegar, oil, salt, and pepper. Steam beans 5 to 8 minutes or until crisp-tender. Toss beans, dressing, and remaining 2 tablespoons nuts in a bowl.

# Arborio Rice Salad

*...best served at room temperature, so ideal for a picnic or buffet*

Plump raisins in water and drain. Add rice and lemon zest to boiling salted water. Cook 15 minutes or until tender. Drain. In a large bowl, combine raisins, rice, lemon juice, scallions, and oil. Season with salt and pepper. Serve at room temperature.

If desired, substitute basmati or white rice for Arborio rice.

1 cup golden raisins
2 cups Arborio rice
zest and juice of 2 lemons
1 cup chopped scallions
¼ cup olive oil
salt and pepper to taste

**Yield: 8 servings**

# Beer Coleslaw

*...if ever there was a town to feature Beer Coleslaw, it's St. Louis!*

Combine cabbage, carrots, onion, and bell pepper in a bowl. In a separate bowl, mix remaining ingredients with a whisk. Pour dressing over vegetables and toss gently but thoroughly. Adjust seasoning as needed. Cover and refrigerate 60 minutes before serving.

1 (2-pound) head cabbage, grated
3 medium carrots, grated
4 tablespoons finely chopped onion
½ red bell pepper, diced
1 cup mayonnaise
1 tablespoon Dijon mustard
1 teaspoon celery seed
¼ cup beer
1 teaspoon salt
black pepper to taste

**Yield: 8 servings**

# Greek Slaw

*...olive trees, with gnarled trunks and silvery-gray foliage, grow everywhere around the Mediterranean*

1 (1½ to 2½ pound) head cabbage, shredded
½ cup sliced stuffed Spanish olives
¾ cup sliced black olives
½ cup chopped green or red bell pepper
1 large onion, chopped
⅔ cup vinegar
¾ cup vegetable oil
1 tablespoon dried oregano
1½ tablespoons Greek seasoning
¾ teaspoon garlic powder

**Yield: 10 to 12 servings**

Combine cabbage, olives, bell pepper, and onion in a large bowl. In a saucepan, bring remaining ingredients to a boil. Pour over vegetables and mix. Allow to cool, stirring frequently.

For best flavor, chill overnight before serving.

# Cumin Vinaigrette

Purée 1 tablespoon chopped fresh cilantro, 2 cloves roasted garlic, 2 tablespoons lemon juice and ¼ cup red wine vinegar in a blender or food processor. Toast 1 tablespoon ground cumin in a dry frying pan until lightly browned, stirring frequently. Whisk into vinegar with ½ cup olive oil, ¼ cup canola or vegetable oil, 1 tablespoon brown sugar and salt to taste.

# Tomato Aspic

*...a Bloody Mary without the vodka*

Dissolve gelatin in water for 5 minutes. In a saucepan, simmer tomato juice, vinegar, sugar, salt, and pepper for 5 minutes. Remove from heat and stir in gelatin until dissolved. Add onion, horseradish, and lemon juice. Pour into a lightly oiled mold. Refrigerate 4 hours or until set. When firm, unmold onto a serving platter.

2 tablespoons unflavored gelatin
½ cup cold water
2 cups tomato juice
½ cup vinegar
½ cup sugar
1 teaspoon salt
pinch of cayenne pepper
1 tablespoon grated onion
1 tablespoon grated fresh horseradish
1 tablespoon lemon juice

**Yield: 6 servings**

# Cucumber Salad

*...serve with a cold poached salmon as a substitute for a highly caloric, creamy sauce*

Heat oil in a small pan until vapors start to rise. Remove from heat, add mustard seed, and cover. The seed will pop in the hot oil. When done popping, combine mustard seed and cucumber in a bowl. Gently mix in remaining ingredients. Chill.

Black mustard seed is available in Asian grocery stores.

2 teaspoons oil
½ teaspoon black mustard seed
2 cucumbers, peeled, seeded, and grated
1 cup low fat yogurt
1 green hot chili pepper, grated (optional)
1-2 tablespoons grated fresh ginger
1 tablespoon finely chopped cilantro
pinch of lemon garlic salt
½ teaspoon salt

**Yield: 4 servings**

# Warm Tuna Salad With Wasabi Dressing

*...wasabi is a Japanese horseradish, usually grated, available to us dried*

## wasabi dressing
  2 tablespoons wasabi
  ¼ cup water
  1 egg yolk
  2 cups vegetable oil
  ¼ cup rice wine vinegar
salt and white pepper to
    taste

## salad
  1 pound angel hair
    pasta or thin
    vermicelli
salt and white pepper to
    taste
  ¼ cup oil
  ¼ cup rice wine vinegar
  ½ cup pimiento, drained
  6 scallions, green only,
    chopped
  1 pound tuna
  ¼ cup soy sauce
  1 medium cucumber,
    peeled, seeded, and
    cut in 2-inch julienne
    strips
  1 teaspoon rice wine
    vinegar
  1 teaspoon sesame
    seeds, toasted
  6 leaves Bibb or Boston
    lettuce
  6 leaves radicchio
  3 medium tomatoes,
    cut in wedges
 12 small broccoli
    flowerets, blanched

**Yield: 6 servings**

To make dressing, blend wasabi and water. Let stand 15 minutes. In a separate bowl, beat egg yolk. Whisk in oil in a thin, steady stream until emulsified. Stir in vinegar, salt, and pepper. Mix in wasabi. To prepare salad, cook pasta according to package directions. Drain, rinse with cold water, and drain. Toss pasta with salt, pepper, oil, vinegar, pimiento, and scallions. Set aside. Cut tuna into ½-inch thick medallions. Rub with soy sauce and marinate 5 minutes. Toss cucumber with vinegar and a pinch of salt. Sprinkle with sesame seeds and toss. Arrange pasta, lettuce, radicchio, tomato, cucumber mixture, and broccoli on individual serving plates. Broil tuna on a baking sheet for 1 minute on each side. Immediately divide tuna medallions among plates. Drizzle dressing over top.

# Mixed Greens With Goat Cheese, Maple Vinaigrette And Toasted Walnuts

*...pure maple syrup is a luxury, but a necessity!*

Blend vinegar, syrup, shallot, oil, salt, and pepper in a food processor. Pour dressing over greens and toss to mix. Arrange salad among individual serving plates. Place goat cheese on side of greens and sprinkle walnuts and chives over top.

*Pulse walnuts in a food processor. Coat cheese slices with finely chopped walnuts.*

¼ cup balsamic vinegar
2 tablespoons pure maple syrup
1 tablespoon minced shallot
¾ cup olive oil
½ teaspoon salt, or to taste
black pepper to taste
6-8 cups mixed salad greens
9 ounces goat cheese, cut into 12 slices
2 cups walnuts, toasted
chopped fresh chives

**Yield: 6 servings**

# Creamy Caesar Salad Dressing

*...worth the trouble!*

Combine all ingredients in a blender. Process on high speed for 45 seconds. Chill at least 2 hours to allow flavors to blend.

Serve on romaine lettuce with seasoned croutons.

1 cup mayonnaise
3 tablespoons milk or cream
1 teaspoon anchovy paste
¼ cup Parmesan cheese
1 tablespoon lemon juice
¼ teaspoon garlic powder, or 1 clove garlic

**Yield: 1½ cups**

# Jones' Salad Dressing

*...the Racquet Club's original recipe from 1934*

cloves garlic
salt and coarsely ground
   black pepper
 4 teaspoons olive oil
 1 teaspoon vinegar
 1 tablespoon Durkee's
   Famous Sauce

**Yield: 1 serving**

Rub a bowl with garlic cloves, being careful to not leave any garlic particles. Sprinkle bowl with salt and pepper. Rub spoon over salt and pepper to saturate seasonings in garlic juice. Add oil and vinegar and mix well. If oil is not cold, add a piece of ice to bowl and stir for a few minutes. Add sauce. Remove ice. Serve over lettuce.

# Mayfair Dressing

*...in 1965, Julia Runge King, manager for many years of the Mayfair Hotel in downtown St. Louis, came to manage the Queeny Tower Hotel and Dining Room at Barnes Hospital, bringing with her The Mayfair's favorite salad*

 1 clove garlic, sliced
 1 stalk celery, diced
½ medium onion, diced
 1 (1-ounce) can
   anchovies in oil,
   drained
 3 eggs
 1 tablespoon coarsely
   ground black pepper
 1 tablespoon seasoned
   salt flavor enhancer
 1 tablespoon prepared
   mustard
 2 cups vegetable oil

**Yield: 1 quart**

Process garlic, celery, onion, anchovies, eggs, pepper, seasoned salt flavor enhancer, and mustard in a blender for 5 seconds. Add oil, ¼ cup at a time, blending after each addition. Store in refrigerator.

# Raspberry Sherry Vinaigrette

*...for blanched fresh asparagus, any spring vegetable, or tossed salad with fruit*

Process vinegar, sherry, parsley, onion, and mustard in a food processor. With machine running, slowly add oil. Season with salt and pepper.

¼ cup raspberry vinegar
⅛ cup dry sherry
4 sprigs parsley
½ small red onion
1 teaspoon dry mustard
1½ cups oil
salt and pepper to taste

**Yield: 2 cups**

# Stilton Dressing

*...for any salad, or as a dip with spicy chicken wings*

In a large mixing bowl, combine mayonnaise, sour cream, and vinegar. Season with salt and pepper. Add cheese, ⅓ cup at a time, stirring after each addition.

2 cups mayonnaise
1 cup sour cream
¾ cup white vinegar
salt and white pepper to taste
1 cup crumbled Stilton cheese

**Yield: 4¾ cups**

# Gorgonzola Dressing

*...tossed with field greens, endive, or of course, chicken*

Combine all ingredients well.

1 cup oil
½ cup white vinegar
½ cup crumbled Gorgonzola cheese
½ shallot, minced
chopped fresh parsley to taste
salt and pepper to taste

**Yield: 2 cups**

# Country Dressing

*...good for a vegetarian salad or a large chef salad*

1 small leek
1 small carrot
½ cup parsley
4 egg yolks
2 tablespoons Dijon
   mustard
½ cup raspberry vinegar
½ cup white vinegar
3½ cups oil
2 tablespoons honey
salt and pepper to taste

Finely chop leek, carrot, and parsley in a food processor. Blend in yolks, mustard, and vinegars. With machine running, slowly add oil. Mix in honey and season with salt and pepper.

**Yield: 5 cups**


# Tarragon Vinaigrette

*...for a seafood salad*

¼ cup prepared
   mustard
salt and pepper to taste
5 tablespoons tarragon
   vinegar
1 egg yolk
¼ cup chopped fresh
   parsley
¼ cup chopped fresh
   tarragon
¼ cup chopped shallots
3½ cups oil

Process mustard, salt, pepper, vinegar, egg yolk, parsley, tarragon, and shallots in a food processor. With machine running, slowly add oil.

Try this dressing on a roast beef sandwich on a baguette bread.

**Yield: 4½ cups**

# Summer Grill

*Roasted Red Pepper with Capers Pizza*

*Gazpacho with Crab Meat*

*Grilled Marinated Swordfish with Artichoke,*
*Kalamata & Sun-dried Tomato Relish*
*Grilled Jumbo Shrimp with Green Mayonnaise*
*Oil-Roasted Summer Vegetables*
*Cucumber Salad*

*Peach Pie*
*Christopher's Blueberry Sherbet*

*MacRostie Chardonnay*
*Cavalchino Bardolino*

# Midwinter Fireside Dinner

*Duck Confit with Plum Chutney*
*Braised Red Cabbage*
*Puréed Lentils*
*Baby Green Beans in Lemon Butter*

*Poached Pears with Brandy Sauce*

*Dubreuil Fontaine Pommard*

# Oven Steamed Halibut In A Ginger Tomato Broth

*...serve halibut on a bed of mashed potatoes, and pour broth over top*

Sauté ginger, garlic, shallots, and leek in a small amount of oil until softened. Add salt, pepper, bay leaf, thyme, and pepper flakes. Stir in wine, water, and tomatoes. Cook until heated through. Place halibut in an ovenproof dish and cover with tomato broth. Bake at 350° for 15 to 20 minutes or until firm to the touch. Remove bay leaf. Place on a serving dish. Spoon broth over top.

*Vary this dish by using shrimp instead of halibut, and serving over angel hair pasta.*

¼ cup minced ginger
5 cloves garlic, minced
4 shallots, minced
½ leek, minced, white part only
vegetable oil
salt and pepper to taste
1 bay leaf
1 sprig fresh thyme, or 1 teaspoon dried
½ teaspoon crushed red pepper flakes
4 cups white wine
4 cups water
1 (28-ounce) can whole tomatoes, coarsely chopped, undrained
6 (6 to 7-ounce) halibut fillets

**Yield: 6 servings**

# Paella

*...paella, a succulent dish from Spain that combines unexpected yet harmonious ingredients - mussels and sausage, chicken and shrimp - is named for the shallow open dish in which it is cooked*

2 chicken breasts, cut
  in 1-inch cubes
1 clove garlic, crushed
1 stick butter
2 cups dry rice
½ teaspoon saffron
½ cup water
4 cups hot chicken
  broth, divided
salt and pepper to taste
2 chorizo links, sliced,
  divided
12 mussels
1 pound shrimp
½ cup diced tomato

**Yield: 6 to 8 servings**

Sauté chicken and garlic in butter in a skillet until browned. Remove chicken. Add rice to skillet and sauté until golden. Soak saffron in water. Strain liquid. Add liquid and 3½ cups broth to skillet. Season with salt and pepper and bring to a boil. Cook until tender. Place half of chicken in a buttered paella pan or Dutch oven. Add half the chorizo and the majority of rice. Top with remaining chicken, chorizo, and remaining rice. Bake, uncovered, at 350° for 45 minutes. Add remaining chicken broth, if needed while baking. Place mussels and shrimp on top and bake 15 minutes longer. Stir in tomato. Discard unopened mussels.

Use steamed clams in place of, or in addition to mussels, if desired.

# Crab Cakes With Red Pepper Coulis

*...fish cakes, like meat loaf, are objects of an unstated affection and often a glimpse of the recent past as they are usually made from leftover fish, extended with potatoes, bread crumbs, or vegetables - a fork or fingers, and a light touch, are a fish cake's best friend, not the food processor!*

Whisk together mayonnaise, salt, pepper, lemon juice, mustard, chives, Worcestershire sauce, and cayenne pepper. Fold in crabmeat. Place cornmeal in a shallow pan for dredging. Form crab mixture into 2½ to 3-inch diameter patties. Coat evenly in cornmeal. Chill until ready to use. Heat oil in a large skillet. Brown patties on both sides. Serve hot with Red Pepper Coulis or a sherry cayenne mayonnaise. To prepare coulis, roast whole peppers over a gas flame, or cut peppers in half and broil, turning frequently, until blackened on all sides. Place in a plastic bag until cool enough to handle. Peel off skin and remove seed and pith. Chop pepper and place in a food processor. Add garlic, basil, and egg yolk. Pulse until well blended. With machine running, slowly add oil. Season with salt and pepper. Chill until ready to use.

Make smaller crab cakes if serving as an appetizer.

## crab cakes

- 1 cup mayonnaise
- 1 teaspoon salt
- ¼ teaspoon black pepper
- 1 teaspoon lemon juice
- 1 tablespoon Dijon mustard
- 1 tablespoon minced chives
- 1 teaspoon Worcestershire sauce
- cayenne pepper to taste
- 1 pound lump crabmeat
- 2 cups cornmeal
- ½ cup vegetable oil

## red pepper coulis

- 2 red bell peppers
- 2 cloves garlic, chopped
- 4 fresh basil leaves, finely chopped
- 1 egg yolk
- ½ cup olive oil
- salt and pepper to taste

**Yield: 10 to 12 cakes, 1 cup coulis**

# Grilled Snapper With Basil Mashed Potatoes

*...snapper is a light fish from the warmer waters of the Atlantic and the Caribbean*

2½ pounds potatoes, peeled and quartered
fresh basil
2 cups olive oil, divided
salt and pepper to taste
2 navel oranges, peeled and cut in segments
2 limes, peeled and cut in segments
6 red snapper fillets

**Yield: 6 servings**

Cook potatoes in lightly salted water until tender. Combine about 20 basil leaves and ½ cup oil in a food processor. Blend until finely chopped. Drain potatoes and mash with about half the basil mixture. Blend in remaining basil mixture and season with salt and pepper. Keep warm. Julienne remaining basil leaves for garnish. Warm orange and lime segments in remaining 1½ cups oil in a sauté pan. Season snapper with salt and pepper. Brush each side with some oil from sauté pan. Grill, skin-side down, for 3 to 4 minutes or until fish flakes easily with a fork. If broiling, broil skin-side up and finish in a 350° oven for 5 minutes. Spoon mashed potatoes onto individual serving plates. Arrange fish on plate and top with citrus segments and oil. Garnish with julienned basil leaves.

# Grilled Swordfish With Artichoke, Kalamata Olive, And Sun-dried Tomato Relish

*...also makes a great focaccia sandwich*

Make relish by combining all ingredients in a bowl. Mix well, cover, and chill. To prepare swordfish, combine salt, pepper, oil, shallots, basil, garlic, lemon juice, and wine. Pour over swordfish and marinate. When ready to cook, remove swordfish from marinade. Place on a lightly oiled grill and cook over medium heat for 5 to 6 minutes on each side. Serve hot with relish.

**relish**
2 (11-ounce) cans artichoke hearts, drained and sliced
½ cup chopped kalamata olives
12 large basil leaves, julienned
10 water-packed sun-dried tomatoes, drained and julienned
6 cloves garlic, sliced
1 red onion, sliced
salt and pepper to taste
½ cup oil

**swordfish**
salt and pepper to taste
1 cup olive oil
2 shallots, minced
2 sprigs basil, minced
2 cloves garlic, minced
1 tablespoon lemon juice
1 tablespoon white wine
6 (6 to 7-ounce) swordfish steaks

**Yield: 6 servings**

# Grilled Tuna With Mango Papaya Relish

*...mango, the choicest of all tropical fruits, was first known in India 4,000 years ago*

**relish**
- 1 mango, peeled, seeded and julienned
- 1 papaya, peeled, seeded and julienned
- ½ green bell pepper, julienned
- ½ red bell pepper, julienned
- 1 red onion, sliced
- 1 tablespoon minced ginger

juice of 3 limes
- ¼ cup minced fresh cilantro

salt and pepper to taste

**tuna**

salt and pepper to taste
- 1 cup olive oil
- 2 shallots, minced
- 2 tablespoons minced fresh cilantro
- 2 cloves garlic, minced
- 2 tablespoons lime juice
- 1 teaspoon Dijon mustard
- 6 (6 to 7-ounce) tuna steaks

**Yield: 6 servings**

Make relish by combining all ingredients in a bowl. Mix well, cover, and chill overnight. To prepare tuna, combine salt, pepper, oil, shallots, cilantro, garlic, lime juice, and mustard. Pour over tuna and marinate at room temperature for 1 to 2 hours. When ready to cook, remove tuna from marinade. Place on a lightly oiled grill and cook over medium heat for 5 to 6 minutes on each side. Serve hot with relish.

# Scallops In Creamy Leek Sauce

*...if in season, use bay scallops*

Cut leeks in half lengthwise, then cut in ½-inch sections. Sauté in 2 tablespoons butter for 3 to 4 minutes. Add broth, wine, salt, and pepper. Simmer until sauce reduces by half. In a separate pan, sauté scallops in remaining 2 tablespoons butter until done. Do not overcook. Add scallops and cream to sauce. Mix well and heat.

This dish is great served on rice.

3 leeks, white part only
4 tablespoons butter, divided
½ cup chicken broth
½ cup white wine
pinch of salt
½ teaspoon black pepper
1 pound sea scallops
½ cup heavy cream

**Yield: 4 servings**

# Lobster Newburg For Two

*...if you prefer to celebrate Valentine's Day at home, try this and hang the cholesterol for one evening*

Boil lobster, cool, and remove meat. Cut meat into chunks. Sauté meat in butter for about 1 minute. Add sherry and cream and simmer 5 minutes. Dilute egg yolks with a small amount of cream sauce. Stir into lobster mixture. Season with salt, pepper, and paprika. Serve hot over wild rice or al dente pasta.

1 (2-pound) lobster
unsalted butter
½ cup imported sherry
1 cup cream
2 egg yolks, beaten
salt and pepper to taste
sweet paprika to taste
cooked wild rice or pasta

**Yield: 2 servings**

# Shrimp With Feta Cheese

*...feta, the most popular of the Greek cheeses, has its origin in the hills above Athens*

1 pound large shrimp, peeled and deveined
2 tablespoons lemon juice
¾ cup diced scallion
2 tablespoons minced fresh parsley
2 cloves garlic, minced
¼ cup olive oil
1½ cups canned Italian tomatoes, drained
½ cup clam juice
3 tablespoons butter
1 fresh tomato, peeled
½ teaspoon dried oregano
¼ cup dry white wine
8 ounces feta cheese, crumbled

**Yield: 4 servings**

Place shrimp in a bowl and sprinkle with lemon juice. In a skillet, sauté scallion, parsley, and garlic in oil until softened. Stir in canned tomatoes and season as desired. Bring to a boil, stirring constantly. Reduce heat and simmer, covered, for 20 minutes. Stir in clam juice and cook 5 minutes. In a separate skillet, sauté shrimp in butter over medium-high heat for 4 minutes or until pink. Pour tomato sauce into a shallow 1½-quart baking dish. Place fresh tomato in center of dish and surround with shrimp. Sprinkle with oregano and pour wine over top. Sprinkle with cheese. Bake at 400° for 15 to 20 minutes.

*For a quicker version, sauté shrimp in oil. Add Italian tomatoes, scallions, 1 teaspoon oregano, and ⅓ cup sherry. When scallions soften, add cheese. Heat through but do not melt cheese. Season with salt and pepper.*

# Shrimp Creole

*...Creole cooking originated with the French and Spanish settlers in the Gulf states*

Make a roux by cooking flour in oil over low heat, stirring constantly until dark brown. Stir in shrimp until thoroughly coated with roux. Add scallions, parsley, bell pepper, and garlic. Sauté lightly. Mix in tomato sauce, water, peppers, salt, and bay leaf. Simmer 30 minutes. Remove bay leaf and serve over steamed rice.

1 cup all-purpose flour
1 cup corn oil
4 pounds shrimp, peeled and deveined
2 cups chopped scallions
¼-⅓ cup chopped fresh parsley
1 cup chopped green bell pepper
1 clove garlic, pressed
4 (8-ounce) cans tomato sauce
½ cup water
1 tablespoon black pepper
½ teaspoon cayenne pepper
salt to taste
1 bay leaf
steamed rice

**Yield: 8 to 10 servings**

A light roux thickens a sauce beautifully - the darker the roux, the less thickening ability, sacrificing thickening for flavor.

# Grilled Jumbo Shrimp With Green Mayonnaise

*...can be a wonderful appetizer or added to a hot or cold pasta*

## shrimp
- 1 teaspoon cayenne pepper
- 1 teaspoon black pepper
- ½ teaspoon salt
- ½ teaspoon crushed red pepper flakes
- ½ teaspoon dried thyme
- ½ teaspoon dried rosemary
- ⅛ teaspoon dried oregano
- 1½ teaspoons minced garlic
- 1 teaspoon Worcestershire sauce
- 1 (12-ounce) can beer
- 3 pounds jumbo shrimp, peeled and deveined

## green mayonnaise
- salt and pepper to taste
- 2 cups cooked spinach
- 2 whole eggs
- 2 shallots
- 4 scallions
- 2 sprigs fresh parsley
- 2 sprigs fresh cilantro
- ¼ cup minced fresh ginger
- 6 cloves garlic, minced
- 1 tablespoon capers, drained
- 1 teaspoon Dijon mustard
- 1 cup olive oil

**Yield: 2 to 3 servings**

Combine peppers, salt, pepper flakes, thyme, rosemary, oregano, garlic, Worcestershire sauce, and beer. Add shrimp. Chill overnight. When ready to cook, remove shrimp from marinade. Grill until done and serve with Green Mayonnaise. To prepare mayonnaise, combine salt, pepper, spinach, eggs, shallots, scallions, parsley, cilantro, ginger, garlic, capers, and mustard in a food processor. Blend until smooth. With machine running, slowly add oil.

*For variety, wrap marinated shrimp in prosciutto and grill. Serve with a spicy black bean sauce.*

# Warm Shrimp And Beans

*...inventive and luxurious - fit for an Italian princess!*

Cover beans with cold water to a depth of 2 inches above beans. Soak for 4 hours or overnight. Drain and place in a saucepan. Cover with cold water to a depth of 2 inches above beans. Bring to a boil and skim surface. Cook over medium heat for 45 minutes or until tender. Drain, reserving ⅓ cup of liquid. Season beans with salt and pepper. Heat 2 tablespoons oil in a large skillet. Add shrimp and sauté 2 to 3 minutes or until pink. Add beans, reserved liquid, garlic, rosemary, and tomatoes. Season with salt and pepper. Cook, stirring gently, for 2 minutes. Remove from heat and add remaining 5 tablespoons oil. Divide shrimp between 4 warm plates, arranging shrimp like spokes on a wheel. Mound bean mixture in center of shrimp. Serve at once.

½ pound dried cannellini beans
salt and pepper to taste
7 tablespoons extra virgin olive oil, divided
20 jumbo shrimp, peeled and deveined
2 large cloves garlic, minced
1 tablespoon chopped fresh rosemary
1 cup diced ripe tomatoes

**Yield: 4 servings**

# Broiled Salmon With Mustard Dill Sauce

*...any variety of fresh herbs can be used to garnish a platter*

**salmon**
2½-3  pounds salmon
    fillets
soy sauce
salt and pepper to taste
fresh bay leaves and
    thyme sprigs for
    garnish

**sauce**
½ cup coarse-grained
    prepared mustard
¼ cup water
½ cup heavy cream
¼ cup olive oil
 4 teaspoons sugar
½ cup fresh dill
black pepper to taste

**Yield: 6 servings**

Arrange salmon, skin-side down, on a foil-lined baking pan. Rub thoroughly with soy sauce and season with salt and pepper. Broil 4 inches from a heat source for 12 to 15 minutes or until cooked through. Transfer to a serving platter and garnish with herbs. Serve warm or at room temperature with Mustard Dill Sauce. To prepare sauce, combine all ingredients and chill. When ready to use, warm to room temperature and whisk before serving.


# Cold Poached Salmon With Dill Créme Fraîche

*...for eight chilled poached salmon fillets*

1½ cups Crème Fraîche
    (page 102)
½ cup minced dill
 1 shallot, minced
½ teaspoon Tabasco
 2 teaspoons lemon
    juice
salt and pepper

**Yield: 8 servings**

Blend all ingredients with hand mixer at a slow speed until firm like whipped cream.

# Pan-fried Trout With Bacon And Sage

*...traditionally a camp fire dinner for the day's catch*

Cook 8 slices bacon until crisp. Drain and crumble. Combine crumbled bacon and sage in a small bowl. Cook remaining 16 slices bacon until translucent and edges start to curl. Drain. Rinse trout and pat dry inside and out with paper towels. Sprinkle sage mixture into fish cavities. Season with salt and pepper. Wrap 2 slices of bacon around each trout and secure, closing cavities, with toothpicks. Coat trout evenly by rolling in cornmeal and shaking off excess. Heat oil over medium-high heat in a skillet. Oil should be hot but not smoking. Fry trout in batches, not allowing fish to touch each other. Cook 3 minutes on each side or until fish is firm and bacon is golden. When done, place in a shallow baking pan. Bake at 375° for 5 minutes. Discard toothpicks. Arrange on a serving platter with lemon wedges and fresh sage. Serve with Tarragon Sauce.

24 slices bacon, divided
3 tablespoons minced fresh sage, or 1 tablespoon dried
8 (10-ounce) trout, cleaned and boned with head and tails intact
salt and pepper to taste
2 cups cornmeal
⅓ cup olive oil
lemon wedges and fresh sage for garnish
Tarragon Sauce (page 230)

**Yield: 8 servings**

# Poached Sole With An Orange Sauce

*...poaching liquid is reduced to make a delicate fennel and orange-flavored sauce*

¼ cup fresh orange juice
¼ cup white wine
1 tablespoon white wine vinegar
2 shallots, minced
½ teaspoon fennel seed
2 strips orange zest, removed with a vegetable peeler
½ cup water
2 (8-ounce) sole or orange roughy fillets
1 tablespoon unsalted butter
salt and pepper to taste

Combine orange juice, wine, vinegar, shallots, fennel seed, and zest in a skillet. Boil and stir until most of the liquid evaporates. Add water and bring to a boil. Reduce heat, add sole, and cover. Poach at a gentle simmer for 10 minutes or until fish flakes easily with a fork. Place fish on individual serving plates, cover, and keep warm. Boil poaching liquid until reduced to about ⅓ cup. Remove from heat and swirl in butter until melted. Season with salt and pepper. Pour over sole and serve.

**Yield: 2 servings**

# Panfried Catfish With Toasted Buttered Pecans

*...the popularity of catfish is such that there are many fish farms solely devoted to raising them for both the wholesale and retail markets*

4 (6-ounce) catfish fillets
½ cup all-purpose flour
salt and pepper to taste
4 tablespoons butter, divided
½ cup pecans
¼ teaspoon cayenne pepper

**Yield: 4 servings**

Lightly coat both sides of fillets with flour, salt, and pepper. Melt 2 tablespoons butter in a skillet over medium heat. Add fillets and cook 2 to 3 minutes per side. Transfer to a serving plate, or individual plates. Add remaining 2 tablespoons butter, pecans, and cayenne pepper to skillet. Cook 2 to 3 minutes or until butter turns golden brown and pecans are toasted. Be careful to not burn. Pour over fish and serve.

# Blackened Catfish

*...spiced and pan-fried in oil and butter, any fish fillet can be served "blackened"*

Combine salt, pepper, paprika, oregano, thyme, cayenne pepper, and sugar in a small bowl. Pat fillets dry. Coat both sides of fillets with seasoning mixture. In a large skillet, sauté garlic in oil over medium-high heat until golden brown. Discard garlic. Add butter and heat until foam subsides. Add fillets and sauté 4 minutes on each side or until cooked through. Place on individual serving plates with lemon wedges and thyme sprigs.

salt and pepper to taste
2 teaspoons paprika
½ teaspoon dried oregano
½ teaspoon dried thyme
cayenne pepper to taste
½ teaspoon sugar
2 (8-ounce) catfish fillets
1 clove garlic, sliced
1 tablespoon olive oil
1 tablespoon unsalted butter
lemon wedges and fresh thyme sprigs for garnish

**Yield: 2 servings**

# Tartar Sauce

*...not to be confused with the stuff in the little plastic packet*

2-3 tablespoons minced
    capers
1 small dill pickle,
    minced
1 ½ cups mayonnaise
2 hard-cooked eggs,
    halved
1 tablespoon minced
    fresh parsley
1 tablespoon minced
    fresh tarragon
1 tablespoon minced
    fresh chives
lemon juice to taste
Dijon mustard to taste
salt and pepper to taste

Squeeze capers and pickle in a towel to remove excess liquid. Combine capers, pickle, and mayonnaise. Remove yolks from eggs and put through a sieve. Chop egg whites. Add yolks and whites to mayonnaise mixture. Blend in remaining ingredients.

**Yield: 2 cups**

# Pipérade

*...a colorful vegetable sauté, of Basque origin, it can also be used in omelets, on pizzas or focaccias, and over chicken breasts*

1 medium onion, sliced
2 tablespoons olive oil
salt and pepper to taste
1 large clove garlic,
    minced
1 medium green bell
    pepper, sliced
1 medium-size red bell
    pepper, sliced
pinch of fines herbes, or
    mixed dried herbs

Sauté onion in oil for 5 minutes or until translucent and softened. Add remaining ingredients. Sauté, stirring occasionally, for 2 to 3 minutes or until bell peppers are crisp-tender.

Stores well in refrigerator for 2 to 3 days, or in the freezer.

**Yield: 1 ½ cups**

# Lemon Butter Sauce

*...a light, lemony sauce that dresses any lean fish such as sole, salmon, trout, turbot, or John Dory*

Combine zest, juice, and broth in saucepan and bring to a boil. Season with salt and pepper. Boil gently for 2 to 3 minutes or until reduced to 3 tablespoons with a syrupy consistency. Chill until ready to use. When ready to serve, bring to a boil over medium heat. Slowly whisk in butter one piece at a time, adding a new piece when previous one is almost melted. Remove from heat immediately after incorporating last piece and whisk in herbs. Adjust seasonings as needed and serve immediately.

zest of ½ lemon
2 tablespoons lemon juice
¼ cup fish or chicken broth
salt and pepper to taste
1¼ sticks unsalted butter, sliced ¼-inch thick
minced fresh parsley, dill, and/or chives

**Yield: ¾ cup**

# Provençal Butter Sauce

*...an extension of the lemon-butter sauce for heartier fish such as shark steaks and red snapper*

zest of ½ lemon
  2 tablespoons lemon
    juice
¼ cup fish or chicken
    broth
salt and pepper to taste
  I large clove garlic,
    minced
pinch of ground
    rosemary
  2 tomatoes, peeled,
    seeded, and finely
    diced
I¼ sticks unsalted butter,
    sliced ¼-inch thick
2-3 tablespoons minced
    parsley

**Yield: I ¼ cups**

Combine zest, juice, and broth in saucepan and bring to a boil. Season with salt and pepper. Boil gently for 2 to 3 minutes or until reduced to 3 tablespoons and a syrup consistency. Add garlic and rosemary. Place a sieve over saucepan. Gently toss tomato with salt and pepper and add to sieve. Let juices drain into saucepan for several minutes. Remove sieve and bring to a boil. Reduce liquid to a syrup. Slowly whisk in butter one piece at a time, adding a new piece when previous one is almost melted. Remove from heat immediately after incorporating last piece and whisk in parsley. Fold in tomato and adjust seasoning as needed. To serve, spoon over fish.

# Hollandaise Sauce

*...can be kept warm for a short period of time over the heat of a pilot light - too warm and the yolks will scramble and the sauce will separate. If sauce refuses to thicken or thins out after you've made it, whisk the sauce and dip out a tablespoon into a mixing bowl. Whisk it with a tablespoon of lemon juice for a moment until it creams and thickens; gradually whisk in little dribbles of the sauce, letting each addition cream and thicken before adding more.*

Beat egg yolks in a saucepan for a minute or until thick and pale yellow. Whisk in lemon juice. Add 2 tablespoons butter. Cook over low heat, gently whisking, until yolks thicken. Remove from heat immediately and beat in another 2 tablespoons butter to stop the cooking. Melt remaining 1¼ sticks butter in a separate pan. By droplets, beat butter into sauce. Sauce should be thick. Whisk in salt, pepper, and extra lemon juice as needed.

*Add whipped cream to sauce to make a "sauce mousseline". For a lighter sauce used with soufflés or vegetables, called "sauce mousseuse", fold in beaten egg whites.*

3 egg yolks
1½ tablespoons fresh
   lemon juice
1¾ sticks cold unsalted
   butter, divided
salt and pepper to taste

**Yield: 1 cup**

# Béarnaise Sauce

*...a hollandaise with the pronounced flavor of vinegar, shallots, and tarragon, goes beautifully with beef tenderloin, or using dill instead of tarragon for poached eggs or fish*

¼ cup white wine vinegar
¼ cup white vermouth
1 tablespoon minced shallot
½ teaspoon dried tarragon
salt and pepper to taste
3 egg yolks
1-1¼ sticks cold unsalted butter, divided

**Yield: 1 cup**

Combine vinegar, vermouth, shallot, and tarragon in a saucepan. Season with salt and pepper. Boil until reduced to 2 tablespoons. Beat egg yolks in a separate saucepan for a minute or until thick and pale yellow. Strain vinegar mixture and whisk into egg yolks. Add 2 tablespoons butter. Cook over low heat, gently whisking, until yolks thicken. Remove from heat immediately and beat in another 2 tablespoons butter to stop the cooking. Melt remaining butter in a separate pan. By droplets, beat butter into sauce until thick. Whisk in salt and pepper as needed.

# Cucumber Sauce

*...for 6 poached salmon or bass fillets either hot or cold*

1 cucumber, peeled, seeded, and finely diced
¼ teaspoon salt
¼ teaspoon sugar
¼ teaspoon wine vinegar
1 cup sour cream
2-3 tablespoons minced fresh dill or watercress

Toss cucumber, salt, sugar, and vinegar in a bowl. Let stand 5 minutes. Fold in sour cream and season to taste. Fold in dill. Cover and chill until ready to serve.

# Chicken Breasts With Apples And Calvados Sauce

*...cider is used to make the distilled apple brandy called Calvados*

Season chicken with salt and pepper. Sauté in oil in a large ovenproof skillet over medium-high heat for 2 to 3 minutes on each side. Pour off fat and add 2 tablespoons butter. Transfer skillet to oven and bake, basting frequently, at 400° for 5 to 7 minutes or until crisp and spongy to the touch. Place chicken on a plate and keep warm. Reserve skillet and fat. Halve apples lengthwise and cut crosswise into thick slices. Cook apple in clarified butter, turning frequently, over medium heat for 8 to 10 minutes or until golden. Keep warm. In skillet used to cook chicken, pour off all but 1 tablespoon fat. Add shallot and cook until softened. Deglaze skillet with Calvados and cook until reduced to 2 tablespoons. Add broth and reduce to ⅓ cup. Stir in cream and reduce, stirring frequently, until thickened. Remove from heat. Cut remaining 6 tablespoons butter into small pieces. Stir in butter, parsley, chives, and tarragon. Season with salt and pepper. Place skillet in a pan of hot water to keep sauce warm. Cut chicken diagonally into ¼-inch slices. Spread sauce on a serving platter. Arrange chicken and apple slices alternately on platter. Place bunches of snow peas on platter in a decorative manner.

6 chicken breasts, boned
salt and pepper to taste
2 tablespoons olive oil
1 stick unsalted butter, softened, divided
3 Golden Delicious apples, peeled
¼ cup clarified butter
½ cup minced shallot
⅓ cup Calvados
⅔ cup chicken broth
1 cup heavy cream
2 tablespoons minced fresh parsley
2 tablespoons minced fresh chives
1½ teaspoons minced fresh tarragon, or ½ teaspoon vinegar-packed
blanched snow peas

**Yield: 6 servings**

# Lobster Chicken Marengo

*...a variation of the dish invented by Napoleon's chef when the emperor defeated the Austrians at Marengo in 1800*

8 chicken breasts, boned
4 tablespoons butter
2 tablespoons sherry
8 ounces mushrooms, sliced
2 tablespoons all-purpose flour
1 ½ cup chicken broth
1 bay leaf, crumbled
1 tablespoon tomato paste
2 tablespoons chopped fresh chives
½ teaspoon salt
pinch of black pepper
1 pound cooked lobster meat
3 ripe tomatoes, quartered

**Yield: 8 servings**

Season chicken breasts. Melt butter in a skillet. Add chicken and cook until browned. Remove chicken from skillet and place in a baking dish. Bake at 300° for 30 minutes. Add sherry and mushrooms to skillet and sauté 8 minutes, adding extra butter if needed. Blend in flour. Stir in broth and bring to a simmer. Add bay leaf, tomato paste, chives, salt, and pepper. Simmer 15 minutes. Mix in lobster and tomatoes and cook 5 minutes. Place baked chicken on a serving platter. Pour lobster sauce over top.

# Chicken Bombay

*...chicken breasts marinated, browned, and baked in an exotic combination of spices*

Place chicken in a large, shallow bowl. Combine lemon juice and salt and pour over chicken. Marinate at room temperature for 10 minutes, turning once. Drain chicken and dredge in flour, coating on all sides and shaking off excess. Heat butter and oil in a large skillet over medium heat. Increase to medium-high heat and add chicken. Brown quickly on both sides. Remove chicken from skillet and place in a 9X13 inch baking dish, skin-side up and about 1 inch apart. Add onion to skillet drippings and sauté about 3 minutes. Remove from heat and stir in yogurt, chilies, garlic, cinnamon, ginger, cloves, turmeric, raisins, and zest. Pour over chicken. Sprinkle with almonds. Bake, uncovered, at 375° for 20 minutes. Cover and bake 20 minutes longer or until a fork is easily inserted into chicken. Garnish and serve on a bed of rice.

6 chicken breasts, boned
¼ cup lemon juice
1 teaspoon salt
½ cup all-purpose flour
2 tablespoons butter
2 tablespoons olive oil
1 onion, chopped
1 (8-ounce) container plain yogurt
1 (4-ounce) can hot green chilies, drained and chopped
2 cloves garlic, minced
½ teaspoon cinnamon
½ teaspoon ground ginger
¼ teaspoon ground cloves
¼ teaspoon turmeric
¼ cup raisins
1 teaspoon orange zest
¼ cup sliced almonds
fresh parsley sprigs and lemon slices for garnish
2 cups cooked white rice

**Yield: 6 servings**

# Five-spice Chicken Stir-fry

*...five-spice powder is often used in Oriental cooking and can be stored with your spices*

**five-spice powder**
- 1 teaspoon cinnamon
- 1 teaspoon crushed anise seed
- 1/4 teaspoon crushed fennel seed
- 1/4 teaspoon black pepper
- 1/8 teaspoon ground cloves

**stir-fry**
- 2 chicken breasts, boned, skinned, and cut in 1-inch cubes
- 3 tablespoons soy sauce
- 1/2 teaspoon Five-spice Powder
- 3 tablespoons sugar
- 2 teaspoons cornstarch
- 3 tablespoons water
- 3 tablespoons white vinegar
- 2 tablespoons canola oil
- 2 dried hot peppers
- 1 teaspoon grated fresh ginger
- 2 cloves garlic, minced
- 1 medium-size sweet potato, julienned
- 1 cup sliced fresh mushrooms
- 12 snow peas, stems removed
- 14 scallions, cut into 1-inch pieces
- hot cooked rice

**Yield: 4 servings**

To make Five-spice powder, combine all ingredients and store in an air-tight container. To prepare stir-fry, combine chicken, soy sauce, and five-spice powder. Marinate 15 minutes. Mix sugar and cornstarch together. Stir in water and vinegar. Heat oil in a wok or large skillet. Sauté hot peppers, ginger, and garlic for 2 minutes. Add potato and mushrooms and cook until tender. Add peas and scallions and stir-fry until peas are crisp-tender. Remove contents of wok. Add extra oil to wok, if needed. Add chicken and marinade to wok and stir-fry 2 minutes. Stir in cornstarch mixture and cook until thickened and bubbly. Add vegetable mixture. Cover and cook 1 to 2 minutes or until heated through. Serve over rice.

Five-spice powder is also available in Oriental grocery stores.

# Stir-fry Cashew Chicken

*...cashew is indigenous to Brazil and was carried to India by the Portuguese - today most cashews come from India*

Combine 1 tablespoon soy sauce, 1 tablespoon sherry, water, and cornstarch. Mix in chicken and marinate 20 minutes or longer. Heat 2 tablespoons oil in a wok or skillet. Add hot peppers and sauté 1 minute. Discard peppers. Add chicken, ginger, mushrooms, bell pepper, scallions, and celery. Stir-fry about 5 minutes. Combine remaining 2 tablespoons soy sauce, 1 tablespoon sherry, and 1 tablespoon oil. Add sugar, black pepper, and vinegar. Pour over chicken mixture. Add cashews and cook 2 to 3 minutes longer. Serve over rice.

3 tablespoons soy sauce, divided
2 tablespoons sherry, divided
2 tablespoons water
1 tablespoon cornstarch
4 chicken breasts, boned, skinned, and cut in strips
3 tablespoons peanut oil, divided
2 whole dried hot red peppers
2 teaspoons finely chopped fresh ginger
1 cup coarsely chopped fresh mushrooms
1 green bell pepper, julienned
4 scallions, sliced ½-inch thick, tops included
2 stalks celery, sliced diagonally in ½-inch pieces
¼ cup sugar
¼ teaspoon black pepper
2 teaspoons vinegar
1 cup lightly salted or unsalted cashews
hot cooked rice

**Yield: 4 servings**

# Curried Fruit-stuffed Chicken Breasts

*...for a fall buffet, serve with Hot Tomato Madrilène, sliced smoked ham, hot buttered rice, and a green salad vinaigrette*

1½ cups golden raisins
3 sticks butter, divided
4 cups finely chopped onions
4 cups finely chopped celery
2 teaspoons minced garlic
8 bay leaves
8 cups peeled and cubed apple
1½ cups chopped chutney
30 chicken breasts, boned
salt and pepper to taste
4 cups heavy cream
3 tablespoons curry powder

**Yield: 24 servings**

Place raisins in a bowl. Add warm water to cover and let stand until raisins swell. Drain. Heat 1 stick butter in a large skillet, or 2 if necessary. Add onions, celery, garlic, and bay leaves and sauté until softened. Add apple and cook and stir for 1 minute. Stir in raisins and chutney. Cool and remove bay leaves. Flatten chicken, skin-side down, on a smooth surface using a mallet or skillet bottom. Season with salt and pepper. Divide raisin mixture among chicken breasts. Fold in edges of breasts to enclose filling in an envelope. Melt remaining 2 sticks butter in shallow baking dishes. Arrange chicken, seam-side down, in dishes. Brush top of breasts with butter and season as desired. Transfer dishes to oven and bake at 425° for 10 minutes, basting once. Blend cream and curry powder and pour over chicken. Bake 10 minutes longer, basting occasionally.

# Chicken Breasts Stuffed With Cheese And Ham

*...Supremes de Volaille Farcies aux Gruyère et Jambon, resembles the Cordon Bleu, but is more refined with Gruyère and prosciutto*

Combine broth and wine in a saucepan. Cook until reduced to 1 cup. Melt butter in another saucepan. Blend in flour. Whisk in broth mixture and cook until thickened and smooth. Stir in cream and season with salt and pepper. Simmer, stirring often, for about 5 minutes. To prepare chicken, remove tenders from breasts. Flatten tenders and breasts, skin-side down, with palm of hand or a mallet. Divide cheese and prosciutto among breasts and press in gently. Place a flattened tender over each breast. Fold sides of breast over tender to make an envelope. Arrange breasts closely together, seam-side down, in a buttered baking dish. Brush with melted butter. Transfer to oven and bake at 425° for 20 minutes. Transfer breasts, using a slotted spoon, to a heated serving platter. Reduce liquid in dish by half. Mix liquid with Cream Sauce. Spoon over chicken breasts and serve immediately.

## cream sauce

- 2 cups chicken broth
- ⅓ cup dry white wine
- 1 tablespoon butter
- 2 tablespoons all-purpose flour
- ½ cup heavy cream
- salt and pepper to taste

## chicken breasts

- 8 chicken breasts, boned
- 4 ounces Gruyère or Swiss cheese
- 4 ounces prosciutto, coarsely chopped
- 1 tablespoon butter, melted
- Cream Sauce

**Yield: 4 servings**

# Chicken Breasts Stuffed With Morels And Wild Rice

*...Farcies aux Morilles et Riz - April in Missouri, fresh morels are readily available and far preferable to dried*

### cream sauce
2 cups chicken broth
1/3 cup dry white wine
1 tablespoon butter
2 tablespoons all-purpose flour
1/2 cup heavy cream
salt and pepper to taste

### chicken breasts
8 chicken breasts, boned
10 fresh morel mushrooms, or dried, rehydrated in warm water to cover
2 tablespoons butter, divided
1/4 cup minced onion
1/2 cup cooked wild rice
salt and pepper to taste
2 tablespoons cognac
1/4 cup finely chopped chives
Cream Sauce

**Yield: 4 servings**

Combine broth and wine in a saucepan. Cook until reduced to 1 cup. Melt butter in another saucepan. Blend in flour. Whisk in broth mixture and cook until thickened and smooth. Stir in cream and season with salt and pepper. Simmer, stirring often, for about 5 minutes. To prepare chicken, remove tenders from breasts. Flatten tenders and breasts, skin-side down, with palm of hand or a mallet. If using dried mushrooms, drain and squeeze out excess moisture. Cut mushrooms in quarters. Heat 1 tablespoon butter in a saucepan. Add onion and sauté until softened. Add mushrooms and cook briefly. Stir in rice, salt, and pepper. Mix in cognac and chives. Cool. Divide mixture among chicken breasts. Place a flattened tender over each breast. Fold sides of breast over tender to make an envelope. Arrange breasts closely together, seam-side down, in a buttered baking dish. Melt remaining 1 tablespoon butter and brush over chicken. Transfer to oven and bake at 425° for 20 minutes. Transfer breasts, using a slotted spoon, to a heated serving platter. Reduce liquid in dish by half. Mix liquid with Cream Sauce. Spoon over chicken breasts and serve immediately.

# Chicken Breasts Stuffed With Tropical Fruits

*...a dish that brings forth visions of white sand beaches, ocean breezes rustling the palm trees, and tall rum drinks with fresh fruit*

Remove tenders from chicken breasts. Flatten tenders and breasts, skin-side down, with palm of hand or a mallet. Combine mango, half of reserved mango juice, pineapples, cantaloupe, pepper, wine, rum, honey, and ginger. Let stand 2 hours or overnight. Drain mixture, reserving juice. Spoon mixture evenly among chicken breasts. Place a flattened tender over each breast. Fold sides of breast over tender to make an envelope. Arrange breasts closely together, seam-side down, in a buttered baking dish. Brush with melted butter. Transfer to oven and bake at 425° for 20 minutes. Transfer breasts, using a slotted spoon, to a heated serving platter. Combine juice from baking dish, remaining reserved mango juice, and reserved juice from filling in a saucepan. Cook until reduced to a sauce. Spoon over chicken breasts.

24 chicken breasts, boned
1 (26-ounce) jar mangoes in light syrup, chopped, juice reserved
3 pineapples, cut in ½-inch chunks
1 large cantaloupe, cut in ½-inch chunks
1 teaspoon white pepper
1 cup white wine
½ cup Malibu rum
¾ cup honey
1 teaspoon ground ginger
melted butter

**Yield: 24 servings**

# Chicken Sauté With Pecans

*...a well-seasoned cast-iron pan has a stick-proof surface, heats slowly, holds heat well, and is easy to clean*

2 (2½ to 3-pound)
 chickens, cut in
 pieces
salt and pepper to taste
4 tablespoons butter
½ cup finely chopped
 onion
½ cup finely chopped
 celery
1 bay leaf
½ teaspoon dried
 thyme, or 2 sprigs
 fresh
2 whole cloves
¼ teaspoon nutmeg
3 cups dry red wine
½ cup heavy cream
½ cup chopped pecans

**Yield: 6 to 8 servings**

Season chicken with salt and pepper. Heat butter in a skillet. Add chicken and brown on all sides. Scatter onion, celery, bay leaf, thyme, and cloves around chicken. Sprinkle with nutmeg. Add wine and cover. Simmer 30 minutes or until chicken is tender. Remove chicken and keep warm. Skim fat from sauce in skillet. Cook sauce to reduce to about 2 cups. Return chicken to skillet and add cream. Bring to a boil and remove bay leaf and cloves. Add pecans and serve hot.

For a smoother appearance, strain reduced sauce before adding chicken and cream.

# Baked Chicken Asian Style

*...fresh ginger and sesame seeds provide the Asian flavor*

Place chicken in a 9X13 inch baking pan. Combine soy sauce, sugar, garlic, ginger , and sesame seed in a saucepan. Bring to a boil and cook until sugar dissolves. Pour over chicken. Bake at 350° for 60 minutes, turning chicken and basting with pan juices every 15 minutes. Garnish with chopped scallions and serve over rice.

1 chicken, cut into pieces
¾ cup soy sauce
¼ cup sugar
2 cloves garlic, chopped
1 teaspoon grated fresh ginger
3 tablespoons sesame seed
1-2 scallions, chopped, for garnish
cooked rice

**Yield: 4 to 6 servings**

# Roast Orange Rosemary Chicken

*...rosemary is the herb of remembrance*

Work fingers between skin and meat of chicken. Cut 2 oranges in thin slices. Sprinkle one side of orange slices with rosemary. Slide slices, herb-side up, under skin. Cut slices in half, if necessary, to completely cover meat, including legs, with orange. Sprinkle chicken cavity with salt and pepper. Quarter remaining orange and add to cavity. Roast at 350° until juices run clear and leg moves easily when shaken.

1 (4-pound) chicken
3 oranges, divided
rosemary
salt and pepper to taste

**Yield: 4 servings**

# Roasted Herbed Baby Chickens With A Spicy Mango Barbecue Sauce

*...when not using a sauce, you can protect the delicate breast meat on a chicken by covering it halfway through the roasting time with some lettuce leaves*

**mango barbecue sauce**
- 2 tablespoons olive oil
- ½ cup finely chopped onion
- 1 tablespoon minced garlic
- salt and pepper to taste
- 1 medium mango, peeled and coarsely puréed
- 1 cup ketchup
- 1 tablespoon Dijon mustard
- 2 tablespoons corn syrup
- 1 teaspoon Worcestershire sauce
- 1 teaspoon Tabasco sauce
- 4 slices lemon

**roasted chickens**
- 3 (2-pound) chickens, trimmed, gizzards and necks reserved
- salt and pepper to taste
- 3 bay leaves
- 6 sprigs fresh thyme
- 1 large clove garlic, cut in thirds
- 3 tablespoons olive oil
- 1 large white onion, halved
- ½ cup Mango Barbecue Sauce

**Yield: 2 cups mango barbecue sauce, 8 servings chicken**

Combine oil, onion, and garlic in a saucepan. Sauté over medium-high heat until softened. Mix in remaining sauce ingredients. Bring to a simmer and cook 5 minutes. Cool. To prepare chickens, season inside and out with salt and pepper. Place a bay leaf, 2 thyme sprigs, and a piece of garlic in each chicken cavity. Brush skin with oil and place chickens in a roasting pan on their sides. Add onion, gizzards, and necks in pan. Roast at 425° for 15 minutes. Turn chickens to other side and roast 15 minutes longer. Turn chickens on their backs and brush with Mango Barbecue Sauce. Roast another 20 minutes, or until done. Cool before carving.

Store unused barbecue sauce in an airtight jar in the refrigerator to use on any barbecued meat or poultry.

# Tarragon Roast Chicken

*...an uncommon roast chicken - serve with wild rice*

Place chicken in a roasting pan. Sprinkle salt, pepper, onion, tarragon, and lemon juice over top. Dot with butter. Bake at 350° for 1 hour, 15 minutes to 1 hour, 30 minutes. Baste with pan juices every 15 minutes. Remove chicken and onion. Heat pan drippings on stove until bubbling. Deglaze pan with cognac. Add cream and season with salt and pepper. Reduce sauce over high heat. Cut chicken into 4 pieces and arrange with onion on a heated serving platter. Garnish with watercress. Pour some sauce over chicken and serve the rest on the side.

1 (3 to 3½-pound) chicken
salt and pepper to taste
1 red onion, thinly sliced
1-2 tablespoons dried tarragon
juice of 1 lemon
2-3 tablespoons butter
¼-½ cup cognac or white wine
1 cup heavy cream
1 bunch watercress for garnish

**Yield: 4 servings**

# Grilled Chicken Breasts With Blueberry Salsa

*...from Maria Estelle's well-known and much loved kitchen*

To make salsa, combine blueberries, onion, jalapeño pepper, lime juice, and salt. Mix thoroughly but gently. Let stand at room temperature for 2 hours. Brush chicken lightly with oil. Place on a medium hot grill and brown on one side. Turn chicken and top with salsa. Cook until chicken browns and is firm to the touch. Serve immediately.

2 cups fresh or frozen blueberries
1 small red onion, chopped
1 jalapeño pepper, seeded and chopped
2 tablespoons lime juice
½ teaspoon salt
6 (8-ounce) boneless, skinless chicken breasts
vegetable oil

**Yield: 6 servings**

# Grilled Lemon And Gin Marinated Chicken With Onions

*...with the aromatic flavor of the juniper berry*

¼ cup fresh lemon juice
¼ cup gin
½ teaspoon dried oregano
½ teaspoon salt
black pepper to taste
½ teaspoon sugar
3 tablespoons vegetable oil
4 chicken breasts, boned and skinned
1 cup thinly sliced onion

**Yield: 4 servings**

Mix lemon juice, gin, oregano, salt, pepper, and sugar in a shallow dish. Whisk in oil in a thin stream until emulsified. Add chicken and coat well. Cover and refrigerate 20 minutes. Remove chicken, reserving marinade. Grill chicken on an oiled rack 6 inches from a heat source. Cook 7 minutes on each side or until cooked through. Meanwhile, combine reserved marinade and onion in a skillet. Cover and bring to a boil over high heat. Cook, stirring occasionally, for 3 minutes or until onion starts to brown. Reduce heat to medium-low and uncover. Cook, stirring constantly, for 5 minutes. Place chicken on a heated serving platter. Use a slotted spoon to scatter onion around chicken.

# Grilled Peppered Chicken With Basil Sauce

*...the social behavior of animals was first discovered with domestic hens - generally referred to as the pecking order*

Combine all sauce ingredients. Blend with an electric mixer on low speed until smooth. Transfer to a serving bowl. To prepare chicken, press black pepper into meaty sides of chicken. Combine melted butter and basil. Stir well and brush lightly over chicken. Grill chicken over medium heat for 8 to 10 minutes on each side. Baste frequently with butter mixture. Garnish with basil sprigs and serve with Basil Sauce.

### basil sauce
- 1 stick butter, softened
- 2 tablespoons minced fresh basil
- 1 tablespoon Parmesan cheese
- 1/4 teaspoon garlic powder
- 1/8 teaspoon salt
- black pepper to taste

### chicken
- 3/4 teaspoon coarsely ground black pepper
- 4 chicken breasts, skinned
- 5 tablespoons butter, melted
- 1/4 cup chopped fresh basil
- fresh basil sprigs for garnish

**Yield: 4 servings**

# Jamaican Jerk Chicken

*...Jerk barbecue is the Jamaican method of marinating and grilling chicken, pork, and fish. The term jerk is thought to be derived from the Spanish word charqui, dried meat, or some say that pork was jerked from side to side on the grill as it was cooked, hence the name jerked pork. The cook is known as a jerk man or jerk woman!*

## marinade

- 2 cups finely chopped scallions
- 2-4 Scotch bonnet or jalapeño peppers, seeded and minced
- ½ cup soy sauce
- ¼ cup fresh lime juice
- 1½ teaspoons dried thyme, or 2 tablespoons minced fresh
- ½ teaspoon ground allspice
- ½ teaspoon ground cloves
- ½ teaspoon nutmeg
- 1 tablespoon English-style dry mustard
- 2 cloves garlic, chopped
- 2 bay leaves, crumbled
- ¼ cup vegetable oil
- ¼ cup packed brown sugar
- 1 teaspoon cinnamon

## entrée

- 3 pounds chicken tenders, or boneless chicken breasts cut into strips
- Marinade
- chili peppers, nasturtiums, or fresh herbs for garnish

**Yield: 10 servings**

Combine marinade ingredients in a food processor. Blend 10 to 15 seconds. Divide chicken between 2 resealable plastic bags and add marinade. Press excess air out of bags and seal. Refrigerate 1 to 2 days, turning bags several times. Remove chicken from marinade. Place on a lightly oiled grill 4 to 6 inches from heat source. Grill, basting occasionally with marinade, for 4 to 5 minutes on each side or until cooked through. Transfer to a heated serving platter and garnish.

Serve with baked bananas. If desired, use 1 tablespoon Scotch bonnet pepper sauce instead of Scotch bonnet peppers.

# Pearl's Lemon Chicken

*...the creation of chef Lee Lum, it consists of boneless chicken breast, coated with water chestnut flour, crisply fried, and served over crisp vegetables in a sweet and pungent lemon sauce*

Place chicken in a glass bowl. Combine soy sauce, sesame oil, salt, and gin. Pour over chicken and toss to coat. Let stand 30 minutes or refrigerate overnight. Drain, discarding marinade. Dip chicken in egg whites, and then in flour. Heat ½ inch of oil in a 350° electric skillet. Add chicken and brown on both sides. Do not overcook. Drain on paper towels and cut crosswise into 1-inch slices. Place lettuce on a serving platter and top with chicken slices. Combine sugar , vinegar, broth, lemon juice, and zest in a saucepan. Bring to a boil. Mix cornstarch and water together and add to saucepan. Cook and stir until thickened. Add carrots, bell pepper, scallions, and pineapple. Remove from heat and stir in lemon extract. Pour over chicken and serve immediately.

Water chestnut flour is available in Oriental grocery stores.

- 8 chicken breasts, boned and skinned
- 2 tablespoons light soy sauce
- ¼ teaspoon sesame oil
- 1 teaspoon salt
- 1 tablespoon gin or vodka
- 3 egg whites, beaten until frothy
- 1 cup water chestnut flour
- peanut or vegetable oil
- ¼ head lettuce, shredded
- ¾ cup sugar
- ½ cup vinegar
- 1 cup chicken broth
- juice of 1 lemon
- zest of 1 lemon
- 1 tablespoon cornstarch
- 2 tablespoons water
- 3 small carrots, julienned
- ½ green bell pepper, julienned
- 3 scallions, julienned
- ½ cup canned pineapple chunks
- 1 (1-ounce) bottle lemon extract

**Yield: 6 servings**

# Mediterranean Chicken

*...one of the earliest mentions (about 570 BC!) of the domestic fowl occurs with Aesop admonishing the foolish milkmaid: 'don't count your chickens before they are hatched'.*

1½ pounds chicken or
    lamb, cubed
3 tablespoons olive oil
1 large onion, chopped
2 cloves garlic, minced
1 cup sliced carrots
1 cup sliced celery
1 cup sliced
    mushrooms
1½ cups slivered almonds
1½ cups cooked
    garbanzo beans
1½ cups tomato sauce
½ cup raisins
¾ cup red wine
¾ cup chicken broth
2 teaspoons curry
    powder
1 bay leaf
¼ teaspoon cayenne
    pepper
1 teaspoon salt
1 teaspoon paprika
hot cooked couscous

**Yield: 6 servings**

Sauté chicken in oil until browned. Add onion, garlic, carrots, celery, mushrooms, and almonds. Cook and stir until vegetables soften. Add remaining ingredients except couscous. Cover and bring to a boil. Reduce temperature and simmer 40 minutes. Remove bay leaf. Serve over couscous.

# Chicken In Tarragon And Champagne Sauce

*...like any Broadway producer, you get the star first and then you write the show*

Melt 1 stick butter in a large saucepan. Blend in flour. Add broth, stirring vigorously. Simmer 10 minutes, stirring often. Add tarragon and cook 45 minutes, stirring frequently. Season chicken with salt and pepper. Divide remaining 6 tablespoons butter between 2 skillets and brown chicken on all sides, cooking 15 to 25 minutes, depending on size of pieces. Remove chicken and keep warm. Deglaze 1 skillet with about ¼ cup champagne and add to other skillet. Add shallots and remainder of champagne to second skillet. Cook and stir over high heat until liquid is almost evaporated. Add tarragon sauce to skillet and cook and stir 5 minutes. Add cream and bring to a boil. Cook 5 minutes, scraping bottom of skillet with spatula while stirring. Strain sauce through a fine sieve. Return chicken to skillets and pour sauce over top. Sprinkle with chopped tarragon for garnish and bring to a boil. Serve piping hot.

1¾ sticks butter, divided
¾ cup all-purpose flour
6 cups chicken broth
⅓ cup coarsely chopped fresh tarragon, or 2 tablespoons dried
6-8 (2½-pound) chickens, cut into pieces
salt and pepper to taste
2 cups dry champagne, divided
6 tablespoons finely minced shallots
3 cups heavy cream
2 tablespoons chopped fresh tarragon for garnish

**Yield: 24 servings**

# Duck Confit

*...served at The Dorset Inn, in Dorset, Vermont, with Plum Chutney, Puréed Cannellini Beans, Braised Red Cabbage, and Hot Buttered Blanched Asparagus - 1996 celebrates the 200th anniversary of The Dorset Inn, New England's oldest, continuously operating inn!*

**entrée**
- 1 duck, quartered
- salt and pepper to taste
- oil
- 6 cloves garlic
- 1 sprig fresh rosemary
- 1 sprig fresh sage
- 1 sprig fresh thyme
- 1 sprig fresh tarragon

**Yield: 2 servings**

**"puréed" cannellini beans**
- 2 cups dried cannellini beans
- 1 leek, coarsely chopped
- 2 stalks celery with tops, coarsely chopped
- 6 cloves garlic, minced
- ¼ cup oil
- 1 sprig fresh sage, leaves chopped
- 3 sprigs fresh tarragon, leaves chopped
- 3 sprigs fresh thyme, leaves chopped
- 3 sprigs fresh rosemary, leaves chopped
- 5-6 cups chicken broth

**Yield: 6 servings**

Season duck with salt and pepper. Place in an ovenproof casserole dish. Add oil to cover. Add garlic and herbs and mix well with hands. Bake at 300° for 3 hours or until done. Cool, cover, and chill until ready to use - up to 2 weeks. Remove duck from fat, scraping off excess fat. Bake at 400° for 15 to 20 minutes or until meat is heated through and skin is crispy. Serve with "Puréed" Cannellini Beans and Plum Chutney.

Soak beans in enough water to cover. Sauté leek, celery, and garlic in oil until softened. Add herbs and continue to cook until softened. Drain beans. Add beans and broth to vegetables. Simmer 1 hour or until beans are semi-soft. Coarsely purée mixture in a food processor, being careful to leave mixture somewhat chunky. Do not overprocess.

Combine plums, apple, onions, raisins, carrot and sugar in a large bowl. Place salt, cloves, ginger, allspice, and chili pepper in a stainless steel saucepan. Stir in vinegars. Slowly bring to a boil. Add fruit mixture and bring to a boil. Reduce heat and simmer about 2 hours or until thickened.

**plum chutney**

2 pounds plums, pitted and coarsely chopped
1 cup peeled and sliced Granny Smith apple
1 cup sliced onions
½ cup raisins
½ cup grated carrot
1 cup packed brown sugar
1 tablespoon salt
1 teaspoon ground cloves
1 teaspoon ground ginger, or fresh, minced
1 teaspoon allspice
1 chipotle chili pepper, seeded and diced
1 cup white vinegar
1 cup raspberry vinegar

**Yield: 6 cups**

Confit, a specialty of Casconne, is an ancient method of preserving meat and poultry - salted and slowly cooked in its own fat, which acts as a sealant and preservative.

# Chicken Curry With Condiments, Chutneys, And Rice

*...a buffet dinner for 24 with a table full of condiments and chutneys, rice, and a big salad - a purist would serve Poppadums, but warm, herbed pita wedges would support an Indian theme*

## chicken curry
3 sticks butter
4 cups finely diced onion
4 cups finely diced peeled Granny Smith apple
5 cloves garlic, pressed
½-¾ cup Madras curry powder
4 teaspoons celery salt
1 teaspoon dried thyme
2 cups chicken broth
1¼ cups dry white wine
½ cup sherry
salt and pepper to taste
3 cups heavy cream
2 cups half-and-half
½ cup puréed mango chutney
2 tablespoons cornstarch (optional)
¼ cup cold water (optional)
4 pounds cooked chicken, cubed

## rice
6 quarts water
2 tablespoons salt
6 cups long-grain rice

## chutney
Plum Chutney, page 201
George's Cranberry Sauce, page 208
Mango Chutney

Melt butter in a large pot. Add onion, apple, and garlic and sauté for 5 minutes. Stir in curry powder, celery salt, and thyme. Cook over medium-low heat. Add broth, wine, and sherry. Bring to a boil. Reduce heat and simmer 15 minutes. Stir in salt, pepper, cream, half-and-half, and chutney. Combine cornstarch and cold water and add to pot. Bring to a simmer and cook 1 to 2 minutes or until thickened. Add chicken and cook until thoroughly heated. To prepare rice, combine water and salt in a 10 to 12-quart pot. Bring to a boil. Slowly sprinkle in rice. Simmer, uncovered and without stirring, for 12 minutes or until tender. Drain in a colander and rinse with cold running water. Drain 30 minutes. Transfer to a buttered baking dish. Cover loosely with foil and refrigerate. When ready to serve, heat, covered, in oven. Fluff with a fork and place in a heated serving dish. Serve with condiments: fresh pineapple, sliced banana, chopped cucumber, chopped scallions, crumbled bacon, chopped hard-cooked egg, sliced avocado, toasted nuts and currants.

# Duck Gumbo

*...serve with Righetti Campolieti, an Italian red wine made from Valpolicella grapes - a soft, full-flavored wine that won't be over-ridden by the gumbo*

Combine flour and oil in a large cast-iron pot. Cook over low to medium heat, whisking frequently at first, and then constantly, for a total of 35 to 45 minutes or until dark chocolate brown. Add onion, scallions, celery, bell pepper, and okra. Cook, stirring frequently, for 15 minutes or until tender. Add garlic and cook 2 minutes. Stir in broth, tomatoes, bay leaves, parsley, and thyme. Bring to almost boiling over medium-high heat. Reduce heat and simmer, uncovered, for 20 minutes. Remove meat from ducks. Shred or chop leg and thigh meat and add to soup. Season with salt, pepper, and Tabasco sauce. Simmer about 35 minutes. Shred or chop breast meat and add to soup. Simmer 5 minutes or until heated through. If not using okra, add filé powder when ready to serve. Let stand 10 minutes and skim fat. Ladle into heated bowls. Top with a scoop of rice and garnish.

Use wild ducks, if available. Store for up to 3 days in refrigerator if preparing ahead. Add filé powder at serving time.

*If desired, add raw shrimp or oysters to gumbo during final 5 minutes of cooking.*

⅔ cup all-purpose flour
⅔ cup safflower oil or other vegetable oil
1 cup chopped yellow onion
½ cup chopped scallions
1 cup chopped celery
1 cup chopped green bell pepper
1 pound fresh okra, sliced ¼-inch thick(optional)
1 tablespoon minced garlic
8 cups chicken broth
2 cups chopped and peeled fresh plum tomatoes, or canned, drained
2 bay leaves, crushed
1 cup minced fresh parsley
1 tablespoon minced fresh thyme, or 1 teaspoon dried
2 (4 to 5-pound) ducks, roasted or smoked
salt and pepper to taste
2 teaspoons Tabasco sauce
1 teaspoon filé powder if not using okra
2 cups hot cooked white rice
minced scallions for garnish

**Yield: 8 side-dish servings, 4 to 5 entrée servings**

# Duck Breasts Condie

*...wild duck breasts sautéed quickly with butter, red wine, and olives, this recipe was adapted from a dinner in a French restaurant in New York City many years ago*

1 stick butter
4 thick slices firm
    bread, toasted
4 mallard duck breasts,
    boned
salt to taste
coarsely ground black
    pepper to taste
16 large pimiento-stuffed
    Spanish olives, halved
    lengthwise
4-6 dashes
    Worcestershire
    sauce
1 cup red wine

**Yield: 4 servings**

Melt butter in a skillet. Use some of butter and a pastry brush to lightly coat toasted bread. Hold toast in a 250° to 300° oven, being careful not to burn. Season breasts on both sides with salt and pepper. Add breasts, olives, Worcestershire sauce, and wine to skillet. Cook and stir over medium heat for 4 minutes or until first bead of blood appears on duck. Turn and cook 4 minutes or until a bead of blood appears or until medium rare. Place toast on four individual heated plates. Arrange duck on toast. Pour sauce over top, dividing olives equally among plates.

Serve with braised red cabbage, mashed potatoes or wild rice pancakes, and a green vegetable or fruit salad.

# Grilled Peking Style Duck

*...can not be done on a gas grill - banking coals and allowing duck fat to drain into pan makes the duck crisp*

Combine ginger, cinnamon, nutmeg, cloves, and pepper. Pierce skin of ducks several times with a fork. Fasten remaining neck skin to back of ducks with a skewer. Sprinkle about ½ teaspoon of ginger mixture in each duck cavity. Rub remaining mixture evenly over outside of ducks. Leave body cavity open to allow for even cooking. Bank about 20 glowing coals on each side of a fire bed and place a deep metal drip pan in center. Place ducks, breast-side up, on an oiled grill 4 to 6 inches above pan. Cover, leaving dampers open to maintain a hot fire. Add 5 to 6 coals to each side of fire every 30 minutes to maintain a constant temperature. Cook for 2 hours to 2 hours, 15 minutes or until thigh meat is soft when squeezed. Combine soy sauce and 2 tablespoons hoisin sauce. Baste ducks with sauce mixture during final 20 minutes of cooking. Meanwhile, lightly dampen tortillas and cut in halves or quarters. Stack and wrap in foil. Heat at 350° for 10 to 15 minutes. Place in a napkin-lined basket and keep warm. Place remaining hoisin sauce, scallions, and cilantro in separate bowls. Serve Peking-style, allowing each guest to slice meat from ducks, spread hoisin sauce on tortilla, top with meat, scallions, and cilantro, and fold tortilla to make an envelope.

1 teaspoon ground ginger
1 teaspoon cinnamon
½ teaspoon nutmeg
¼ teaspoon ground cloves
¼ teaspoon black pepper
2 (4½ to 5-pound) ducks, trimmed with giblets removed
¼ cup soy sauce
1 cup hoisin sauce, divided
18 flour tortillas
1½ cups slivered scallions
½-1 cup coarsely chopped fresh cilantro

**Yield: 6 servings**

# Roast Quail With Oysters And Wild Rice In A Wild Mushroom Sauce

*...both a sportsman's and epicure's delight, being as tasty on the table as it is honest in the field*

## wild rice

4 cups wild rice
12 cups water
salt and pepper to taste
5-8 tablespoons butter, melted

## roast quail

4 sticks butter
16 sprigs fresh parsley
32 oysters
16 slices lemon
16 quail
16 slices bacon, halved
salt and pepper to taste

## wild mushroom sauce

1 pound fresh wild mushrooms, trimmed and sliced
4 tablespoons butter
brandy
1 cup heavy cream
chicken broth

**Yield: 16 servings**

Bring water to boil in a saucepan, adding salt to taste. Add rice, cover, and bring to a boil. Stir and reduce heat to a low simmer. Cover and cook 55 minutes or until tender. Drain. Season with salt and pepper. Add butter and toss with a fork. To prepare quail, place 2 tablespoons butter, 1 sprig parsley, 2 oysters, and 1 lemon slice in cavity of each bird. Top each with 2 bacon halves and arrange on a rack in a shallow roasting pan. Bake at 450° for 15 minutes. Remove bacon and baste birds with pan juices. Add melted butter if there is not enough fat in pan for basting. Sprinkle with salt and pepper. Roast 5 to 6 minutes longer and baste again. Place birds on a hot serving platter and keep warm while making sauce. To make sauce, sauté mushrooms in butter in a large skillet. Deglaze skillet with brandy and bring to a boil. Stir in cream and cook until smooth. Add chicken broth or degreased juices from quail roasting pan, if needed, to thin sauce. To serve, pour sauce over quail and serve wild rice on side.

Try shiitake, morel, or chanterelle mushrooms, or a combination of all.

# Nortie's Dove

*...gently cooked, these dove remain moist and tender*

Dredge dove in flour. Season with salt and pepper. Melt butter in a skillet. Add dove and quickly brown. Add lemon zest and juice and cover. Simmer 45 minutes. Place 1 tablespoon mustard on each dove. Cover skillet and cook until heated through.

Serve with currant jelly and wild rice.

12 dove, boned
all-purpose flour for
    dredging
salt and pepper to taste
1 stick butter
zest of 6 lemons
1 cup fresh lemon juice
¾ cup Dijon mustard

**Yield: 6 servings**

# Grilled Goose Boobs

*...a luncheon specialty at The Hager Hinge Co.*

Use a mallet to carefully flatten goose breasts to ¼-inch thick. Place goose breasts in a glass bowl and cover with milk. Refrigerate 8 hours. Drain goose. Rinse in salt water and then in fresh water. Pat dry. Prepare a marinade by combining soy sauce and remaining ingredients. Combine goose and marinade and refrigerate 8 hours. Remove goose from marinade. Cook on a lightly oiled grill over medium heat for 5 minutes or until medium-rare. Slice across the grain and serve.

boneless, skinless goose
    breasts
milk
½ cup soy sauce
½ cup red wine
2 tablespoons
    Worcestershire
    sauce
2 tablespoons garlic
    powder
2 tablespoons black
    pepper
½ cup Andria's steak
    sauce

**Yield: 1¾ cups
    marinade**

# Wild Rice, Apricot, And Pecan Stuffing

*...perfect for a wild turkey, as the meat of a stuffed bird is moister and more flavorful than that of an unstuffed bird*

1 cup wild rice
1 stalk celery, chopped
2 onions, chopped
1 stick butter
1 cup white rice
1 teaspoon dried rosemary
1 teaspoon salt
½ teaspoon black pepper
2 cups chicken broth
½ teaspoon nutmeg
1 cup pecan halves
1 cup chopped dried apricots

Cook wild rice in water for 45 minutes or until tender. Drain. Cook celery and onions in butter for 5 minutes or until soft. Add white rice and rosemary. Cook and stir 1 minute. Add salt, pepper, broth, and nutmeg. Bring to a boil. Reduce heat and cover. Simmer until rice is tender and liquid is absorbed. Stir in pecans, apricots, and wild rice. Place mixture in a casserole dish. Bake at 325° for 20 to 30 minutes, or stuff turkey.

**Yield: 8 servings**

# George's Cranberry Sauce

*...cranberries grow in turfy bogs in New England and are the traditional accompaniment to roast turkey and chicken*

1 pound cranberries
1 tablespoon orange zest
¼ teaspoon diced ginger
½ cup orange juice
1 tablespoon lemon zest
¼ cup water
½ teaspoon cinnamon
1 cup sugar

Combine all ingredients in a saucepan. Cover and cook until berries soften and sauce thickens. Cool and serve.

*Vary flavor by adding pineapple chunks or strawberries. For a sweeter taste, add extra sugar.*

**Yield: about 4 cups**

# Easter Dinner

*Asparagus with Orange Sauce*

*Herbed Rack of Lamb*
*Crisp Baked Acorn Squash Rings*
*Scalloped Potatoes*

*Mixed Greens with Goat Cheese, Maple*
*Vinaigrette & Toasted Walnuts*

*Haddie's Rum Pie*

*Honig Sauvignon Blanc*
*Jayson Meritage*

# Veal Stew

*...there's an autumn edge to the air, and appetites that languished through the summer are once again craving hot and rib-sticking meals*

Sauté veal in 4 tablespoons butter in an ovenproof skillet. Remove veal from skillet. Add garlic and onion and sauté. Add remaining 4 tablespoons butter and mushrooms and sauté. Stir in veal, salt, pepper, broth, tomato paste, and water chestnuts. Cover and place in oven. Bake at 350° for 1 hour, 30 minutes. Remove from oven and stir in cream and brandy. Simmer on stove for 15 minutes. Combine cornstarch and water. Mix into stew. Top with parsley.

To prepare ahead, refrigerate after stew is removed from oven. When ready to serve, reheat before adding cream.

2½ pounds veal, cut in
    1½-inch cubes
1 stick butter, divided
1 clove garlic, minced
1 medium onion,
    chopped
1 pound fresh
    mushrooms, sliced
salt and pepper to taste
1 cup beef broth
3 tablespoons tomato
    paste
2 (8-ounce) cans water
    chestnuts, drained
    and sliced
2 cups heavy cream
¼ cup brandy
1½ tablespoons
    cornstarch
3 tablespoons water or
    wine
chopped fresh parsley

# Halooshki Dumplings

*...a Czechoslovakian dumpling to accompany any meat stew*

Combine flour, eggs, salt, and baking powder. Salt water to taste and bring to a boil. Add butter to water. Drop in flour mixture by teaspoonfuls. Boil 15 minutes. Add cream and remove from heat. Serve hot.

1 cup all-purpose flour
2 eggs
1 teaspoon salt
½ teaspoon baking
    powder
4 cups water
1 stick butter
1 cup cream

**Yield: 6 servings**

# Veal And Ham Pie

*...a mildly seasoned, country-style, pâté mixture for a traditional summer or tailgate picnic before the steeple chase*

1½ pounds boneless veal shoulder, divided
1½ pounds smoked ham, divided
2 teaspoons salt
½ teaspoon black pepper
¼ teaspoon ground allspice
1 teaspoon lemon zest
½ teaspoon dried thyme
⅛ teaspoon nutmeg
2 tablespoons cognac
2 eggs, lightly beaten
2 pastry crusts, divided
2 hard-cooked eggs
3-4 pickled walnuts
1 (¼-ounce) package unflavored gelatin
2 cups chicken broth, divided

**Yield: 8 to 10 servings**

Grind together ½ pound veal and ½ pound ham. Finely dice remaining pound of veal and pound of ham and add to ground meat. Add salt, pepper, allspice, zest, thyme, nutmeg, cognac, and eggs and mix lightly. Place 1 pastry crust in a pie pan. Add meat mixture until half full. Place hard-cooked eggs in center of pie pan. Arrange walnuts between and on either side of eggs. Pack remaining meat mixture around and on top of eggs. Top with remaining pastry crust. With a sharp knife, cut a 1-inch diameter hole in center of crust to allow steam to escape. Crimp edges to seal. Bake at 425° for 40 minutes. Place a pan below pie in oven to catch drips. Reduce heat to 350° and bake 1 hour, 30 minutes to 2 hours or until done. Cover crust with foil to prevent overbrowning. Heat gelatin and ¼ cup broth until dissolved. Add to remaining 1½ cups broth. Use a funnel through the steam hole to fill broth mixture into all spaces of pie where meat has shrunk from pastry. Add more, if desired, as pie cools. Allow pie to cool to room temperature before serving.

# Veal Scallops With Brandy And Sour Cream

*...the best brandies are always known by the name of the district where the wine from which they were distilled was made: Cognac brandy, Armagnac brandy, etc.*

Pat veal with paper towels to dry. Sprinkle to taste with salt and pepper. Dredge in flour. Heat 2 tablespoons butter in a chafing dish until bubbly. Add veal in batches so as to not crowd dish. Cook 3 minutes on each side. Transfer to a warm plate. Add more butter as needed to cook each batch. Add onion to dish. Sauté 2 to 3 minutes, stirring with a wooden spoon. Stir in 2 tablespoons butter and mushrooms. Cover and cook 5 minutes, stirring occasionally. Add brandy and shake to ignite, or use a match. Stir in sour cream and ½ teaspoon salt when flames subside. Bring to just boiling. Return veal to dish. Spoon sauce over veal, bringing mixture to just boiling. Reduce heat to keep warm until ready to serve.

Serve over buttered noodles.

12 (8X4X¼ inch) veal scallops
salt and pepper
all-purpose flour for dredging
6-8 tablespoons unsalted butter, divided
1 cup minced onion
1 pound fresh mushrooms, sliced
¼ cup brandy
1 cup sour cream
½ teaspoon salt

**Yield: 6 servings**

# Veal Scallops Almondine

*...not a dish to attempt for a crowd as the scallops are sautéed very quickly and served immediately*

6 (4-ounce) veal scallops
salt and pepper to taste
2½ cups dry breadcrumbs
⅓ cup minced fresh parsley
3 tablespoons lemon zest
1½ cups sliced blanched almonds, lightly toasted
3 egg whites, lightly beaten
¾ cup clarified butter
lemon slices for garnish

**Yield: 6 servings**

Flatten veal between sheets of wax paper to a ¼-inch thickness. Season with salt and pepper. In a shallow bowl, combine breadcrumbs, parsley, zest, and almonds. Place egg whites in a separate shallow bowl. Dip veal in egg whites and then in breadcrumb mixture, pressing mixture onto surface. Chill on a baking sheet for at least 30 minutes. Sauté veal in butter in a large skillet for 1 to 2 minutes on each side or until thoroughly cooked and golden. Place on a heated serving platter and garnish with lemon slices.

# Grilled Sirloin Steak With Stilton Sauce

*...this is the meal for the crested velvet slippers, hunt hound at your feet in front of a glowing fire with the bottle of red wine you've put down for the occasion*

1 stick butter, melted
6 tablespoons Worcestershire sauce
8 ounces Stilton cheese, crumbled
1 clove garlic, crushed
1 (3-inch thick) beef sirloin steak, at room temperature
salt and pepper to taste

**Yield: 6 to 8 servings**

Combine butter, Worcestershire sauce, cheese, and garlic to make a sauce. Heat and stir until cheese melts. Season sirloin with salt and pepper. Cook on a grill until rare. Pour a fourth of sauce over steak. Turn steak and pour another fourth over top. Grill to desired degree of doneness. Place on a serving platter and top with half of remaining sauce. Serve remainder of sauce on the side.

# Carbonnades à la Flamande

*...a Belgian beef stew with humble ingredients - beef, onions, and beer - needs lively appetites for a hearty mid-winter meal.*

Cut beef into ½-inch thick slices. Cut slices into 1X2 inch pieces. Dredge in flour and brown, a few at a time, in hot oil in a skillet. Place in a 6 to 8-quart casserole dish. Add onion and garlic to skillet. Cook until lightly browned, adding extra oil if needed. Place over beef in casserole dish. Stir 2 tablespoons vinegar, sugar, parsley, bay leaves, thyme, salt, and pepper into casserole dish. Pour off any oil remaining in skillet and add broth. Heat over low heat, stirring to loosen browned bits from skillet. Pour over beef mixture. Add beer. Cover and bake at 325° for 2 hours. Meanwhile, prepare dumpling batter by combining flour, milk, and butter. Mix lightly. Transfer stew to stove top. Stir in remaining 2 tablespoons vinegar and bring to a simmer over medium heat. Drop batter by teaspoonfuls over hot stew. Reduce heat and cover. Simmer 15 minutes or until a toothpick inserted in dumplings comes out clean. Do not remove cover or allow stew to come to a full boil during this time.

4 pounds lean beef
½ cup all-purpose flour
½ cup vegetable oil
2 pounds large onions, thickly sliced
6 cloves garlic, crushed
¼ cup red wine vinegar, divided
3 tablespoons packed brown sugar
½ cup chopped fresh parsley
2 small bay leaves
2 teaspoons thyme
1 tablespoon salt
black pepper to taste
2 (10¾-ounce) cans beef broth
3 cups beer
2 cups sifted self-rising cake flour
¾ cup milk
2 tablespoons butter, melted

**Yield: 6 servings**

# Racquet Club Charbroiled Steak With Magil's Salt'n Pepper Mix And Steak Butter

*...from the recipe book of Robert Magil, first manager of The Racquet Club*

## magil's salt'n pepper mix

- 1 (1-pound) container salt
- 6 teaspoons crushed black pepper
- 4 teaspoons garlic powder
- 1 teaspoon liquid smoke

## steak butter

- 3 cloves garlic, minced
- 2 sticks butter
- 2½ tablespoons prepared mustard
- 2½ tablespoons tomato sauce
- dash of Worcestershire sauce
- salt and pepper to taste
- paprika to taste

## steak

- 3 pounds beef sirloin
- ½ cup olive oil
- 4 teaspoons Worcestershire sauce, or to taste
- Magil's Salt'n Pepper Mix

**Yield: 4 servings**

To prepare mix, combine all mix ingredients. Store in an airtight container. Mix all steak butter ingredients in a food processor. Chill until ready to use. To prepare steak, marinate beef in oil and Worcestershire sauce. Sprinkle with Magil's Salt'n Pepper Mix. Grill 2 minutes on each side or until rare. Bake at 500° to desired degree of doneness, 12 to 15 minutes for medium-rare. Cut into ½-inch slices across the grain. Serve topped with Steak Butter.

# Lebanese Hamburgers

*...typical Lebanese spices - cinnamon, paprika, and cayenne - flavor the hamburgers and the onions. Since the onions require a long, slow cooking, they could be done ahead and reheated. The Yogurt Sauce is a nice accompaniment.*

Combine cinnamon, paprika, salt, and cayenne pepper. Melt 6 tablespoons butter in a large skillet over low heat. Add onion and cook, stirring often, for 40 minutes or until softened and starting to brown. After 20 minutes of cooking, mix in 4 teaspoons of spice mixture. When done cooking, remove from heat and keep warm in an oven, or refrigerate and reheat when ready to use. In a large skillet, melt remaining 2 tablespoons butter. Add tomatoes and cook 1 to 2 minutes on each side. Place tomatoes and any juice from skillet on top of onions. In a bowl, combine remaining spice mixture, beef, and water. Shape into 12 patties. Place on an oiled grill, 4 to 6 inches above a heat source. Cook 6 to 8 minutes on each side or to desired degree of doneness, turning only once. After turning patties, toast buns by arranging them, cut-side down, around the outer edge of grill. Serve patties in buns with warm vegetable mixture and Yogurt Sauce on the side.

1 tablespoon cinnamon
1 tablespoon paprika
1 tablespoon salt
¾ teaspoon cayenne pepper
1 stick butter, divided
4 large onions, halved lengthwise and sliced
4 small tomatoes, sliced ½-inch thick
3 pounds lean ground beef
½ cup water
12 hamburger buns, split and buttered
Yogurt Sauce (page 132)

**Yield: 12 servings**

# Venison Burgers

*...there's little fat in the meat, so it's best grilled and if you can taste the cinnamon, it's too much*

1½ pounds ground
    venison
1 medium onion,
    minced
pinch of cinnamon
½ teaspoon
    Worcestershire
    sauce
1 clove garlic, pressed
black pepper to taste

Combine all ingredients. Form into patties and grill to desired degree of doneness.

**Yield: 4 servings**

# Lamb Burgers

*...serve with grilled vegetables and mozzarella slices topped with Sun-dried Tomato Dressing*

⅓ cup dry rice
⅔ cup chicken broth
1 cup minced onion
2 tablespoons butter
1 egg
1 clove garlic, mashed
1 pound lean ground
    lamb shoulder
salt and pepper to taste
dried rosemary or thyme
    to taste
olive oil for frying
    (optional)
Sun-dried Tomato
    Dressing (page 258)

Cook rice in broth until tender. Sauté onion in butter until softened. Purée rice, onion, egg, and garlic in a food processor. Blend puréed mixture, lamb, salt, pepper, and rosemary together. Form into patties and grill, or fry in olive oil. Serve with Sun-dried Tomato Dressing.

**Yield: 4 servings**

# Lamb With Dill

*...the favorite meat of the Arab countries, lamb is cooked with dill, an herb powerful enough to ward off the Evil Eye when carried in a packet over the heart*

Pat lamb dry with paper towels. Melt butter in a large skillet. Add lamb in batches, cooking only a single layer at a time. Cook and stir over medium-high heat until lightly browned. Place in a bowl. Add onion to skillet and sauté 1 to 2 minutes. Return lamb and any juices in bowl to skillet. Sprinkle with flour and mix until coated. Add broth, wine, and dill seed. Bring to a boil, stirring occasionally. Reduce heat, cover, and simmer 60 minutes. Cool. Refrigerate, covered, for several hours or overnight. Skim fat from top. When ready to serve, reheat stew. Add mushrooms and cover. Cook gently for 20 minutes, stirring occasionally. Season as desired. Stir in sour cream and heat thoroughly without boiling.

Serve with rice pilaf.

3½ pounds boneless leg of lamb, cut in 1½-inch cubes
3 tablespoons butter
½ cup chopped onion
5 tablespoons all-purpose flour
1¾ cups beef broth
⅓ cup red wine
1½ teaspoons dill seed
1 pound mushrooms, trimmed and quartered
½ cup sour cream

**Yield: 6 servings**

# Mediterranean Lamb Couscous

*...national dish of the North African countries, couscous is a fine semolina made from wheat grain*

1 ½ pounds lamb or
    chicken, cubed
1 onion, chopped
2 cloves garlic, minced
1 cup sliced carrots
1 cup sliced celery
1 cup sliced
    mushrooms
1 ½ cups slivered almonds
3 tablespoons olive oil
1 ½ cups garbanzo beans,
    cooked or canned
1 ½ cups tomato sauce
½ cup raisins
¾ cup red wine
¾ cup chicken broth
2 teaspoons curry
    powder
1 bay leaf
¼ teaspoon cayenne
    pepper
1 teaspoon salt
1 teaspoon ground
    cumin
1 teaspoon paprika
hot cooked couscous

**Yield: 6 servings**

Sauté lamb, onion, garlic, carrots, celery, mushrooms, and almonds in oil in a large pan. Add garbanzo beans, tomato sauce, raisins, wine, broth, curry powder, bay leaf, cayenne pepper, salt, cumin, and paprika. Cover and bring to a boil. Reduce heat and simmer 40 minutes. Remove bay leaf. Serve over couscous.

# Moussaka

*...called the cottage pie of the Balkans, this moussaka is of Greek origin and is equally as good made with leftover lamb*

Brown eggplant quickly in 4 tablespoons butter in a skillet. Set aside. Heat 4 tablespoons butter in same skillet. Add onions and sauté until brown. Add lamb and cook and stir 10 minutes. In a bowl, combine salt, pepper, tomato paste, wine, parsley, and cinnamon. Stir mixture into skillet. Simmer over low heat, stirring frequently, until all liquid is absorbed. Remove from heat and set aside. Prepare a white sauce by melting remaining 1 stick butter in a pan. Blend in flour. In a separate pan, bring milk to a boil. Slowly whisk milk into flour mixture. Cook and stir until thickened and smooth. Cool slightly. Beat eggs until frothy. Add eggs, nutmeg, and ricotta cheese to white sauce. To assemble, lightly sprinkle the bottom of a buttered 11X16 inch pan with some of breadcrumbs. Arrange alternate layers of eggplant and meat mixture in pan. Sprinkle each layer with Parmesan cheese and breadcrumbs. Pour sauce over top. Bake at 375° for 60 minutes or until golden. Cool at room temperature for 20 to 30 minutes before serving. Cut into squares and serve.

The flavor improves if refrigerated overnight. Reheat or serve at room temperature.

3 medium eggplants, peeled and sliced ½-inch thick
2 sticks butter, divided
3 large onions, finely chopped
2 pounds ground lamb or beef
salt and pepper to taste
3 tablespoons tomato paste
½ cup red wine
½ cup chopped fresh parsley
¼ teaspoon cinnamon
6 tablespoons all-purpose flour
4 cups milk
4 eggs
nutmeg
2 cups ricotta or cottage cheese
I cup fine breadcrumbs
I cup Parmesan cheese

**Yield: 8 to 10 servings**

# Herbed Rack Of Lamb

*...served with Crisp Baked Acorn Squash Rings and a Warm Green Bean Salad at a luncheon to celebrate a christening*

1 (1 to 1¼-pound)
  4-rib rack of lamb
2 teaspoons olive oil
¼ teaspoon dried
  rosemary, crumbled
salt and pepper to taste

**Yield: 2 servings**

Trim lamb of all but a thin layer of fat. Shorten bones as needed. Rub lamb with oil and rosemary. Season with salt and pepper. Let stand at room temperature for 60 minutes. Cook, fat-side up, in a small roasting pan at 500° for 10 minutes. Reduce heat to 400° and bake 8 minutes for a medium-rare doneness. Remove from heat and let stand 10 minutes before cutting into chops.

# Marinated And Grilled Lamb Chops

*...the fair weather that insures a steady supply of good produce also suggests a more carefree, casual ambiance of entertaining*

8 (1-inch thick) lamb
  loin chops, trimmed
2 tablespoons red wine
  vinegar
1 tablespoon lemon
  juice
2 teaspoons Dijon
  mustard
3 tablespoons olive oil
1 clove garlic, minced
¼ teaspoon ground
  ginger
1 tablespoon chopped
  fresh rosemary, or 1
  teaspoon dried
¼ teaspoon salt
1 small onion, sliced

**Yield: 8 servings**

Place chops in a deep ceramic or glass bowl. Combine vinegar and remaining ingredients and pour over chops. Cover and refrigerate 4 to 5 hours. Grill or broil chops. Cooking 5 minutes on each side should achieve a medium-rare doneness.

# Raspberry Pork Tenderloin With A Raspberry, Dijon, And Maple Sauce

*...with many thanks to Sidney Street Cafe, which is located in a century-old storefront building in colorful Benton Park, creating contemporary American and continental cuisine since 1986*

Combine mustard, brandy, syrup, vinegar, rosemary, parsley, sage, thyme, and marjoram. Spread over tenderloin and let stand 60 minutes. Sprinkle with salt, pepper, and garlic. Roll tenderloin in crushed cracker, patting crumbs on to help them stick. Refrigerate at least 30 minutes to allow coating to harden. Sauté quickly in butter, rolling tenderloin until crisp and golden. Bake at 400° for 12 to 15 minutes or until cooked to desired degree of doneness. Serve with Raspberry, Dijon, and Maple Sauce. To make sauce, combine Merlot, liqueur, and broth in a pan. Bring to a boil and reduce by half. Add cream, syrup, and mustard. Cook until reduced by half.

¼ cup Dijon mustard
1 tablespoon brandy
1 tablespoon maple syrup
½ tablespoon raspberry vinegar
¼ teaspoon dried rosemary
¼ teaspoon dried parsley
¼ teaspoon dried sage
¼ teaspoon dried thyme
¼ teaspoon dried marjoram
1 (1½ to 2-pound) pork tenderloin
coarse salt
cracked black pepper
crushed fresh garlic
4 cups crushed buttery crackers
butter for sautéing

**raspberry, dijon, and maple sauce**
1 cup Merlot
¼ cup raspberry liqueur
1 cup veal broth
1 cup heavy cream
¼ cup maple syrup
1 tablespoon Dijon mustard

**Yield: 4 servings**

# Fruit-stuffed Pork ^Tender Loin With Bourbon Orange Glaze

*...serve with gingered carrots and scalloped potatoes or sautéed snap peas*

1 (3-pound) pork tenderloin
2-3 cups chopped dried fruit
2 teaspoons salt
black pepper to taste
½ cup orange juice
½ cup bourbon
½ cup packed light brown sugar
1 tablespoon ground ginger
1 tablespoon orange zest
¼ teaspoon powdered cloves

**Yield: 6 servings**

Lay tenderloin on counter and with hands on each end, push together so tenderloin is as short as it can get. With a long bread knife, pierce one end of tenderloin and gently continue to push knife through tenderloin to other end, being careful not to poke out top or bottom when creating a lengthwise "pocket". When a "tunnel" has been established end to end, take knife and gently widen pocket, creating a "smile" at each end. With the handle of a wooden spoon, work from both ends towards the middle and firmly stuff dried fruit into the pocket. Rub tenderloin with salt and pepper. Bake at 325° for about 60 minutes. Do not overcook. Meanwhile, combine orange juice and remaining ingredients in a small saucepan to make a glaze. Simmer 30 minutes. During the final 30 minutes of baking time, baste tenderloin with glaze. Slice tenderloin, arrange on a serving plate, and top with remainder of glaze.

Use any combination of dried fruits, such as prunes, apricots, peaches, and pears. If desired, use ⅓ cup orange juice and ⅔ cup bourbon.

*Score a fully-cooked ham. Baste with glaze during the final 30 minutes of cooking.*

# Pork Tenderloin With Mustard Cream Sauce

*...port is a blend of wine, brandy, and unfermented grape juice. Vintage port is made in 1 year, shipped, and bottled 2 years later, and then aged in the bottle for 12 to 20 years to get the desired strength, delicacy, sweetness, and flavor. Tawny port is a blend of wines from several years' grapes, is matured in wood, aging more rapidly than early-bottled vintage port, and is shipped when ready to drink*

Place pork on wax paper. Spread with mustard and dredge carefully in flour. Combine oil and 2 tablespoons butter in a large, ovenproof skillet. Place over medium-high heat until foam subsides. Add pork and sear, turning carefully with tongs, until a golden coating forms. Place skillet on center rack in oven and bake at 450° for 12 to 15 minutes or until internal temperature reaches 155°. Transfer to a large plate and cover loosely with foil. Melt 2 tablespoons butter in skillet. Add shallots and sauté for 1 minute. Deglaze skillet with port. Cook until liquid reduces by half. Remove from heat and add remaining 2 tablespoons butter and cream. Stir until butter melts. Divide sauce among 4 individual plates. Slice pork and place on plates. Garnish with parsley.

2 (¾-pound) pork tenderloins, trimmed
½ cup Dijon mustard
⅓ cup all-purpose flour
2 tablespoons vegetable oil
6 tablespoons unsalted butter, divided
6 shallots, minced
1 cup Tawny port
½ cup heavy cream
chopped fresh parsley for garnish

**Yield: 4 servings**

# Caribbean Pork Loin With Baked Bananas

*...for a quick trip to the islands, serve with black beans and rice*

**pork loin**
- 3 cloves garlic
- 2 scallions, minced
- ¼ cup pine nuts
- 1 jalapeño pepper, seeded and minced
- 1 cup minced fresh cilantro leaves
- ⅓ cup olive oil
- 5 tablespoons fresh lime juice
- 2 tablespoons minced kalamata olives
- salt and pepper to taste
- 1 (4-pound) boneless pork loin
- ½ cup hot pepper jelly

**baked bananas**
- 4 ripe bananas, peeled and halved lengthwise
- 4 tablespoons butter
- 2 tablespoons sherry
- 1 tablespoon fresh lime juice
- ⅓ cup packed brown sugar
- 1 teaspoon cinnamon

**Yield: 8 servings**

Combine garlic, scallions, pine nuts, jalapeño pepper, and cilantro in a food processor. Blend to form a thick paste. With machine running, add oil in a slow, steady stream. Blend in lime juice, olives, salt, and pepper. Place pork in a glass baking dish. Pour marinade over top and cover. Refrigerate 24 hours, turning occasionally. Grill pork over medium-high heat, or bake at 375° for 1 hour, 30 minutes. Baste occasionally with marinade while cooking. Brush with jelly during final 15 minutes of cooking. Remove from heat and let stand 10 to 15 minutes before slicing. Serve with baked bananas. To prepare bananas, arrange halves in a single layer in a shallow casserole dish. Melt butter in a saucepan. Stir in sherry and lime juice and heat thoroughly. Pour over bananas. Sprinkle sugar and cinnamon on top. Bake at 375° for 12 to 15 minutes.

# Sausage And Leek Pie

*...a unique tailgate or picnic entrée*

Place crust in a 9-inch pie pan. Trim edge, leaving a 1-inch overhang. Fold up overhang and crimp to make a decorative edge. Prick crust several times with a fork and chill 60 minutes. Line crust with wax paper and fill with dry rice. Bake at 400° for 10 minutes. Carefully remove paper and rice. Bake 10 to 15 minutes longer or until lightly browned. Cool on a rack. Place leeks and butter in a saucepan and cover with buttered wax paper and a lid. Cook over low heat for 45 minutes or until softened. In a skillet, sauté sausage in oil over medium-high heat until browned. Stir in leek, sage, salt, and pepper. Allow to cool. Sprinkle ¼ cup cheese in crust. Add sausage mixture. Lightly beat cream and egg together. Pour over sausage. Sprinkle remaining ¼ cup cheese over top. Bake at 350° for 35 minutes.

1 pastry crust
dry rice
3 cups chopped leeks
6 tablespoons butter
8 ounces sausage
1 tablespoon oil
½ teaspoon dried sage
salt and pepper to taste
½ cup grated Gruyère cheese, divided
½ cup heavy cream
1 egg

**Yield: 6 servings**

# Provençal Spice Mix

For any meat bound for the grill: with food processor motor running, put in zest of 2 lemons. Add ⅓ cup thinly sliced garlic, ⅓ cup fresh rosemary, ⅓ cup kosher salt, ¼ cup fresh sage leaves and ¼ cup freshly ground pepper.

# BBQ Rub

*...dryly described in various dictionaries as "social gatherings where animal carcasses are roasted whole" - the institution of the barbecue has become a way of life*

- 1 tablespoon salt
- 1 tablespoon granulated sugar
- 1 tablespoon packed brown sugar
- 1 tablespoon ground cumin
- 1 tablespoon chili powder
- 1 tablespoon black pepper
- ½ tablespoon cayenne pepper
- 2 tablespoons paprika

Combine all ingredients. Store in an airtight container until ready to use.

**Yield: ½ cup**

# Bourbon Barbecue Sauce

*...great with pork*

- 3 slices bacon
- 1½ cups ketchup
- ¼ cup molasses
- 2 tablespoons cider vinegar
- 2 tablespoons Worcestershire sauce
- 2 tablespoons bourbon
- 2 tablespoons strong brewed coffee
- 1 teaspoon prepared mustard
- ½ small onion, minced

Cook bacon until crisp. Drain and mince. Combine all ingredients in a saucepan. Bring to a boil. Reduce heat and simmer 30 minutes.

**Yield: 2 cups**

# BBQ Sauce

*...on fine days, especially in the hot summer months, the smoke from barbecue fires has become a familiar sight and smell throughout the city and county*

Sauté onion, garlic, and peppers in oil until browned. Add vinegar, sugar, ginger, paprika, chili powder, cumin, mustard, molasses, and Worcestershire sauce. Cook for a few minutes. Add tomatoes and paste.

2 large onions, chopped
6 cloves garlic, minced
2 jalapeño peppers, seeded and minced
oil for sautéing
½ (8½-ounce) bottle balsamic vinegar
1 cup packed brown sugar
½ tablespoon minced fresh ginger
1 tablespoon paprika
1½ tablespoons chili powder
1 tablespoon ground cumin
2 tablespoons dry mustard
¼ cup molasses
⅔ cup Worcestershire sauce
1 (4-pound) can tomatoes
½ cup tomato paste

**Yield: 3 quarts**

# Tarragon Sauce

*...excellent sauce for filet mignon, sautéed veal scallops, or substitute sage for the tarragon, call it a sage sauce and serve it with Pan-fried Trout*

¼ cup chopped shallot
1 tablespoon olive oil
½ cup white wine
2 tablespoons heavy cream
1 tablespoon minced fresh tarragon
pinch of minced fresh oregano
½ teaspoon Dijon mustard
1 teaspoon fresh lemon juice
4 tablespoons unsalted butter, softened
salt and pepper to taste

**Yield: 4 servings**

Sauté shallots in oil until softened. Add wine and cook until reduced to a glaze. Blend in cream, tarragon, oregano, mustard and lemon or lime juice. Slowly whisk in butter, 1 tablespoon at a time. Season lightly with salt and pepper.

# Raisin Cider Or Beer Sauce

*...serve with hot/cold ham or smoked tongue*

¾ cup packed brown sugar
1½ tablespoons cornstarch
⅛ teaspoon salt
1 cup cider or beer
¼ cup raisins, halved
8 whole cloves
1 cinnamon stick
1 tablespoon butter

**Yield: 1½ cups**

Combine sugar, cornstarch, and salt in a saucepan. Add cider, raisins, cloves, and cinnamon. Cook over medium heat, stirring constantly, for 10 minutes. Stir in butter. Remove from heat and discard cloves and cinnamon. Serve very hot.

Vegetables

# Game Dinner

*Goat Cheese Ravioli With Garlic Tomato Sauce*

*Mussel Bisque or Consommé Madrilene*

*Cider Sorbet with Red Wine Sauce*

*Nortie's Dove*
*Roast Quail with Oysters & Wild Rice in a Wild Mushroom Sauce*
*The Best Brussels Sprouts*
*Puréed Garlic & Leek with Mashed Potatoes*

*Stilton & Pear Salad*

*Crème Brûlée*

*Welsh Rabbit*

*Dagueneau Pouilly Fumé*
*Chateau Lynch Bages*

# Broccoli Soufflé

*...the son of Tiberius one day ate so much broccoli that his father chided him for his greediness. Considering the extraordinary eating habits of wealthy Romans in those times, it makes one wonder how much broccoli the young man did, in fact, consume!*

Steam broccoli until tender, if using fresh broccoli. Drain and place in a bowl. Add butter and ½ cup cheddar cheese. Mix in flour. In a separate bowl, combine cottage cheese and eggs. Add broccoli mixture, onion, salt, and pepper. Pour into a buttered 1-quart casserole dish. Top with remaining ½ cup cheddar cheese. Bake at 350° for 60 minutes.

4 cups fresh broccoli flowerets, or 1 (10-ounce) package frozen
4 tablespoons butter, cut in small pieces
1 cup grated cheddar cheese, divided
3 tablespoons all-purpose flour
8 ounces cottage cheese
3 eggs, lightly beaten
½ cup minced onion
salt and pepper to taste

**Yield: 4 servings**

# Asparagus with Orange Sauce

Reduce 3 cups freshly squeezed orange juice to 1½ cups over low heat, stir in 2 teaspoons champagne vinegar and then ¼ cup lemon juice bit by bit until a delicate sweet and sour balance is achieved. Season to taste and spoon onto hot individual dishes, arrange asparagus on the sauce and sprinkle with slivers of orange and lemon zest.

# The Best Brussels Sprouts

*...there are many people so confirmed in their dislike of this member of the cabbage family that it would be useless to try to convert them. However, this version should win over the undecided.*

2½ pounds Brussels
　sprouts, halved and
　cored (8 cups)
6 slices bacon, cut into
　¼-inch pieces
½ cup pine nuts
2 teaspoons minced
　garlic
I cup finely diced
　carrots
2 teaspoons salt
black pepper to taste
¼ cup chopped fresh
　Italian parsley

**Yield: 10 to 12
　servings**

Cut each Brussels sprout half into quarters. Cook bacon in a large skillet until fat is rendered. Add pine nuts and cook 1 minute or until bacon is crisp and nuts are golden. Add sprouts, garlic, and carrots. Cover pan and sauté 1 minute or until sprouts wilt but are still bright green. Stir in salt, pepper, and parsley. Serve warm.

# Winter Vegetable Mélange

*...a favorite of the winter kitchen, its flavor is the perfect foil for a roast of duck, lamb, or beef, and the diced carrot sweetens them*

½ pound Brussels
　sprouts, halved and
　cored (2 cups)
3 tablespoons butter
I leek, sliced ½-inch
　thick
2 large carrots, sliced
　½-inch thick
I tablespoon water
¼ teaspoon caraway
　seed
¼ teaspoon salt
black pepper to taste

**Yield: 4 servings**

Sauté Brussels sprouts in butter over medium heat for 3 minutes. Stir in leek and carrot and sauté 2 minutes longer. Add water. Cover and steam 5 minutes. Sprinkle with caraway seed and season with salt and pepper.

# Braised Red Cabbage

*...when cooking red cabbage, add an acidic ingredient (like vinegar) to help the cabbage hold its color*

Sauté onion in oil over medium heat for 5 minutes. Stir in remaining ingredients. Mix well and cover. Bring to a boil, stirring occasionally. Reduce heat to low and simmer 40 minutes, stirring occasionally. Uncover and cook 5 minutes longer to reduce liquid.

*Substitute 6 allspice berries plus ⅔ cup red wine for the white wine and the vinegar.*

1 medium onion, sliced
2 tablespoons olive oil
1 medium head red cabbage, sliced ½-inch thick
1 large cooking apple, peeled and chopped
½ cup dry white wine
¼ cup red wine vinegar
6 tablespoons packed light brown sugar
½ teaspoon salt
¼ teaspoon black pepper

**Yield: 8 servings**

# Crisp Baked Acorn Squash Rings

*...can make a Sunday lunch elegant, served with Herbed Rack of Lamb*

In a shallow dish, whisk eggs, milk, and honey together. In a separate shallow dish, combine cornmeal, breadcrumbs, salt, and pepper. Slice squash into ½-inch thick rings and seed. Dip squash rings into egg mixture and then into cornmeal mixture. Coat rings well, patting on crumbs as needed. Arrange rings in a single layer on 2 well-buttered baking sheets. Drizzle butter over top. Bake at 400° for 30 minutes or until tender. Turn rings half-way through cooking time. Season with salt to taste and arrange on a heated platter.

2 eggs, lightly beaten
¼ cup milk
2 teaspoons honey
¾ cup yellow cornmeal
1½ cups breadcrumbs
salt and pepper
2 acorn squash
3 tablespoons butter, melted

**Yield: 6 servings**

# Sicilian Stuffed Artichokes

*...in the 17th century, artichokes had acquired a reputation for being an aphrodisiac; the mere mention of them aroused a snicker*

4 artichokes
½ small onion, chopped
1 clove garlic, chopped
1 tablespoon chopped
   fresh parsley
¾ cup Romano or
   Parmesan cheese
¾ cup dried
   breadcrumbs
½ teaspoon salt
½ teaspoon black
   pepper
6 tablespoons olive oil,
   divided
2 tablespoons water

**Yield: 4 servings**

Remove stalks, tough outer leaves, and leaf tips from artichokes. Spread remaining leaves open and remove choke with silver teaspoon. Combine onion, garlic, parsley, cheese, breadcrumbs, salt, and pepper in a bowl. Moisten with 4 tablespoons oil, or more if needed, and water. Fill each leaf and center of each artichoke with mixture. Place artichokes in a glass baking dish. Drizzle remaining 2 tablespoons oil over top. Add a small amount of water to the bottom of dish. Bake at 325° for 45 minutes or until bottom of artichokes are soft.

# Crisp Braised Celery

*...a wonderful winter vegetable that's often forgotten and when seen, has played a supporting role in stews and large chowders*

1½ large bunches celery
   with leaves
2 tablespoons vegetable
   oil
1 tablespoon butter
½ teaspoon salt
1 teaspoon sugar
¾ teaspoon celery seed
⅓ cup chicken broth

**Yield: 10 servings**

Trim celery, reserving leaves. Cut stalks diagonally into ⅛-inch thick slices. This should result in about 8 cups sliced celery. In a large skillet, heat oil and butter over medium-high heat. Add celery, salt, sugar, and celery seed. Sauté for 1 minute. Add broth and reserved leaves. Bring to a boil. Reduce heat and simmer 3 to 5 minutes or until celery is crisp-tender.

# Carrot Turnip Gratin

*...turnips are at their best when so young that they can be eaten raw, as they are in Greece as an hors d'oeuvre*

In a large mixing bowl, combine 3 tablespoons cornstarch, carrots, turnips, scallion greens, and parsley. Spread mixture in a buttered, shallow 1½-quart baking dish. Press vegetables down, smoothing into place. In a small saucepan, dissolve remaining 1 tablespoon cornstarch in ¼ cup milk. Add cream and remaining 1¾ cup milk. Bring to a boil over medium-high heat, whisking constantly. Reduce to medium heat. In a medium mixing bowl, beat egg, salt, and pepper. Add egg to milk mixture in a slow, steady stream, beating until combined. Pour over vegetables. Sprinkle with cheese. If desired, refrigerate up to 24 hours before ready to serve. Dot butter over gratin. Bake in middle of oven at 375° for 45 minutes or until gratin is bubbly and golden. Let stand 10 minutes before serving.

4 tablespoons cornstarch, divided
¾ pound carrots, grated
¾ pound turnips, grated
½ cup thinly sliced scallion greens
2 tablespoons minced fresh parsley
2 cups milk, divided
½ cup cream or half-and-half
1 egg
salt and pepper to taste
½ cup Parmesan cheese
1 tablespoon cold butter

**Yield: 6 servings**

It is said that the ladies of King Charles I of England's court used to wear the foliage of the carrot as a decoration instead of feathers.

# Dijon Carrots

*...in France, moutarde de Dijon is made by moistening the mustard powder with "verjus" (sour grapes) and moutarde de Bordeaux with unfermented wine*

  1 pound carrots, sliced
  ¼ cup Dijon mustard
  1 tablespoon butter, melted
  3 tablespoons packed brown sugar
coarsely chopped cashews

Cook carrots until just tender and drain. Combine mustard, butter, and sugar. Pour over carrots. Sprinkle cashews on top.

**Yield: 4 servings**


# Gingered Carrots

*...puréeing vegetables isn't strictly for babies*

  2 pounds carrots, sliced
  ½ teaspoon salt
black pepper to taste
  6 tablespoons butter, melted
  1 teaspoon ground ginger

**Yield: 6 servings**

In a saucepan, cook carrots in boiling salted water for 15 to 20 minutes or until soft. Drain and purée until smooth. Return to saucepan. Add remaining ingredients. Cook over low heat until hot.

Can be made ahead and frozen.

*Variation: Spread puréed carrots in a baked pie crust. Arrange 1 to 1½ cups blanched carrot slices over top in overlapping spiral design. Sprinkle chopped scallions over top and bake at 350° until heated through.*

# Cauliflower With Cheddar Sauce And Rye Breadcrumbs

*...may be prepared a day in advance and kept covered and chilled, then brought to room temperature before preparing the breadcrumbs*

Cut cauliflower into 2-inch flowerets. Cut cauliflower greens into thin slices. Grind bread in a food processor to make fine crumbs. Toast crumbs at 350° for 3 to 5 minutes or until golden. Cool. In a saucepan, sauté onion in 3 tablespoons butter until softened. Stir in flour and cook and stir over low heat for 3 minutes. Remove pan from heat. Add milk in a steady stream, whisking until mixture is thick and smooth. Simmer 10 minutes, stirring occasionally. Add cheese and cook and stir until melted. Season with salt and pepper. Cover and keep warm, or cover surface with plastic wrap and refrigerate up to 2 days. Reheat stored sauce when ready to serve. Cook cauliflower flowerets in boiling salted water for 5 minutes. Add greens and cook 3 to 4 minutes longer or until flowerets are tender. Drain and plunge into a bowl of ice water. Drain well and pat dry. Refrigerate overnight, if desired. Place cauliflower in a buttered 2-quart baking dish and bring to room temperature. Melt remaining 1 tablespoon butter and toss with breadcrumbs in a bowl. Pour warm cheese sauce over cauliflower and sprinkle with breadcrumb mixture. Brown breadcrumbs under a broiler.

1½ heads cauliflower with greens
1 slice rye bread
1 tablespoon minced onion
4 tablespoons unsalted butter, divided
¼ cup all-purpose flour
1 quart milk, scalded
2 cups grated sharp cheddar cheese
salt and white pepper to taste

**Yield: 8 servings**

# Corn Pudding

*...best made with fresh corn, scraped from the cob with the "milk"*

2 cups corn
2 eggs, beaten
1 teaspoon sugar
1½ tablespoons butter, melted
2 cups milk, scalded
1 teaspoon salt

**Yield: 4 servings**

Combine all ingredients and place in a well-buttered shallow 8X8 inch baking dish. Place dish in a larger pan. Add water to pan half way up side of dish. Bake at 325° for 45 minutes.


# Curried Corn With Red And Green Peppers

*...colors speak for themselves*

4 ears fresh corn
⅓ cup chopped scallions
1 teaspoon finely chopped garlic
1 teaspoon curry powder
1 tablespoon butter
1 green bell pepper, julienned
1 red bell pepper, julienned
salt and pepper to taste
2 teaspoons chopped fresh cilantro or parsley

**Yield: 4 servings**

Remove kernels from ears of corn. Sauté scallions, garlic, curry powder, and butter until scallions wilt. Add corn, bell peppers, salt, and pepper. Mix well. Cover and cook over medium heat for about 2 minutes. Blend in cilantro.

# "Sweated" Cucumbers In Dill

*..."sweating" - a technique in which an ingredient is cooked in a very small amount of butter over low heat, covered with a buttered circle of wax or parchment paper - it keeps moisture in so ingredients soften and don't burn*

Cut cucumbers into ½-inch slices. Place in a bowl and sprinkle with salt. Let stand 30 minutes. Drain and pat dry. In a saucepan, combine cucumbers and 5 tablespoons butter. Cover with a buttered round of wax paper and cook over medium low heat for 10 minutes or until slightly translucent but still crisp. Swirl in remaining tablespoon butter. Sprinkle with dill and season to taste with salt and pepper.

8 cucumbers, peeled, halved, and seeded
1 tablespoon salt
6 tablespoons butter, divided
fresh dill
white pepper

**Yield: 8 servings**

# Eggplant Patties

*...serve with a butterflied leg of lamb*

Place eggplant in a saucepan with a small amount of water. Cook, drain well, and mash eggplant. Stir in remaining ingredients except oil. Shape mixture into eight (3-inch diameter) patties. Fry in hot oil for 3 minutes on each side or until golden brown.

1 medium eggplant, peeled and cubed
1¼ cups round buttery cracker crumbs
1¼ cups grated sharp cheddar cheese
2 eggs, lightly beaten
2 tablespoons fresh parsley
2 tablespoons sliced scallions
1 clove garlic, minced
½ teaspoon salt
½ teaspoon black pepper
2 tablespoons olive oil

**Yield: 4 servings**

# Jo's Baked Eggplant

*...the late Jo Tichacek, Plaza Shop, originated this recipe*

### sauce

- 1 large onion, diced
- 1 clove garlic, diced
- 3 tablespoons olive oil
- 1 (28-ounce) can Italian-style tomatoes, chopped
- 1/3 cup tomato paste
- 2 teaspoons sugar
- 1/2 teaspoon salt
- 1/4 teaspoon black pepper
- 3 large fresh basil leaves, chopped

### eggplant

- 2 medium or 4 small eggplants
- 1/2 cup coarse salt
- olive oil for frying
- Sauce
- 6 tablespoons imported Parmesan cheese
- 2 tablespoons imported Romano cheese
- 1 tablespoon diced garlic
- table salt and pepper to taste

**Yield: 6 servings**

To prepare sauce, sauté onion and garlic in oil until golden brown. Add tomatoes, tomato paste, sugar, salt, and pepper. Simmer 15 to 30 minutes or until thickened. Stir in basil near end of cooking time. To prepare eggplant, cut lengthwise in 1/2-inch slices. Sprinkle with coarse salt. Lay slices on a tilted drain board for 30 minutes or longer. Wash off salt and bitter liquid and partially dry on paper towels. Fry eggplant until brown in 1/2-inch of hot oil. Drain on paper towels. In a buttered 9X13 inch pan, form 3 layers of ingredients in the following order: Eggplant, Parmesan cheese, Romano cheese, garlic, and sauce. Season each layer with salt and pepper to taste. Press together with a spatula. Broil until top browns.

Serve warm with meat or pasta, or at room temperature as an appetizer with toasted bread rounds.

# Ratatouille Pie

*...it's the cheese that holds the pie together when sliced into wedges*

Sauté eggplant in oil in a large ovenproof skillet for about 5 minutes. Stir in zucchini, onion, and green bell peppers. Add salt, pepper, garlic, thyme, and bay leaf. Cook and stir 4 minutes. Add tomatoes and parsley and cook another 5 minutes. Place skillet in oven and bake at 425° for 30 minutes. Stir in olives and bake 10 minutes longer. Remove bay leaf and let stand until thoroughly cooled. Line a 10-inch pie plate with a pie crust, allowing 1 inch of crust to hang over side. Add ⅓ of vegetable mixture. Layer ⅓ of fontina cheese and ⅓ of Parmesan cheese on top. Repeat vegetable and cheese layers twice. Beat together egg yolk and water. Brush portion of bottom crust still exposed with yolk mixture. Place remaining pie crust on top of layers. Roll edge of bottom crust over top, seal, and crimp. Use a small biscuit cutter to make a hole in center of top crust. Decorate with leftover pastry, using yolk mixture to get pieces to stick. Bake at 425° for 30 minutes. Reduce heat to 375° and bake 15 to 20 minutes longer or until crust is golden brown.

1 (1¾-pound) eggplant, peeled and cubed
¼ cup olive oil
2 (10-ounce) zucchini, halved and sliced
1 large onion, cubed
2 green bell peppers, cubed
salt and pepper to taste
2 tablespoons minced garlic
1 teaspoon minced fresh thyme
1 bay leaf
1 pound tomatoes, peeled and quartered (2½ cups)
1 cup coarsely chopped fresh parsley
½ cup pitted black olives
2 pie crusts, unbaked, divided
2 cups grated fontina cheese, preferably imported
¾ cup Parmesan cheese
1 egg yolk
2 teaspoons water

**Yield: 8 servings**

# Horseradish Creamed Leeks

*...leeks are mostly thought of when making soups, but sauced and broiled stand beautifully on their own*

8 leeks (1 pound)
4 tablespoons butter
⅔ cup chicken broth
⅔ cup heavy cream
2 tablespoons
horseradish, or to
taste
salt and pepper to taste
6 tablespoons grated
Gruyère cheese

**Yield: 4 servings**

Leaving whole, trim leeks with white and pale green parts remaining. Cut a slit down one side of each leek to within 1 inch of base. In a large bowl of cold water, fan out leaves, rinse well, and pat dry. In a large skillet, heat butter over medium heat until foamy. Add leeks and toss to coat. Add broth and cream and bring to a boil. Reduce heat and simmer, uncovered, 25 to 30 minutes or until tender. Stir occasionally. Transfer leeks with a slotted spoon to a gratin dish. Add horseradish to skillet and season with salt and pepper. Pour sauce over leeks and sprinkle with cheese. Broil, 4 inches from the heat source, for about 2 minutes.

# Sage And Onion Bread Pudding

*...an exquisite accompaniment to baked ham for a winter brunch*

Melt butter in a skillet over low heat. Add garlic, onions, and leeks and cover with a wax paper round to fit skillet. Cook gently for 12 minutes. Remove paper and cook, stirring occasionally, for 8 minutes or until liquid evaporates. Combine sage and cheese in a food processor and mince. Add ⅔ cup milk, eggs, mustard, salt, and pepper. Blend 5 seconds. Add sautéed vegetables and pulse until well combined. Transfer to a large mixing bowl and stir in remaining 1 cup milk. Place bread in a buttered, shallow 8-cup baking dish. Pour mixture over bread, using a fork to evenly distribute onion. Let soak 30 to 45 minutes or until liquid is absorbed, or cover and refrigerate overnight. Bring to room temperature before baking. Place on center rack of oven and bake at 300° for 45 minutes. Increase temperature to 450° and bake 15 minutes or until puffy and browned. Remove from oven and let stand 15 minutes before serving.

2 tablespoons butter
1 large clove garlic, minced
3 medium-size red onions, thinly sliced
2 medium leeks, white only, thinly sliced
2 teaspoons fresh sage
5 ounces Muenster cheese, cubed
1⅔ cups milk, divided
3 eggs
2 teaspoons Dijon mustard
¾ teaspoon salt
¾ teaspoon black pepper
4 cups cubed whole wheat bread

**Yield: 8 servings**

# Puréed Garlic And Leek With Mashed Potatoes

*...never cuisinart mashed potatoes unless you need to do some tuck pointing!*

6 large leeks
2 pounds red-skinned potatoes, peeled
1½ sticks unsalted butter, divided
2 cloves garlic, minced
½ cup heavy cream
salt and pepper to taste

**Yield: 6 servings**

Trim leeks, cutting away most of green leaves, so that each leek is about 7 inches long. Split down to, but not through, base. Wash thoroughly. Cook in boiling water for 15 minutes or until tender. Drain and chop. Cover potatoes with salted cold water in a saucepan. Bring to a boil. Reduce heat and cook 20 to 40 minutes or until tender. Drain. Melt 3 tablespoons butter in a skillet over low heat. Add garlic and sauté 5 to 10 minutes or until lightly colored. Add leeks and 3 tablespoons butter and continue to cook, stirring occasionally, for 15 minutes. Transfer to a food processor and purée until smooth. Mash potatoes, adding cream as needed. Stir leek purée and remaining 6 tablespoons butter into potatoes. Season with salt and pepper. Reheat gently until steaming.

# Indian Style Potatoes With Sesame Seeds

*...black mustard seeds keep well and can be found in Indian ethnic groceries*

Cook potatoes in boiling water until just tender. Drain, cool, and cut into ¾-inch cubes. Heat oil in a skillet until very hot. Add cumin, mustard seed, and sesame seed. When seeds start to pop, add potatoes. Sauté about 5 minutes. Add salt, pepper, and lemon juice. Cook another 3 to 4 minutes or until browned.

2 pounds potatoes, peeled (8 medium)
6 tablespoons vegetable oil
2 teaspoons cumin seed
2 teaspoons black or yellow mustard seed
2 tablespoons sesame seed
2 teaspoons salt
⅛-½ teaspoon cayenne pepper
1 tablespoon lemon juice

**Yield: 6 to 8 servings**

# Parmesan Potatoes

*...a roasted potato with a cheesy crust*

Cut each potato into six wedges. Combine flour, cheese, salt, and pepper in a paper bag. Moisten potatoes with water. Add potatoes to bag and shake to coat. Melt butter in a 9X13X2 inch baking pan. Place potatoes in a single layer in pan. Bake at 375° for 60 minutes or until browned. Turn once during baking.

4 large potatoes, peeled
½ cup all-purpose flour
½ cup Parmesan cheese
1½ teaspoons salt
¼ teaspoon black pepper
1⅓ sticks butter

**Yield: 4 to 6 servings**

# Scalloped Potatoes

*...the fat content is alarming, but the results are worth a splurge*

3 pounds potatoes,
 peeled and thinly
 sliced
2 cloves garlic
salt and pepper to taste
6 tablespoons unsalted
 butter
3 cups heavy cream

**Yield: 12 servings**

Rinse potato slices in cold water and pat dry. Rub garlic cloves over inside of a shallow earthenware dish and butter dish well. Arrange potatoes in layers, seasoning each layer with salt and pepper, and dotting with butter. Pour cream over top layer. Bake at 325° for 1 hour, 20 minutes. Increase heat to 400° and bake 10 minutes longer or until browned.

# Swedish Roesti Potatoes

*...unusual presentation for a family favorite*

14 small baking potatoes,
 peeled
2 sticks butter, melted,
 or 1 cup olive oil
Krazy Salt or any
 seasoned coarse salt
 to taste
¼cup Parmesan cheese

**Yield: 8 to 10 servings**

Slice potatoes ⅛ to ¼-inch thick, two-thirds of the way through. Roll potato in butter and sprinkle with salt. Reserve butter. Place on a baking sheet cut side up. Bake at 400° for 1 hour, 30 minutes or until browned. Drizzle with reserved butter and sprinkle with cheese.

Use a vegetable cutter with an accordion-type blade to slice potatoes. To prevent cutting through the potato when slicing, place the handle of a wooden spoon behind potato so that vegetable cutter is stopped by handle.

# Baked Sesame Potato Balls

*...can be made ahead; were once served at a lunch for 150*

Cook potatoes in boiling water for 15 to 20 minutes or until soft. Drain well. Return potatoes to pan and mash with butter and oil. Cool to room temperature. Stir in egg yolks, scallions, and pepper. Line a baking sheet with foil. In a small bowl, beat egg whites. Place sesame seeds in a separate bowl. Form potato mixture into 1½ to 2-inch balls. Dip in egg white and then sesame seeds. Place on baking sheet. Bake at 450° for 12 minutes or until golden.

4 large baking potatoes, peeled and cubed
2 tablespoons unsalted butter
2 tablespoons sesame oil
2 eggs, separated
⅓ cup minced scallions
black pepper to taste
½ cup sesame seeds

**Yield: 8 servings**

# Scalloped Cheese Tomatoes

*...adds a splash of summer color to any dinner*

Layer ingredients in order listed in a shallow baking dish. Bake at 350° for 30 minutes.

½ cup herb-seasoned bread stuffing
1 (28-ounce) can tomatoes, drained and chopped
1½ tablespoons butter, melted
½ teaspoon garlic salt
¾ cup grated cheddar cheese
¼ teaspoon dried oregano
1 cup thinly sliced onion
2 teaspoons sugar

**Yield: 8 servings**

# Spaghetti Squash With Tomatoes, Basil, And Parmesan

*...an alternative to pasta*

1 (3-pound) spaghetti
  squash, halved
  lengthwise and
  seeded
½ cup water
6 tablespoons
  Parmesan cheese,
  divided
¼ cup olive oil
½ cup chopped fresh
  basil
½ teaspoon dried
  oregano
2 cups thinly sliced
  cherry tomatoes
salt and pepper to taste
fresh basil sprigs for
  garnish

**Yield: 4 servings**

Place squash halves, cut side down, in a glass baking dish. Add water to dish. Cover tightly with plastic wrap. Microwave on high power for 15 minutes or until soft when pressed. Let stand, covered, 5 minutes. In a large bowl, whisk 4 tablespoons cheese, oil, basil, and oregano together. Stir in tomatoes and season with salt and pepper. Scrape squash with a fork to form strands. Add to tomato mixture. Toss to mix well. Sprinkle with remaining 2 tablespoons cheese and garnish with basil sprigs.

# Creamed Spinach Ring

*...colorful addition to any buffet, with limitless possibilities for the center*

Finely chop or purée spinach in a food processor. Sauté onion in butter in a large skillet until golden. Blend in flour. Slowly stir in half-and-half. Cook and stir until smooth and thickened. Reduce heat to low. Beat egg yolks. Stir a small amount of cream mixture into yolks and return to skillet. Cook 1 minute, stirring constantly. Add spinach and season with salt, pepper, and nutmeg. Remove from heat. Beat egg whites until stiff. Fold into mixture. Turn into a buttered 7-inch ring mold. Set mold in a pan of hot water. Bake at 325° for 30 minutes or until set. Invert onto a heated platter.

Fill ring with Wild Rice in a Wild Mushroom Sauce (page 206) or Dijon Carrots (page 238).

1 (10-ounce) package spinach, cooked and drained
1 tablespoon chopped onion
3 tablespoons butter
3 tablespoons all-purpose flour
1 cup half-and-half
3 eggs, separated
salt and pepper to taste
nutmeg to taste

**Yield: 4 servings**

# Fried Spinach

*...from the Dogtown Cafe*

Wash spinach and pat dry. Heat oil in a fryer to 350°. Drop a few leaves at a time into fryer basket. Lower basket into oil for 1 to 2 minutes. Drain leaves on paper towels. Sprinkle with salt, pepper, and cheese.

Use as an appetizer, a side dish, or as a base for salmon or polenta.

8 ounces fresh spinach leaves
2 cups vegetable or olive oil
salt and pepper to taste
Parmesan cheese to taste

**Yield: 4 servings**

# Sweet Potato Soufflé

*...topping caramelizes during baking*

**soufflé**
4 medium to large
    sweet potatoes,
    peeled
1 cup sugar
1 stick butter
⅓ cup milk
2 eggs
½ teaspoon salt
1 teaspoon vanilla

**topping**
1 cup packed light
    brown sugar
⅓ cup self-rising flour
1 cup chopped pecans
5 tablespoons butter,
    melted

Cut potatoes into large chunks and cook until tender. Drain, mash, and measure 3 cups into a mixing bowl. Add sugar, butter, milk, eggs, salt, and vanilla. Mix well and pour into a buttered 2-quart baking dish. To make topping, combine all ingredients. Crumble over potatoes. Cover and bake at 350° for 30 minutes or until topping is bubbly and caramelized.

**Yield: 8 to 12 servings**

# Sweet Potatoes And Onions

*...onions and spices provide unusual flavor for an old favorite*

1 large yellow onion,
    sliced
2 tablespoons olive oil
2 tablespoons butter
pinch of allspice
½ teaspoon cinnamon
salt and pepper to taste
5 medium sweet
    potatoes, cooked,
    peeled, and diced
¼ cup chopped fresh
    parsley

Sauté onion in oil and butter until translucent. Mix in allspice, cinnamon, salt, and pepper. Add potatoes and sauté until lightly browned. Toss with parsley.

**Yield: 4 to 6 servings**

# Yam Fritters Harris Tweed

*...for a new flavor with your Thanksgiving dinner*

Boil yams until just starting to soften, but still somewhat firm. Cool and grate yams. Combine flour , baking powder, salt, cinnamon, nutmeg, and egg in a bowl. Mix in yams. Form into 1½ to 2-inch balls and dredge in flour. Deep-fry in 350° oil for 4 minutes or until brown.

2 pounds yams, peeled (4 yams)
1 tablespoon all-purpose flour, plus extra for dredging
½ teaspoon baking powder
½ teaspoon salt
½ teaspoon cinnamon
½ teaspoon nutmeg
1 egg, beaten
oil for frying

**Yield: 6 servings**

# Oven Roasted Winter Vegetables

*...rutabaga is called the Swedish turnip, though less watery than its cousin; but it's the fennel that makes this dish distinctive*

Trim away top of fennel bulb. Remove brown and tough outer layers. Halve bulb lengthwise and cut in ¼-inch slices. Combine fennel bulb and remaining ingredients in a bowl. Toss well. Spread evenly on a baking sheet. Bake at 475° for 8 to 10 minutes. Turn vegetables and bake 5 to 7 minutes or until slightly crisp and tender.

1 large fennel bulb
1 celery root, peeled, halved, and sliced ¼-inch thick
2 parsnips, peeled and sliced ¼-inch thick
1 large turnip, peeled, quartered, and sliced ¼-inch thick
1 large rutabaga, peeled, quartered, and sliced ¼-inch thick
2-3 tablespoons olive oil
1 teaspoon salt
½ teaspoon black pepper

**Yield: 4 to 6 servings**

# Oil-roasted Winter Squash

*...can also be made with a combination of winter squashes*

8 cups peeled and
  cubed butternut
  squash
¼ cup all-purpose flour
2 teaspoons ground
  ginger
salt and pepper to taste
6 cloves garlic, minced
½ cup minced fresh
  parsley
2 tablespoons minced
  fresh rosemary
⅓ cup plus 2
  tablespoons olive oil,
  divided
fresh rosemary sprigs for
  garnish

**Yield: 8 servings**

Combine squash, flour, and ginger in a large mixing bowl. Toss to coat well. Mix in salt, pepper, garlic, parsley, and rosemary. Add ⅓ cup oil and stir to coat evenly. Transfer to a shallow 2-quart baking dish. Drizzle remaining 2 tablespoons oil over top. Cover with foil. Bake at 325° for 1 hour, 30 minutes. Uncover and bake 45 to 60 minutes longer, or until top is crusty and brown. Garnish with fresh rosemary sprigs.

*For added color and tang, combine 3 cups peeled and diced acorn or butternut squash, 3 cups diced red apples, and 3 cups cranberries in a buttered 9X13-inch baking dish. Stir in 1 cup maple syrup and 4 tablespoons melted butter. Sprinkle ½ teaspoon cinnamon over top. Cover and bake at 400° for 1 hour, 15 minutes. Stir and serve warm. Serves 10 to 12.*

# Oil-roasted Summer Vegetables

*...a colorful sampling of the best of summer's vegetables right out of the garden*

Arrange potatoes in a single layer in a large baking dish. Drizzle lightly with some of oil. Sprinkle with salt and pepper. Cut eggplant, zucchini, squash, and bell peppers in half lengthwise. Cut each half into ½-inch slices. Cut onions in half lengthwise and then into ¼-inch slices. Arrange vegetables, standing on their flat edge, in alternating rows over potatoes. Drizzle with ½ cup oil and season with salt and pepper. Cover lightly with foil. Bake at 375° for 1 hour, 15 minutes. Remove foil and insert tomato wedges randomly between the rows of vegetables. Sprinkle basil over top. Drizzle with more oil if dish appears dry. Bake, uncovered, 30 to 40 minutes longer. Serve warm or at room temperature.

3 large red potatoes, thinly sliced
¾-1 cup olive oil, divided
coarse salt and pepper to taste
1 medium eggplant
2 medium zucchini, unpeeled
2 medium summer squash
2 yellow bell peppers, seeded
2 red bell peppers, seeded
2 medium-size red onions
3 medium-size ripe tomatoes, seeded and cut into ½-inch wedges
¼ cup chopped fresh basil

**Yield: 8 to 10 servings**

# Curried Root Vegetable Stew With Dumplings

*...healthy, spicy Sunday Night Supper when it's cold and snowy*

## dumplings
1 cup all-purpose flour
1½ teaspoons baking powder
¾ teaspoon salt
½ teaspoon ground mace
2 tablespoons butter, cold
¼ cup currants
6 tablespoons milk

## stew
1½ teaspoons butter
1 small onion, chopped
3 cloves garlic, minced
1½ teaspoons curry powder
4 cups vegetable broth
2 medium carrots, halved lengthwise and sliced ½-inch thick
2 large parsnips, peeled, halved lengthwise and sliced ⅛-inch thick
1 small celery root, peeled and diced
1 medium sweet potato, peeled and cubed
3 tablespoons all-purpose flour
2 teaspoons salt
black pepper to taste
1 tablespoon chopped fresh Italian parsley

**Yield: 6 servings**

To prepare dumplings, combine flour, baking powder, salt, and mace in a bowl. Cut in butter until mixture resembles coarse meal. Mix in currants. Stir in just enough milk to combine into a dough. On a floured surface, shape dough into 1-inch balls. Make stew by melting butter in a large pot over medium heat. Add onion and cook 3 minutes. Stir in garlic and curry and cook 30 seconds. Add broth, carrots, and parsnips. Bring to a boil. Reduce heat, cover, and simmer 15 minutes. Add celery root and sweet potato and cook 10 minutes. Stir ¼ cup of simmering stew broth into flour. Mix until smooth. Stir into stew. Season with salt and pepper. Place dumplings on top of stew. Cover and cook 15 minutes. Sprinkle parsley over top.

# Fresh Pickled Vegetables

*...if you don't have a cheesecloth, you can use a coffee filter to make the spice bag, cutting away excess paper after tying it shut.*

Place basil in a cheesecloth and tie securely with a string. In a 1-pint jar or a medium bowl, combine vinegar, sugar, salt, and garlic. Stir until dissolved. Add spice bag and carrots. Cover and refrigerate overnight or up to one week. Turn or toss occasionally. When ready to serve, remove vegetables with a slotted spoon.

Use this as an antipasto, a side dish, or in a tossed salad.

*Instead of carrots, substitute 2 cups cauliflower flowerets, 3 small, thinly sliced zucchini, or a mixture of any of the above.*

2 teaspoons chopped fresh basil
⅓ cup white wine vinegar
4 teaspoons sugar
1¼ teaspoons salt
1 clove garlic, minced
3 medium carrots, sliced lengthwise

**Yield: 1 pint**

# Chilled Sliced Beets

*...beets require careful treatment and should not be cut before cooking or they will bleed while cooking and become pale and anemic*

Combine ¼ cup beet juice, vinegar, sugar, salt, and cloves. Heat to a boil. Add beets, onion, cinnamon stick, and bay leaf. Cover and simmer 5 minutes. Remove cinnamon stick and bay leaf. Chill.

2 cups cooked sliced beets, juice reserved, or 1 (16-ounce) can
⅓ cup vinegar
¼ cup sugar
¼ teaspoon salt
¼ teaspoon ground cloves
1 small onion, sliced
1 whole cinnamon stick
1 bay leaf

**Yield: 4 to 6 servings**

# Grilled Vegetables

*...as a kebab or added to pasta, couscous, or rice*

Tender, quick cooking vegetables, such as bell peppers, asparagus, squashes, mushrooms, and corn (peel back and tie husk, remove silk, and soak in water 30 minutes) are easiest to grill because they will cook thoroughly. Leeks develop wonderful pink colors, baby onions on a skewer caramelize, and red onions (held together with a toothpick) tossed with olive oil and rosemary are a delicious accompaniment to any meat. Brush vegetables with oil to prevent sticking to the grill. Adding fresh herbs, salt, and pepper gives extra flavor. Vegetables can be marinated for several hours in oil seasoned with ginger, chilies, garlic, or dried spices such as cumin or coriander. Skewered vegetables are easy to move around on a grill. If using bamboo skewers, soak them in water 20 minutes to prevent breaking and to keep tips from burning. Cook vegetables over direct, medium heat, moving them to the side as they finish cooking to keep moist and warm. Most vegetables are best grilled uncovered. Slower cooking vegetables, such as whole eggplants, artichokes, or large potatoes, do best with a cover.

Serve with Sun-dried Tomato Dressing.

# Sun-dried Tomato Dressing

*...also great on grilled fish or chicken*

⅔ cup sun-dried tomatoes, rehydrated, cooked and drained
1 shallot
2 coves garlic
6 fresh basil leaves
2 teaspoons balsamic vinegar
1 cup oil
salt and pepper to taste

**Yield: 1½ to 2 cups**

Blend tomatoes, shallot, garlic, basil, and vinegar in a food processor. With machine running, slowly add oil. Season with salt and pepper.

Slice fresh mozzarella cheese onto hot grilled vegetables and top with dressing.

# Valentines Day Tea

*Chocolate Orange Eclairs*     *Macaroons*          *Choclate Roulade*

*White Chocolate Raspberry Cheesecake*

*Lemon Buttermilk Cake with Lemon Curd Sauce*

*Hot Chocolate*     *Percolator Punch*          *Tea*

# Bread Pudding With Rum Sauce Or Whiskey Sauce

*...cooked with egg and milk, flavored with nutmeg and raisins and served with a rum or whiskey sauce*

Scald milk. Melt butter in hot milk. Stir in sugar. Place bread cubes and raisins in a large bowl. Pour milk mixture over bread. Let stand 15 minutes. Add remaining pudding ingredients. Pour into a buttered 1½-quart baking dish. Bake at 350° for 35 to 45 minutes. To prepare rum sauce, cream butter and sugar. Slowly add rum. Cook until heated through. Make whiskey sauce by melting butter in a double boiler. Combine sugar and egg. Add mixture to butter. Cook and stir 3 to 4 minutes or until sugar dissolves. Cool. Stir in bourbon. Serve sauce of choice with bread pudding.

*For added flavor, soak raisins in rum or bourbon before adding to pudding.*

**pudding**
- 2 cups milk
- 4 tablespoons butter
- ½ cup sugar
- 4 cups day-old French bread cubes
- ½ cup raisins
- 2 eggs, beaten
- ⅛ teaspoon salt
- ½ teaspoon nutmeg
- 1 teaspoon vanilla

**rum sauce**
- 1 stick butter
- 2 cups powdered sugar
- ¼ cup dark rum

**whiskey sauce**
- 1 stick butter
- 1 cup sugar
- 1 egg, beaten
- ½ cup bourbon

**Yield: 6 to 8 servings**

# Peach Bread Pudding

Add 4 to 5 peaches peeled and sliced to the Bread Pudding. Serve with Rum Sauce.

# Chocolate Orange Eclairs

*...don't be alarmed by the length of the recipe - it's a 3-step process: make the pastry cream and refrigerate it; make the eclairs or puffs, bake them, and allow them to cool; and finally the assembly - the end result is better than a bakery!*

## orange pastry cream
- ¼ cup all-purpose flour
- ¼ cup sugar
- 1 cup half-and-half
- 2 egg yolks, lightly beaten
- 1 tablespoon butter
- 2 tablespoons orange zest
- 1 tablespoon orange liqueur
- ⅓ cup heavy cream, whipped

## eclair shells
- ½ cup water
- 4 tablespoons butter, cut in pieces
- ¼ teaspoon salt
- ½ cup all-purpose flour
- 2 eggs

## chocolate glaze
- 2 ounces semi-sweet chocolate
- 1 tablespoon unsalted butter, softened

**Yield: 18 small eclairs or puffs**

To make pastry cream, whisk together flour and sugar in a small saucepan. Slowly stir in half-and-half until smooth. Place over medium heat and bring to a simmer, stirring constantly. Mixture will be thick. Remove from heat. Stir a small amount of sauce into egg yolks, then gradually whisk yolk mixture into saucepan. Place over low heat and cook for 1 to 2 minutes or until thick and smooth. Mix in butter, zest, and liqueur. Transfer to a bowl and cover with plastic wrap, placing wrap directly on surface of pastry cream. Chill thoroughly. When ready to assemble, fold in whipped cream. To prepare shells, bring water, butter, and salt to a boil in a small saucepan. Stir in flour all at once. Cook and stir over low heat until mixture is smooth, glossy, and leaves sides of pan. Transfer mixture to a bowl or a food processor. Add eggs, one at a time, beating well after each addition with an electric mixer or in food processor. Fit a pastry bag with a large plain or star tube. Pipe 2-inch lengths of dough, placing them 1½ inches apart, onto a buttered and floured baking sheet. For puffs, use pastry bag or a teaspoon to form 1½-inch diameter circles on baking sheet. Bake at 400° for 20 minutes or until golden brown and until small beads of fat no longer bubble on surface. Remove from oven and quickly cut a small slit in the side of each shell. Return to oven and turn off heat. Dry shells in oven for 15 minutes. Remove from oven and cool completely. Make chocolate glaze by melting chocolate in a double boiler over simmering water. Remove from heat and whisk in butter. Cut a large slit in the side of each shell. Fill with cream. Brush tops with chocolate glaze.

# Grapefruit Alaska

*...a dramatic dessert that requires some last minute fuss, it's a "baked Alaska" served in a grapefruit shell*

3 grapefruit, halved crosswise
½ cup Triple Sec
4 egg whites, at room temperature
½ cup sugar
1 quart vanilla ice cream

**Yield: 6 servings**

Spoon grapefruit segments into a bowl, removing all membrane and seeds. Reserve grapefruit shells. Drain juice from bowl. Add Triple Sec and toss gently. Cover and refrigerate. Remove membrane from grapefruit shells. Invert shells onto paper towels to drain. Whip egg whites until doubled in volume. Mix in sugar, 2 tablespoons at a time. Beat until meringue is stiff but not dry. Divide grapefruit segments among shells. Place a scoop of ice cream in each shell. Spread meringue around ice cream. Bake at 450° for 5 minutes or until lightly browned.

# Crème Brûlée

*...neither difficult nor time consuming, it requires some attention - but well worth it!*

Combine cream, vanilla, and salt in a saucepan. Cook over medium heat for 5 minutes or until mixture begins to simmer. Mix together egg yolks and granulated sugar in a bowl. Add cream mixture and stir until dissolved. Strain into another bowl. Skim air bubbles off top. Pour into 10 individual serving ramekins and skim air bubbles. Place ramekins in a pan of hot water and cover pan tightly with foil. Bake at 300° for 55 to 60 minutes. Chill at least 6 hours. When ready to serve, sprinkle each ramekin with 1 tablespoon natural sugar. Broil about 30 to 45 seconds.

4 cups heavy cream
1 vanilla bean, or 1 teaspoon vanilla
pinch of salt
9 egg yolks
¾ cup plus 2 tablespoons granulated sugar
10 tablespoons natural sugar or brown sugar

**Yield: 10 servings**

# Wild Rice Pudding

*...a custard as rich as crème brûlée, baked over wild rice and brandy-soaked currants*

Soak currants in brandy. Combine currants and rice in a buttered 9X13 inch baking dish. In a bowl, whisk together remaining ingredients. Pour over rice mixture. Place dish in a pan of hot water. Bake at 275° for 1 hour, 30 minutes.

1 cup currants
brandy
2 cups cooked wild rice
6 cups heavy cream
12 egg yolks
⅔ cup sugar
¼ cup honey
1 teaspoon vanilla

**Yield: 10 to 12 servings**

# Poached Pears With Brandy Sauce

*...lesser fruits may be more rugged, but when pears are perfect, they soar - fortunately, this dessert does not depend on finding the ultimate pear*

4 Bartlett pears, cored and peeled
½ teaspoon mace or nutmeg
½ cup packed brown sugar
1 stick butter
½ cup brandy
1 cup heavy cream

**Yield: 4 servings**

Place pears in a baking dish. Dust with mace. Sprinkle brown sugar over top. Dot with butter. Pour brandy over pears. Bake, covered, at 375° for 45 minutes. Carefully remove pears to a serving dish. Pour pan juices into a small saucepan. Bring to a boil. Reduce heat and add cream. Simmer 15 minutes, stirring occasionally to prevent burning. Pour over warm or room temperature pears.

If cream sauce does not thicken enough during cooking, add a mixture of cornstarch and water. Simmer 5 minutes longer.

# Palm Beach Brownies

*...so named because they are so rich*

1 stick butter
4 (1-ounce) squares unsweetened chocolate
2 cups sugar
4 eggs
1 cup all-purpose flour
1 teaspoon vanilla
1 cup chopped nuts (optional)

**9 servings**

Melt butter and chocolate. Mix in sugar. Add eggs, one at a time, beating well after each addition. Mix in flour all at once. Stir in vanilla and nuts. Pour batter into a 9X9 inch buttered baking pan. Bake at 350° for 35 minutes or until a toothpick inserted in the center comes out clean.

If doubling or tripling recipe, double or triple baking time as well.

# Apple Baklava

*...a crisp, light, and delicate inspiration from Turkey, but Americanized with the apple!*

Brush 6 sheets of phyllo dough with about a third of melted butter. Place in a buttered 10X15 inch baking pan. Keep remaining phyllo dough covered with a damp towel until ready to use. Combine apples, walnuts, almonds, sugar, raisins, zest, juice, and cinnamon. Sprinkle half of apple mixture in pan. Top with 6 sheets of phyllo dough that have been brushed with melted butter. Add remaining apple mixture. Brush remaining phyllo dough sheets with melted butter and place on top. Trim edges and score into diamonds. Bake at 350° for 35 to 40 minutes. Warm honey and drizzle over top. Cool.

18 (18X16 inch) sheets frozen phyllo dough, thawed and divided
2½ sticks unsalted butter, melted
2 cups coarsely grated peeled Jonathan apples
1 cup chopped walnuts or pecans
1 cup toasted almonds
⅔ cup sugar
¼ cup golden raisins
1 teaspoon lemon zest
2 tablespoons fresh lemon juice
2 teaspoons cinnamon
½ cup honey

**Yield: 40 servings**

# Tiramisu

*...a traditional Italian dessert enhanced by a zabaglione topping*

1 pound mascarpone
  cheese
¼ cup sugar
2 tablespoons light rum
24 Italian ladyfingers
1 cup brewed espresso,
  cooled
4-Egg Zabaglione
2 tablespoons
  unsweetened cocoa
  powder

**4-egg zabaglione**
4 egg yolks
¼ cup sugar
½ cup Marsala

**Yield: 8 servings**

Process cheese, sugar, and rum in a food processor until smooth. Place 6 ladyfingers side by side, flat side up, on a plate or in a decorative bowl. Moisten lightly with espresso. Spread a third of cheese mixture over ladyfingers. Repeat layers two more times, ending with cheese mixture. Cut remaining ladyfingers in half lengthwise. Pour Zabaglione over top and around sides of plate. Press halved ladyfingers around edge to form a "fence". Sprinkle cocoa powder over top. To prepare Zabaglione, combine yolks and sugar in the top of a double boiler. Cook and beat until pale and fluffy. Add Marsala and continue to beat until mixture thickens to the consistency of a batter. Remove from heat and beat a few more seconds.

# Strawberries With Amaretto Butter Cream

*...prepared in individual custard cups or in a shallow baking dish, it's a "super, easy, and delicious dessert"*

Toast almonds and granulated sugar over low heat. Toss until sugar dissolves and almonds are coated, being careful not to burn almonds. Cool and break apart. Beat together butter and almond paste in a small bowl. Mix in powdered sugar. Add egg, amaretto, and vanilla and blend well. If mixture is not thick, add extra powdered sugar. Divide mixture among 8 individual ovenproof dishes. Cut large strawberries in half, leaving smaller ones whole. Stand up berries in butter mixture. Bake at 325° for 5 to 7 minutes or until heated through. Sprinkle with toasted almonds. Garnish with mint sprigs and serve immediately.

Prepare this dish a day ahead of time, cover, and refrigerate. Remove from refrigerator just before serving main course and bake when ready to serve dessert.

½ cup slivered blanched almonds
2 tablespoons granulated sugar
6 tablespoons butter
2 tablespoons almond paste
¾ cup powdered sugar
I egg
¼ cup amaretto
I teaspoon vanilla
2 quarts strawberries
fresh mint sprigs for garnish

**Yield: 8 servings**

# Chocolate Loaf

*...when cocoa was first imported into Mexico, the beans were used as local currency as well as for making a cocoa drink*

3 sticks butter
3 tablespoons cocoa powder
1½ teaspoons instant coffee
¾ teaspoon vanilla
1 egg, beaten
1½ (16-ounce) packages powdered sugar
2 (10-ounce) boxes Lorna Doone cookies

**Yield: 20 servings**

Melt butter in a saucepan. Remove from heat and stir in cocoa, coffee, vanilla, egg, and sugar. Line a loaf pan with foil. Layer chocolate mixture and cookies, starting and ending with chocolate mixture. Cool in refrigerator for several hours. Invert onto a serving plate. Let stand at room temperature for a few minutes. Cut into thin pieces with a very sharp knife.

# Lorraine's Chocolate Sauce

*...serve over ice cream, or make a brownie sundae with brownie, vanilla ice cream, and chocolate sauce - keeps well in the freezer*

1 cup cocoa powder
2 cups sugar
¾ cup cornstarch
1 cup water
1 cup corn syrup
4 ounces unsweetened chocolate
2 sticks butter

**Yield: 4 cups**

Mix cocoa powder, sugar, and cornstarch in a saucepan until well blended. Stir in water and syrup until smooth. Bring to a boil over medium heat. Add chocolate and stir until melted. Reduce heat and cook and stir 5 minutes. Add butter and stir until melted.

# White Chocolate Raspberry Cheesecake

*...for a white chocolate cheesecake, omit the raspberries*

Process crumbs and almonds in a food processor until finely ground. Mix in butter. Press into the bottom and two-thirds of the way up the sides of a 10-inch springform pan. Melt chocolate in a double boiler. Stir until smooth and remove from heat. Beat cream cheese until smooth and fluffy. Add sugar. Beat in eggs and egg yolks. Add flour and vanilla. Mix until smooth. Beat in melted chocolate in a slow, steady stream. Scatter raspberries over graham cracker crust. Pour cream cheese mixture over top. Bake at 250° for 60 minutes or until top is firm to the touch. Cool completely, cover and chill overnight. Carefully remove from pan. Garnish with raspberries and whipped cream.

2 cups graham cracker crumbs
1 cup slivered almonds
4 tablespoons clarified butter
8 ounces white chocolate
4 (8-ounce) packages cream cheese, softened
⅔ cup sugar
4 eggs
2 egg yolks
2 tablespoons all-purpose flour
1 teaspoon vanilla
1 quart fresh red raspberries, plus extra for garnish
whipped cream for garnish

**Yield: 8 to 12 servings**

# Pumpkin Cheesecake With Sour Cream Topping

*...the French make pumpkin jams and the Italians use pumpkin as a filling for sweet ravioli; we have our famous pumpkin pie - but this could become a holiday tradition*

**crust**
- ¾ cup graham cracker crumbs
- ½ cup finely chopped pecans
- ¼ cup packed brown sugar
- ¼ cup granulated sugar
- 4 tablespoons unsalted butter, melted and cooled

**filling**
- 1½ cups pumpkin pack
- 3 eggs
- 1½ teaspoons cinnamon
- ½ teaspoon nutmeg
- ½ teaspoon ground ginger
- ½ teaspoon salt
- ½ cup packed brown sugar
- 3 (8-ounce) packages cream cheese, softened
- ½ cup granulated sugar
- 2 tablespoons heavy cream
- 1 tablespoon cornstarch
- 1 teaspoon vanilla
- 1 tablespoon bourbon

**topping**
- 2 cups sour cream
- 3 tablespoons granulated sugar
- 1 tablespoon bourbon
- 16 pecan halves for garnish

**Yield: 12 servings**

Combine crust ingredients and press into the bottom of a 9-inch springform pan. Combine all filling ingredients in a large bowl. Beat well with an electric mixer until thoroughly blended. Pour into pan. Bake at 350° for 60 minutes or until set. Chill thoroughly. When ready to serve, remove sides of pan. Combine sour cream, sugar, and bourbon to make topping. Spread over cheesecake and bake an additional 5 minutes. Garnish with pecans.

# Amaretto Bourbon Pecan Pie

*...amaretto and bourbon, rum, or chocolate contribute to variations of an already perfect pie!*

Arrange pecan halves over bottom of pie crust. Combine sugar and butter in a medium bowl. Stir vigorously to dissolve sugar. Mix in eggs. Stir in corn syrup, amaretto, bourbon, and vanilla. Pour mixture over pecans. Bake at 350° for 50 to 55 minutes or until center is set but not completely firm. Cool at least 30 minutes before cutting. Serve with whipped cream and chocolate shavings.

*To make Rum Pecan Pie, substitute ¼ cup rum for the amaretto and bourbon.*

*To make Chocolate Pecan Pie, melt and slightly cool 4 ounces semi-sweet chocolate. Add with eggs.*

1 cup halved pecans
1 (9-inch) pie crust, unbaked
⅔ cup sugar
4 tablespoons butter, melted
3 eggs, lightly beaten
1 cup dark corn syrup
2 tablespoons amaretto
2 tablespoons bourbon
1 teaspoon vanilla
whipped cream (optional)
chocolate shavings (optional)

**Yield: 8 servings**

# Apple Crisp

*...the apple actually preceded the settlers west. Indians had apple orchards near their villages by the time the settlers moved into this area*

15 apples, peeled and sliced
3 tablespoons lemon juice
1¼ cups sugar
½ teaspoon ground cloves
1¼ teaspoons cinnamon
2 cups all-purpose flour
½ teaspoon salt
2 sticks butter
1¼ cups packed brown sugar
1 cup chopped walnuts
1 cup oatmeal

Toss apples and lemon juice together. Combine sugar, cloves, and cinnamon. Add to apples and toss. Place in a 9X13 inch baking pan. Mix together flour and salt. Cut in butter. Mix in brown sugar, walnuts, and oatmeal. Spread over apple mixture. Bake at 350° for 60 minutes to 1 hour, 30 minutes. Serve warm.

**Yield: 14 servings**

# Rhubarb Strawberry Crisp

*...although considered a fruit, rhubarb is actually a vegetable*

1 stick butter, melted
1⅓ cups all-purpose flour, divided
3 pounds rhubarb, sliced ½-inch thick
3 cups strawberries
1 cup granulated sugar
½ teaspoon cinnamon
1 cup packed dark brown sugar
½ cup rolled oats
¾ cup chopped pecans

Cover bottom of a 9X13 inch baking dish with butter. Combine ⅓ cup flour, rhubarb, strawberries, granulated sugar, and cinnamon. Place in baking dish. Mix remaining 1 cup flour, brown sugar, oats, and pecans. Sprinkle over rhubarb mixture. Bake at 375° for 35 to 45 minutes.

**Yield: 10 servings**

# Plymouth Cranberry Pie

*...Plymouth, the Mayflower, and cranberries, what better way to celebrate Thanksgiving*

Combine cranberries, sugar, and cornstarch. Mix egg and almond extract together. Add to cranberry mixture. Line a 9-inch pie pan with a pastry crust. Pour in cranberry mixture. Cut remaining pastry crust into strips. Arrange strips over pie in a lattice design. Seal edges. Bake at 400° for 10 minutes. Reduce heat to 350° and bake 35 minutes longer or until cranberries soften and pastry browns.

4 cups cranberries, chopped
1½ cups sugar
3 tablespoons cornstarch
1 egg, lightly beaten
½ teaspoon almond extract
2 pastry crusts, divided

**Yield: 8 servings**

# Rum-flavored Pumpkin Pie

Combine squash, sugars, and cream in a mixing bowl. Beat in eggs, one at a time, until well blended. Reserve a small amount of one egg white for later use. Stir in ginger, salt, cloves, rum, allspice, cinnamon, and nutmeg. Line a 9-inch pie pan with pastry crust. Brush with reserved egg white and trim edges. Fill with squash mixture. Bake at 450° for 10 minutes. Reduce heat to 300° and bake 45 minutes or until firm.

1½ cups cooked winter squash or puréed pumpkin
1 cup granulated sugar
1 tablespoon packed brown sugar
1 cup heavy cream or evaporated milk
3 eggs
½ teaspoon ginger
½ teaspoon salt
⅛ teaspoon ground cloves
2 tablespoons rum
⅛ teaspoon ground allspice
1 teaspoon cinnamon
1 teaspoon nutmeg
1 pastry crust

**Yield: 8 servings**

# Raspberry Meringue Pie

*...it's delightful, it's delicious, it's delovely - it's divine my dear*

## meringue crust
3 egg whites
¼ teaspoon baking powder
¼ teaspoon salt
¼ teaspoon cream of tartar
1 cup sugar
¾ cup quick-cooking oats
½ cup chopped walnuts
½ teaspoon vanilla

## filling
1 (10-ounce) package frozen raspberries, thawed
1 tablespoon cornstarch
whipped cream
grated coconut (optional)

**Yield: 8 servings**

Beat egg whites, baking powder, salt, and cream of tartar until stiff. Slowly add sugar and beat until stiff but not dry. Combine oats and walnuts. Blend into egg white mixture. Fold in vanilla. Spoon meringue into an 8 or 9-inch pie pan, leaving a depression in center and edges thicker, to make a crust. Bake at 325° for 25 minutes or until lightly browned. Cool. For filling, drain raspberries over a saucepan to collect juice. Blend cornstarch into juice and cook over medium heat until thickened. Cool slightly and stir in raspberries. Spoon into cooled meringue crust. Spread whipped cream over top and sprinkle with coconut. Chill several hours.

# Chocolate Cake With Coffee Frosting

*...just what it says it is - sublime!*

Melt chocolate in a saucepan over low heat. Whisk in ½ cup buttermilk until smooth. Add granulated sugar and 1 egg yolk. Stir 3 minutes or until thick and smooth. Cool. Cream butter and brown sugar. Add 2 egg yolks, one at a time. Sift together flour, baking soda, and salt. Alternately, in three parts, mix dry ingredients and remaining ¾ cup buttermilk to creamed mixture. Stir in cooled chocolate mixture and vanilla. Beat egg whites until stiff but not dry. Fold into batter. Pour into two (9-inch) buttered cake pans. Bake at 350° for 25 to 30 minutes or until cake begins to pull away from sides of pan and center springs back when pressed. Cool completely in pans. To prepare frosting, dissolve coffee in hot water. Combine with butter and remaining ingredients. Beat until smooth. Remove cooled cake from pans. Frost between cake layers and around outside of cake.

## cake

- 5 ounces unsweetened chocolate
- 1 ¼ cups buttermilk, divided
- 1 cup granulated sugar
- 3 eggs, separated, divided
- 1 stick butter, softened
- 1 cup packed light brown sugar
- 2 cups sifted cake flour
- 1 teaspoon baking soda
- ¼ teaspoon salt
- 1 teaspoon vanilla

## coffee frosting

- 2-3 tablespoons instant coffee
- ¼ cup hot water
- 2 sticks butter, softened
- ¼ teaspoon salt
- 3 cups powdered sugar
- 2 teaspoons rum or brandy

**Yield: 12 servings**

# Double Mocha Chocolate Cake

*...if more is better "spread a thin layer of raspberry jam between layers"*

**coffee syrup**
1 cup water
½ cup ground coffee
2 tablespoons sugar

**cake**
4 ounces unsweetened
  chocolate
½ cup shortening
½ cup Coffee Syrup
2 cups sugar
2 cups cake flour
¾ teaspoon salt
1 teaspoon baking soda
¾ cup sour milk
2 eggs
2 teaspoons vanilla
cocoa powder

**frosting**
½ cup shortening
1 (16-ounce) package
  powdered sugar
1 teaspoon vanilla

**Yield: 8 to 10 servings**

To prepare coffee syrup, combine water, coffee, and sugar in a saucepan. Bring to a boil and strain. Make cake by melting chocolate and shortening in a saucepan over low heat. With an electric mixer on medium speed, combine chocolate mixture, coffee syrup, and sugar in a bowl. In a separate bowl, mix flour, salt, and baking soda. Alternately, add dry ingredients and milk to chocolate mixture. Add eggs and vanilla. Beat 2 minutes. Butter two (8-inch) round cake pans and dust with cocoa powder. Divide batter between pans. Bake at 350° for 30 to 35 minutes. Cool 10 minutes before removing from pans. Cool completely on a rack. To make frosting, combine shortening, sugar, and vanilla. Blend well. Spread over cooled cake.

# Lemon Buttermilk Cake With Lemon Curd Sauce

*...a very light cake, the Lemon Curd Sauce can either be served traditionally with sauce over cake, or sauce the plate and lay the cake on top - either way, it's great for a "ladies' lunch" to follow Broiled Chicken Breasts with Mixed Salad*

Cream butter with an electric mixer. Add 2 cups sugar. Beat in eggs, one at a time. Sift together flour, baking soda, and salt. Alternately, starting and ending with dry ingredients, add dry ingredients and buttermilk. Fold in zest and 3 tablespoons lemon juice. Butter a Bundt pan and coat with breadcrumbs. Pour batter into pan. Bake at 350° for 1 hour, 15 minutes. Combine remaining ⅓ cup sugar and remaining ½ cup lemon juice in a saucepan. Heat until sugar dissolves. Poke holes in hot cake and pour lemon juice mixture over top of cake. Let stand a few minutes. To make sauce, combine lemon zest and juice, eggs, and sugar in the top of a double boiler. Whisk over low heat until mixture coats spoon. Remove from heat. Whisk in butter, a small amount at a time. Serve sauce with cake.

*Fold whipped cream into sauce for an instant lemon mousse. Top with fresh blueberries.*

### cake
- 2 sticks butter, softened
- 2⅓ cups sugar, divided
- 3 eggs
- 3 cups all-purpose flour
- ½ teaspoon baking soda
- ½ teaspoon salt
- 1 cup buttermilk
- zest of 2 or 3 lemons
- ½ cup plus 3 tablespoons lemon juice, divided
- breadcrumbs

### lemon curd sauce
- zest and juice of 6 lemons
- 6 eggs
- 2 cups sugar
- 1½ sticks butter, softened

**Yield: 10 to 12 servings**

# Coconut Cake

*...the coconut palm, one of the most important trees of the tropics, can produce 100 or more "nuts" a year*

## cake

- 1 cup shortening
- 2 cups sugar
- 5 eggs
- 2 cups all-purpose flour
- 1½ teaspoons baking powder
- 1 teaspoon salt
- 1 cup buttermilk
- 1 teaspoon coconut extract
- 1 (7-ounce) can shredded coconut

## syrup

- 1 cup sugar
- ½ cup water
- 1 teaspoon coconut extract

**Yield: 12 to 16 servings**

In a large bowl, cream shortening, sugar, and eggs. In a separate bowl, combine flour, baking powder, and salt. Alternately, add dry ingredients and buttermilk to creamed mixture. Stir in coconut extract and coconut. Pour into a buttered and floured Bundt pan. Bake at 350° for about 60 minutes. Meanwhile, make syrup by combining sugar, water, and coconut extract in a saucepan. Boil for 2 minutes. When done baking, invert cake onto a serving platter. Use a knife to poke several holes into cake. Pour syrup over hot cake.

# Scotch Cake

*...the cake is iced while still hot, therefore absorbing the icing*

Sift together flour, sugar, and salt in a large bowl. In a saucepan, combine butter, shortening, water, and cocoa powder. Bring to a boil. Pour over dry ingredients. Add eggs, buttermilk, baking soda, cinnamon, and vanilla. Beat with an electric mixer until just smooth. Immediately pour into a buttered 9X13 inch pan. Bake at 350° for 40 to 45 minutes or until surface springs back when gently pressed with a fingertip. While baking, prepare icing. Combine butter, cocoa, and milk in a saucepan. Bring to just boiling and remove from heat. Beat in sugar and vanilla with a spoon until smooth. Stir in coconut and pecans. Spread over cake immediately after removing from oven. Cool in pan on a rack.

Cut cake in small pieces as it is very rich.

### cake
- 2 cups all-purpose flour
- 2 cups sugar
- ½ teaspoon salt
- 1 stick butter
- ½ cup shortening or margarine
- 1 cup water
- ¼ cup cocoa powder
- 2 eggs, lightly beaten
- ½ cup buttermilk
- 1 teaspoon baking soda
- 1 teaspoon cinnamon
- 1 teaspoon vanilla

### icing
- 1 stick butter
- ¼ cup cocoa powder
- 6 tablespoons milk
- 1 (16-ounce) package powdered sugar
- 1 teaspoon vanilla
- 2 cups flaked coconut
- 1 cup chopped pecans

**Yield: 24 servings**

# Teresa's Biscotti

*..."biscotti" means twice cooked and are good any time of day, particularly with a cup of tea in front of a fire on a cold winter afternoon*

5 eggs
1-1¼ cups sugar
2½ sticks butter, melted
1 teaspoon almond extract
2 teaspoons vanilla
2 teaspoons anise extract
1 cup chopped almonds
6 cups all-purpose flour
5 teaspoons baking powder

**Yield: 3 dozen**

Whisk together eggs and sugar in a large mixing bowl. Stir in butter, almond extract, vanilla, and anise extract. Mix well. Blend in almonds, flour, and baking powder. Roll dough into 12-inch ropes on a floured board. Place ropes 2 inches apart on a baking sheet. Bake at 375° for 20 minutes or until lightly browned. Remove from oven and let stand 2 minutes. Cut into slices. Bake on baking sheet for 10 minutes longer.

# Ginger Cookies

*...a sublime ginger-flavored cookie with a particularly firm yet crisp consistency*

2 cups all-purpose flour
1 cup sugar, plus extra for rolling balls
2 teaspoons ground ginger
2 teaspoons ground cloves
2 teaspoons cinnamon
2 teaspoons baking soda
½ teaspoon salt
1 egg
½ cup plus 1 tablespoon molasses
¾ cup shortening

**Yield: 2 to 3 dozen**

Combine all ingredients. Shape into 1-inch balls and roll in sugar. Bake at 350° for 11 to 13 minutes or until cracked on top.

# Praline Cookies

*...praline traditionally indicates almonds or pecans covered with a coating of sugar syrup, flavored, and colored*

Melt margarine in a saucepan. Cool slightly and add sugar and molasses. Mix well. Beat in eggs and vanilla. In a separate bowl, sift together flour, baking soda, and salt. Stir into molasses mixture. Add pecans and mix well. Drop by scant teaspoonfuls, 2 inches apart, onto a buttered baking sheet. Bake at 375° for 8 to 10 minutes. Remove from pan immediately.

1⅓ sticks margarine
1 cup sugar
½ cup molasses
2 eggs
½ teaspoon vanilla
1¾ cups all-purpose flour
½ teaspoon baking soda
¼ teaspoon salt
2 cups chopped pecans

**Yield: 6 dozen cookies**

# Angel Cookies

*...a flaky, crispy, melt-in-your-mouth goodness!*

Cream shortening and sugars. Add eggs and vanilla. Sift together flour, baking powder, salt, and baking soda. Blend dry ingredients into creamed mixture. Stir in coconut, pecans, and oats. Drop by teaspoonfuls onto a foil-lined baking sheet. Bake at 325° for 10 to 12 minutes or until flaky and crispy.

1 cup shortening
1 cup packed brown sugar
1 cup granulated sugar
2 eggs, beaten
2 tablespoons vanilla
1 cup all-purpose flour
1 teaspoon baking powder
1 teaspoon salt
1 teaspoon baking soda
2 cups coconut
1 cup pecans
2 cups quick-cooking oats

**Yield: 4 dozen cookies**

# Oatmeal Lace Cookies

*...a very elegant and delicate cookie*

1½ cups quick-cooking oats
¾ cup sugar
1 tablespoon all-purpose flour
1 teaspoon baking powder
pinch of salt
1 stick butter, melted
1 teaspoon vanilla
1 egg, beaten
½ cup chopped nuts

**Yield: 6 dozen cookies**

In a bowl, combine oats, sugar, flour, baking powder, and salt. Add remaining ingredients. Line a baking sheet with foil, shiny-side up. Shape dough into walnut-size balls. Place on baking sheet, allowing plenty of room for cookies to spread. Bake at 350° for 10 to 11 minutes. Do not brown. Cool 5 minutes before removing from sheet.

# Koodree

*...Russian pastry flakes usually served at weddings and baby showers*

6 eggs, beaten
2 heaping tablespoons sour cream
dash of salt
½ cup sugar, or to taste
1 teaspoon vanilla
2½ cups all-purpose flour
powdered sugar

Combine eggs, sour cream, salt, sugar, vanilla, and flour to make a stiff dough. Roll dough paper-thin on a board. Cut into 3 to 4-inch triangles. Cut a 1½-inch slit in center of each triangle. Pull a corner of triangle through the slit. Fry in hot oil until both sides are golden brown. Drain and cool on paper towels. Sprinkle with powdered sugar.

# Sherry Freeze

*...Xavier and Anna Bourquenot, natives of France, settled in Springfield, Missouri and opened a confectionery on South Street - they soon became known for their delicious ice cream, a real treat in the days before home refrigeration*

Mix together egg, milk, and sugar. Fold in whipped cream and sherry. Add food coloring until pale pink. Freeze in an ice-cream maker. To improve flavor, let stand at room temperature until slightly softened before serving.

1 egg, beaten
2 cups milk
2 cups sugar
2 cups heavy cream, whipped
½ cup sweet sherry
pink food coloring

**Yield: 1½ quarts**

# Six Three's Ice Cream

*...E. A. Hamwi had a waffle stand at the 1904 Louisiana Purchase Exposition, better known as the World's Fair, next to an ice cream concession - and serendipitously developed the ice cream cone. Hamwi went on to found the Missouri Cone Co. and became a multimillionaire*

Combine milk, cream, and sugar. Stir until sugar dissolves. Place in an ice-cream maker and freeze until frozen to a soft consistency. Add lemon and orange juices and banana. Continue to freeze in ice-cream maker until firm. Remove dasher and pack in salt and ice for several hours.

3 cups milk
3 cups cream
3 cups sugar
juice of 3 lemons
juice of 3 oranges
3 bananas, mashed

**Yield: about 1 gallon**

# Cantaloupe Ice With Blueberries

*...the color, the taste, and the texture of cantaloupe resulting in an absolutely sensational dessert*

1¼ cups simple syrup
3½ cups puréed
    cantaloupe (1 large
    cantaloupe)
1 tablespoon fresh
    lemon juice
zest of ½ lemon
1 pint blueberries

**Yield: 3 cups**

Chill all ingredients. Combine syrup, cantaloupe, juice, and zest. Pour into a metal pan. Cover and freeze. When almost frozen, place in a food processor or a blender and pulse a few times. Transfer back into pan, cover, and freeze. When almost frozen, pulse as before in food processor. Freeze 60 minutes before serving. Serve on a bed of blueberries.

Simple syrup: combine 1¼ cups water with 1¼ cups sugar. Bring to a boil. Remove from heat and chill until ready to use.

# Christopher's Blueberry Sherbet

*...conceived with coconut milk leftover in the refrigerator, you can substitute water if that's not what's leftover in your refrigerator*

¾ cup coconut milk or
    water
½ cup sugar
1 teaspoon lemon juice
1 pint fresh blueberries,
    puréed
6 small slices melon of
    choice for garnish

**Yield: 6 servings**

Combine coconut milk, sugar, and lemon juice in a saucepan. Bring to a boil. Turn off heat and cool. Mix in blueberries. Freeze in an ice-cream maker. Garnish each serving with a melon slice.

# Cranberry Raspberry Sherbet

*...serve with Oatmeal Lace Cookies for a refreshing summer luncheon dessert*

Combine cranberries in 2½ cups water in a saucepan. Cook over high heat for 5 minutes or until skins pop. Meanwhile, sprinkle gelatin over remaining ½ cup water. Force cranberries and water through a sieve. Discard skins. Force raspberries through sieve. Discard seeds. Combine cranberry and raspberry juice in a saucepan. Add gelatin mixture and heat. Stir in sugar until dissolved. Remove from heat and mix in lemon juice. Freeze in an ice-cream maker. Beat egg whites until stiff peaks form. While sherbet is still soft, fold in egg white. Place in freezer to harden. Garnish with mint sprigs and fresh raspberries.

3 cups fresh cranberries
3 cups water, divided
1 (¼-ounce) package unflavored gelatin
1 (10-ounce) package frozen raspberries, thawed
1½ cups sugar
3 tablespoons fresh lemon juice
2 egg whites
12 sprigs fresh mint and fresh raspberries for garnish

**Yield: 6 servings**

# Betsy Buddy Bombe

*...iced bombes are made by freezing ice cream in a "melon" mold - so named for its shape*

Slowly beat sugar and kirsch into whipped cream until it holds a definite shape. Fold in almonds and cherries. Line a 6-cup melon mold with cream mixture, reserving some for over sherbet. Leave a large well in the center. Fill with sherbet. Spread remaining cream mixture over top. Cover with foil or plastic wrap and freeze for 4 to 5 hours or until solid. Unmold onto a chilled platter.

1½ cups powdered sugar
2 tablespoons kirsch
2 cups heavy cream, whipped
½ cup finely chopped almonds
¼ cup finely chopped candied cherries
1 quart raspberry sherbet

**Yield: 8 servings**

# Cider Sorbet With Red Wine Sauce

*...what a wonderful dessert for an elegant winter dinner*

**red wine sauce**
  2 cups red wine
  ½ cup sugar
  3 cinnamon sticks

**sorbet**
  2 cups cider
  ¾ cup plus I tablespoon
    sugar
  2 tablespoons lemon
    juice
  I tablespoon vodka
crème fraîche or
    whipped cream for
    topping

**Yield: 6 servings**

Combine wine, sugar, and cinnamon sticks in a saucepan. Cook until reduced by half. Remove cinnamon sticks and chill until ready to use. To prepare sorbet, combine cider, sugar, lemon juice, and vodka in a stainless steel saucepan. Cook over low heat until sugar dissolves. Chill thoroughly. Freeze in an ice-cream maker. Top each serving with red wine sauce and a dollop of Crème Fraîche (page 102).

# Chocolate Sorbet

*...sweet oranges are excellent with chocolate*

  I cup sugar
  3½ cups water, divided
  ½ cup light corn syrup
  2½ ounces semi-sweet
    chocolate, chopped
  1¼ cups Dutch cocoa
    powder
  3 tablespoons dark rum

**Yield: 5 cups**

Combine sugar, 1½ cups water, and corn syrup in a saucepan. Bring to a boil, stirring to dissolve sugar. Cool. Melt chocolate in a double boiler over simmering water. Cool. Mix cocoa powder into syrup mixture. Whisk in chocolate and rum until smooth. Whisk in remaining 2 cups water. Strain through a fine sieve. Freeze in an ice-cream maker.

Comfort Food

# Sunday Night Dinner with Grandmother

*Cheese Pennies*

*Chicken Pot Pie    Meat Loaf*
*"The Best" Mashed Potatoes    Creamed Spinach Ring*
*Raspberry Salad on Shredded Iceberg Lettuce*
*Oma's Rolls*

*Grandma Taylor's Chocolate Cake with Chocolate Frosting*

*Chenin Blanc*
*Beaujolais Villages*

# Cheese Pennies

...probably named for their shape and size

Combine all ingredients until well blended. Form into small balls and place on an unbuttered baking sheet. Crosshatch and flatten balls with a fork. Bake at 325° for 10 to 12 minutes or until just browned on top. Remove from sheet with a spatula and serve.

1 stick butter, softened
8 ounces sharp cheddar cheese, grated
1 cup all-purpose flour
½ teaspoon salt

**Yield: 6 servings**

# Deviled Eggs

...if the egg dish went in the garage sale, line a plate with bunches of fresh dill or lettuce to keep the eggs from sliding

Remove yolks from egg halves, reserving egg white shells. Combine yolks, salt, pepper, mayonnaise, butter, and dill in a food processor. Blend until smooth. Fill each shell with mixture. Cover loosely with plastic wrap and chill up to 3 hours. Top each shell with a few grains of caviar. Arrange in an egg dish.

10 hard-cooked eggs, peeled and halved lengthwise
salt and pepper to taste
3 tablespoons mayonnaise
2 tablespoons butter, melted
1 tablespoon finely chopped fresh dill
1 ounce large salmon roe caviar (optional)

**Yield: 20 servings**

# Fluffer-nutter Sandwich

...a heavenly blend of marshmallow fluff and creamy peanut butter, generously spread and sandwiched on any bread!

# Rach's Vichyssoise

*...generally considered to be American, but in fact a refinement of a French country soup, Louis Diat is undeniably credited for its introduction to America in 1940*

1 cup chopped onions
2 cups chopped leeks,
  white only
4 tablespoons butter
2 cups diced potatoes
4 cups chicken broth
salt and pepper to taste
1 cup light cream
2 tablespoons chopped
  fresh chives

**Yield: 8 servings**

Sauté onions and leeks in butter until yellow. Add potatoes and broth. Season with salt and pepper. Cook until potatoes are soft. While hot, purée in a blender. Chill thoroughly. Mix in cream and garnish with chives.

# Chris's Baked Eggs

*...still gives us the essence of comfort*

1 loaf French bread,
  torn into pieces
6 tablespoons butter
12 ounces Swiss cheese,
  grated
8 ounces Monterey
  Jack cheese, grated
16 eggs
3¼ cups milk
½ cup dry white wine
4 scallions, chopped
1 tablespoon mustard
¼ teaspoon black
  pepper
⅛ teaspoon cayenne
  pepper
1½ cups sour cream
1 cup Parmesan cheese

**Yield: 8 servings**

Spread bread pieces in the bottom of a buttered 9X13 inch baking dish. Dot with butter. Sprinkle Swiss and Monterey Jack cheeses over top. In a bowl, beat together eggs, milk, wine, scallions, mustard, and peppers. Pour into baking dish. Refrigerate overnight. Bake, covered, at 325° for 60 minutes. Spread sour cream over top and sprinkle with Parmesan cheese. Bake, uncovered, 10 minutes longer.

# Fondue Bourguignonne

*...inspired by cheese fondue, although nothing is "fondu", or melted, it is do-it-yourself cookery at its most lively, as each diner, armed with a spear-like utensil, sits around a cannibal pot! Guests help themselves to sauces and meat (a 5 to 6-compartment plate, such as an artichoke or an oyster plate would be perfect, although the sauces can sit on a regular dinner plate); serve with Swedish Roesti Potatoes, a tossed salad, and a good bottle of red wine to mollify the combatants!*

Fill a fondue pot three-fourths full with oil. Heat on top of stove. When hot, place over an alcohol burner in center of the dinner table. Invite guests to spear meat cubes with a fondue fork and cook in hot oil to desired degree of doneness. Serve with a variety of sauces.

**Horseradish Sauce**: combine ¼ cup horseradish with remaining ingredients.

**Mustard Sauce**: combine mustard, white wine, sugar, and salt in a saucepan. Bring to a boil over medium heat, stirring constantly. Mix flour with water and stir into mustard mixture. Reduce heat, simmer, and stir 10 minutes or until thickened. Serve hot or cold.

**Herb Sauce**: Stir 1 cup chopped fresh herbs with 1 tablespoon grated onion into 1½ cups homemade mayonnaise. Season to taste.

**Currant Sauce**: heat a jar of currant jelly.

vegetable or peanut oil for frying
8-10 ounces beef tenderloin per person, cut in ¾ to 1-inch cubes
sauces for dipping

**horseradish sauce**
 ¼ cup horseradish
 2 cups sour cream
 2 tablespoons lemon juice
dash of Tabasco sauce
 1 teaspoon salt

**mustard sauce**
1½ cups mustard
 ½ cup white wine
 2 tablespoons sugar
 1 teaspoon salt
 2 tablespoons flour
 ¼ cup water
Tartar Sauce, page 176
Béarnaise Sauce, page 180
BBQ Sauce, page 229

# Sour Cream Noodle Bake

*...many memorable family evenings have been shared with this dish*

2 pounds ground beef
1 teaspoon salt
⅛ teaspoon black pepper
¼ teaspoon garlic salt
1 (8-ounce) can tomato sauce
1 (8-ounce) package medium noodles, cooked al dente and drained
1 cup cottage cheese
1 cup sour cream
½ cup chopped onion
¾ cup grated sharp cheddar cheese

**Yield: 6 servings**

Brown ground beef and drain fat. Add salt, pepper, garlic salt, and tomato sauce to beef. Simmer 5 minutes. Combine noodles, cottage cheese, sour cream, and onion in a bowl. Alternate layers of noodle mixture and beef mixture in a 2-quart casserole dish, beginning with noodles and ending with beef. Top with cheddar cheese. Bake at 350° for 20 to 25 minutes or until cheese browns.

# Ziti With Meatballs And Sausage In Tomato Sauce

*...for one who's completely at home in the kitchen, this is a recipe!*

Sauté Italian sausage and sliced onions in a small amount of oil. Add canned tomatoes and bring to a boil. Reduce heat and simmer. Soak bread in water. Squeeze dry and crumble. To make meatballs, combine bread, ground pork or sirloin, chopped onion, minced garlic, Romano or Parmesan cheese, 3 eggs, salt, and pepper. Form into balls and chill until ready to cook. Sauté meatballs in a small amount of oil. Add meatballs, cooked ziti, and fresh basil or Italian parsley to tomato mixture.

# Pot Roast

*...describes the process of cooking which combines braising and steaming and requires a heavy pan. It is usually done on top of the stove over a gentle heat. This method is used for tougher meats and is a good way of roasting smaller meat joints, as there is less shrinkage - noodles or mashed potatoes are traditional accompaniments*

**B**rown roast in oil in a Dutch oven. Add sherry, soy sauce, broth, sugar, soup mix, and cinnamon and mix thoroughly. Cover and simmer 2 hours to 2 hours, 30 minutes. Remove roast from Dutch oven and keep warm. Add vegetables to Dutch oven and simmer until tender. Surround roast with vegetables and serve with broth.

For assorted vegetables, add your favorites or try any combination of the following: onions, carrots, new potatoes, green beans, celery, turnips, or parsnips.

1 (6-pound) beef bottom round or chuck roast, trimmed
¼ cup olive or vegetable oil
2 cups dry sherry or red wine
1 cup soy sauce
1 cup beef broth
½ cup sugar
1 (1½-ounce) envelope onion soup mix
cinnamon (optional)
assorted vegetables

**Yield: 8 servings**

# Hubert's Meat Loaf

*...the fact remains that meat loaf is an object of mom-and-apple-pie-type nostalgia*

1 medium onion, finely chopped
1 green bell pepper, finely chopped
5 stalks celery, finely chopped
4 cloves garlic, minced
3 slices bread
⅓ cup milk
3 eggs
salt and pepper to taste
3 pounds ground beef
¾ cup chili sauce
3 tablespoons Worcestershire sauce

Sauté onion, bell pepper, celery, and garlic until tender. Soak bread in milk in a mixing bowl. Mix thoroughly. Beat in sautéed vegetables and eggs. Add remaining ingredients. Mix well. If mixture is too moist, adjust consistency by adding bread or cracker crumbs. Form into loaves. Bake at 350° for 60 minutes.

**Yield: 8 servings**

# Shepherd's Pie

*...although equally as good when made from scratch, it is a wonderful way to use leftovers. The potatoes should be creamy, so an addition of milk may be necessary and the lamb, if grilled, will have enough seasonings, but chopped onion and/or peppers could be added and, as the name would indicate, it should be lamb!*

2 cups cooked and seasoned ground lamb
2 cups seasoned mashed potatoes
butter
grated cheese

**Yield: 6 servings**

Spread lamb in the bottom of a buttered casserole dish. Top with potatoes. Dot with butter and sprinkle with cheese. Bake at 400° until heated through and browned on top.

*For a variation, separate 2 eggs. Beat egg whites until stiff. Beat yolks into mashed potatoes and then fold in egg white. Serve with gravy.*

# Eggs Baked With Creamed Chicken

*...serve with brioche, croissants, or buttered English muffins for an informal brunch*

Melt 2 tablespoons butter in a saucepan. Blend in flour. Add broth and cook, stirring until thick and smooth. In a skillet, sauté mushrooms and shallot in remaining 1 tablespoon butter for 2 minutes. Add sherry and cook 10 seconds. Blend in white sauce and ½ cup cream. Add chicken. Season with salt and pepper. Simmer 1 minute. Divide mixture evenly among four (1½-cup) buttered ramekins or soufflé dishes. Top each dish with 2 eggs and sprinkle with salt, pepper, and nutmeg. Set dishes in a pan of water. Bring water to a boil. Transfer pan to oven and bake at 400° for 20 minutes. Divide remaining ¼ cup cream over individual servings.

3 tablespoons butter, divided
2 tablespoons all-purpose flour
¾ cup chicken broth
4 ounces mushrooms, sliced
1 tablespoon finely chopped shallot
2 tablespoons sherry
¾ cup heavy cream, divided
1½ cups cubed cooked chicken
salt and pepper to taste
8 eggs
nutmeg

**Yield: 4 servings**

# Chicken Fricassee With Cheese-herb Dumplings

*...The creamy richness of this traditional chicken stew comes from the roux, which is cooked slowly to a golden brown - and the crusty topped dumplings are easily adapted to beef stew by substituting rosemary and thyme for chervil and omitting the cheese*

## stew

1 (4½-pound) chicken, cut up
nutmeg
white pepper
½ teaspoon paprika, plus extra to season chicken
2½ tablespoons vegetable oil
3 tablespoons all-purpose flour
3 cups water
1 cup dry white wine
2 large shallots, slivered
1 medium onion, finely chopped
3 leeks, cut in ½-inch pieces
4 carrots, sliced ½-inch thick
1 cup celery, sliced ½-inch thick
2 tablespoons butter
½ teaspoon dried thyme
1 tablespoon dried chervil
1 teaspoon salt

Sprinkle chicken on both sides with nutmeg, pepper, and paprika. Brown in hot oil in a large pot. Remove chicken and stir in flour. Reduce heat and cook and stir until smooth and lightly browned. Whisk in water and wine. Add chicken and cover. Simmer 45 to 60 minutes. Strain and reserve broth. Cool chicken in a colander over a bowl. In a Dutch oven, sauté shallots, onion, leeks, carrots, and celery in butter until vegetables soften. Add reserved broth, ½ teaspoon paprika, thyme, chervil, and salt. Simmer, skimming fat as it rises. Remove meat from chicken and add with any drippings to Dutch oven.

To prepare dumplings, sift together flour, salt, baking powder, and chervil. Stir in cheese. Combine egg, butter, and milk. Stir into flour mixture to form a moist, stiff batter. Drop batter by heaping teaspoonfuls into simmering stew. Cover and simmer 15 minutes. Uncover and cook 5 minutes longer.

**cheese-herb dumplings**

2 cups all-purpose flour
1 teaspoon salt
4 teaspoons baking powder
1 teaspoon chervil
⅓ cup grated cheddar cheese
1 egg, beaten
3 tablespoons butter, melted
⅔ cup milk

**Yield: 6 servings**

# Turkey Tetrazzini

*...many would be disappointed if this wasn't part of the Thanksgiving weekend*

8 ounces fresh mushrooms, sliced

6 tablespoons butter, divided

¼ cup all-purpose flour

2 cups chicken broth

1 cup heavy cream, heated

2 tablespoons sherry

¾ cup Parmesan cheese

3 cups cooked, cubed turkey

8 ounces spaghetti, cooked al dente and drained

¼ cup breadcrumbs

**Yield: 4 to 6 servings**

Sauté mushrooms in 4 tablespoons butter for 5 minutes. Remove mushrooms with a slotted spoon and reserve. Add flour to butter and stir until bubbly. Slowly stir in broth and cook until thickened. Remove from heat. Add cream, sherry, and cheese. Stir until cheese melts. Add mushrooms and turkey. Mix in spaghetti. Pour into a buttered 9X13X2 inch pan. Melt remaining 2 tablespoons butter and mix with breadcrumbs. Sprinkle over casserole. Bake at 375° for 30 minutes.

*For added flavor and color, sauté ⅔ cup sliced onion with mushrooms, and add 2 tablespoons chopped pimiento and ½ cup blanched, slivered almonds with the cream.*

# "21" Chicken Hash

*...there's probably not a social luminary in this country who hasn't sampled the legendary chicken hash at New York's "21" Club*

Melt butter in a saucepan. Add flour and stir 2 minutes. Gradually blend in milk. Cook and stir until thickened. Add white pepper, salt, Tabasco sauce, and Worcestershire sauce. Stir in cheese and mix well. Cover saucepan and bake at 300° for 1 hour, 30 minutes. Strain sauce into another saucepan. Add cream to sauce and whisk until fluffy. Mix in sherry. Bring to a simmer over low heat. Dice one of the bell peppers. Stir in diced pepper and chicken. Bring to a simmer and remove from heat. In a medium bowl, beat together egg yolks and ½ cup of chicken mixture. Stir back into saucepan. Let mixture rest while cutting remaining bell pepper into quarters. Arrange bell pepper on a serving dish. Spoon chicken mixture around quarters. Garnish with a border of puréed peas.

Serve with toast or wild rice.

2 tablespoons butter
2 tablespoons all-purpose flour
2 cups milk, scalded
¼ teaspoon white pepper
1 teaspoon salt
½ teaspoon Tabasco sauce
1 teaspoon Worcestershire sauce
½ cup Parmesan cheese
½ cup heavy cream
¼ cup sherry
2 red bell peppers, divided
3 cups cubed cooked chicken
2 egg yolks
2 cups cooked and puréed peas

**Yield: 4 to 6 servings**

# Chicken Pot Pie

*...the seductive power of comfort food - the key to making a great chicken pot pie is to make each element in the dish taste good enough to eat on its own*

5 tablespoons butter, divided

2 (2½-pound) chickens, cut into pieces

salt and pepper to taste

½ cup coarsely chopped carrot

½ cup coarsely chopped celery

1 cup pearl onions, peeled

8 ounces fresh mushrooms, thinly sliced

3 sprigs fresh parsley

2 whole cloves

3 sprigs fresh thyme, or ½ teaspoon dried

¼ cup flour

1 cup dry white wine

4 cups chicken broth

Tabasco sauce

3 hard-cooked eggs, cut into sixths

5 strips bacon, cut into 2-inch lengths, cooked crisp, and drained

1 cup heavy cream

1 teaspoon Worcestershire sauce

1 pastry crust

1 egg, beaten

**Yield: 6 servings**

Melt 3 tablespoons butter in a large skillet. Add chicken, skin side down. Sprinkle with salt and pepper. Cook over low heat without browning for about 5 minutes, turning once. Scatter carrot, celery, and onions over top. Heat remaining 2 tablespoons butter in a separate skillet. Add mushrooms and cook and stir until liquid cooks out of mushrooms and evaporates. Add mushrooms to chicken. Combine parsley, cloves, and thyme in a cheesecloth and tie shut. Add to chicken. Cook, stirring frequently, for about 10 minutes, being careful not to burn. Sprinkle flour over top and stir to evenly distribute. Add wine, broth, and a few dashes of Tabasco sauce. Cover and simmer 30 minutes. Discard cheesecloth bag. Remove chicken. Discard skin and bones of chicken. Cube or shred meat. Arrange meat and vegetables in a 16X10½X2 inch baking dish. Reserve cooking liquid. Arrange eggs in baking dish. Sprinkle bacon over top. Skim fat from cooking liquid. Bring liquid to a boil. Stir in cream and return to a boil. Reduce heat and simmer about 20 minutes. Add Worcestershire sauce and season with salt and pepper. Pour sauce over chicken mixture. Top with crust. Brush beaten egg over crust. Bake at 400° until crust is golden brown.

# Granny's Ham And Potato Gratin For A Crowd

*...needs only a copious salad, a loaf of bread, and a jug of light red wine to make the meal*

Melt butter in a saucepan. Stir in flour and cook 2 minutes but do not allow to brown. Remove from heat and whisk in half of the milk. When blended, whisk in remaining milk. Simmer and stir for 3 minutes. Remove from heat and add salt, pepper, nutmeg, garlic, mustard, and thyme. Bring to a simmer and adjust seasoning as needed. To prepare gratin, slice potatoes ¼-inch thick into a kettle containing cold water. Cover kettle and bring to a boil. Uncover and cook 3 to 4 minutes or until barely cooked through. Drain and cover kettle. Let stand 3 to 4 minutes. Uncover. To assemble, spoon a 1/16-inch layer of sauce into a buttered 3-quart baking dish. Set aside 3 cups of sauce and 1 cup of cheese for final layer. Arrange in four layers, starting with a quarter of potatoes, and a quarter of ham. Add a third of remaining sauce and a third of remaining cheese. Continue in layers, using the reserved sauce and cheese in the final layer. Bake in upper third of oven at 375° for 45 minutes or until sauce is bubbly and top is browned.

If desired, assemble dish up to a day in advance and refrigerate. Bake when ready to serve.

**garlic and mustard sauce**

1¼ sticks butter
1 cup all-purpose flour
6½ cups milk, heated, divided
salt and pepper to taste
pinch of nutmeg
2 large cloves garlic, mashed
¼ cup Dijon mustard
½ teaspoon dried thyme or sage

**gratin**

10 pounds boiling potatoes, peeled
4 cups cold water
Garlic and Mustard Sauce
4 cups coarsely grated Swiss cheese
6-8 cups diced, sliced, or ground ham

**Yield: 18 to 24 servings**

# Macaroni And Cheese

*...bears no resemblance to what comes in the box*

7 tablespoons unsalted butter, divided
6 tablespoons all-purpose flour
4 cups milk
1½ teaspoons dry mustard
⅛ teaspoon cayenne pepper, or to taste
salt and black pepper to taste
1 (16-ounce) package elbow macaroni, cooked al dente and drained
3 cups coarsely grated extra-sharp cheddar cheese
1⅓ cups Parmesan cheese, divided
1 cup fresh breadcrumbs

**Yield: 6 to 8 entrée servings, 8 to 10 side dish servings**

Melt 6 tablespoons butter over medium-low heat. Stir in flour and cook 3 minutes. Slowly whisk in milk and bring to a boil. Add mustard, cayenne pepper, salt, and black pepper. Simmer sauce, stirring occasionally, for 2 minutes or until thickened. In a large bowl, combine sauce, macaroni, cheddar cheese, and 1 cup Parmesan cheese. Pour into a buttered 3 to 4-quart shallow baking dish. In a small bowl, combine remaining ⅓ cup Parmesan cheese and breadcrumbs. Sprinkle evenly over casserole. Dot with remaining 1 tablespoon butter. Bake at 350° for 25 to 30 minutes or until golden and bubbling.

*If desired, add 1 tablespoon Dijon mustard and 1 cup diced ham.*

# Welsh Rabbit

*...the origin of the name Welsh Rabbit, where there's not even the hint of fur, is a joke of sorts - a Welsh hunter returned home empty-handed, so his wife concocted a dish with melted cheese and dubbed it "rabbit" - the British serve "savouries", one being Welsh Rabbit, at the end of the meal to "clear the palate" of the taste of sweets before the port is served*

Melt butter in a large stainless steel saucepan. Blend in flour and dry mustard. Cook and stir over low heat for 5 minutes. Whisk in beer and cook 8 to 10 minutes or until thickened. Add remaining ingredients. Cook over very low heat for 8 to 10 minutes, stirring occasionally with a wooden spoon.

Serve on toasted bread or English muffins accompanied by tomato or apple slices.

3 tablespoons butter
3 tablespoons whole wheat flour
1 teaspoon dry mustard
1½ cups beer or ale, at room temperature
1 pound cheddar cheese, grated
½ teaspoon prepared horseradish
Tabasco sauce to taste
black pepper to taste

**Yield: 6 servings**

# Chipped Beef In Sour Cream

*...a staple breakfast for the American GI of World War II - perhaps what put it out of favor for so long*

8 ounces chipped beef, shredded
2 tablespoons butter
2 cups sour cream
1 (6½-ounce) jar artichoke hearts, drained and thinly sliced
cayenne pepper to taste
½ cup dry white wine
1 tablespoon Parmesan cheese

**Yield: 4 servings**

Cook beef in boiling water for 2 minutes. Drain. Melt butter over low heat in a skillet. Add sour cream and stir until smooth. Add beef, artichokes, and remaining ingredients. Cook and stir over medium heat until smooth and hot.

Serve over hot buttered white toast with extra Parmesan cheese sprinkled on top. If sauce is too thin, thicken with flour. If too thick, thin with white wine.

# Cheddar Garlic Grits

*...served with memories of entertaining in a grand southern style with large bone-in baked hams and beaten biscuits with sweet butter and homemade preserves*

3 cups water
¾ cup old-fashioned grits
1½ teaspoons minced garlic
2 tablespoons butter, divided
1½ cups grated sharp white cheddar cheese
salt and pepper to taste

**Yield: 6 servings**

Bring water to a boil and stir in grits. Cover and cook over low heat, stirring occasionally, for 30 minutes or until thick and creamy. In a small skillet, sauté garlic in 1 tablespoon butter for 1 minute. Stir into grits along with remaining 1 tablespoon butter and cheese. Season with salt and pepper. Place in a buttered 1½-quart baking dish. Bake at 375° for 35 to 40 minutes or until the edges turn golden.

# "The Best" Mashed Potatoes

*...the inspiration is nostalgia for 1950's home-cooking, lumps and all - serve with Hubert's Meat Loaf, of course! - or under Oven Baked Halibut*

Boil potatoes in salted water until tender. Drain well and dry by tossing potatoes in a pan over low heat. Add remaining ingredients. Mash with a potato masher.

*Variations of this dish are limitless. Try adding a combination of equal amounts of puréed parsnips, rutabaga, carrot, cauliflower, celery root, turnip, pumpkin, or winter squash to the potatoes. To prepare a trendy Southwestern dish, add corn, chili powder, and chopped fresh cilantro. For a different flavor, substitute olive oil for the butter, ½ cup of the cooking liquid for the milk and cream, and add 1 tablespoon fresh herbs. To make garlic mashed potatoes, add 4 to 6 roasted and mashed cloves garlic. For those on heart-healthy diets, replace higher fat ingredients, such as cream or butter with low fat cottage cheese or sour cream.*

2 pounds russet
 potatoes, peeled and
 cubed or sliced
salt and pepper to taste
 ¼ cup heavy cream or
 crème fraîche
 ¼ cup milk
 1 stick butter, cut into
 pieces

**Yield: 6 servings**

# Roasted Garlic

Trim tops of garlic heads and remove loose "paper". Place in ovenproof dish, tightly arranged. Add enough chicken broth to cover ¾ of garlic heads. Drizzle olive oil over top, add fresh herbs and bake at 375° for 35 minutes or until soft.

# Boston Baked Beans

*...cooked long and slow so the beans literally caramelize in their juices, a crock pot is ideal for this dish - no soaking, no fussing, dump it all in and walk away*

1 (2-inch) square salt pork, rind intact
8 cups water
2 cups dried small white beans, soaked and drained
1½ teaspoons salt
1 cup thinly sliced onion
2 large cloves garlic, minced
2 tablespoons dark molasses
2 tablespoons Dijon mustard
½ teaspoon dried thyme
2 bay leaves
½ tablespoon grated fresh ginger
black pepper to taste

**Yield: 6 servings**

Cut salt pork into ¼-inch thick strips. Simmer salt pork in 8 cups water for 10 minutes. Drain and rinse with cold water. Combine salt pork, beans, and remaining ingredients in a pot or slow cooker. Cover and bring to a simmer. Bake at 250° to 275° in the oven, or over low heat in the slow cooker for 12 to 14 hours or until beans are a dark-reddish brown. Check beans occasionally while cooking and add boiling water if needed.

If desired, prepare beans a day or more ahead of time and reheat when ready to serve. In Boston, this dish is served on Saturday nights with coleslaw and Boston brown bread.

*Variation: Combine 3 cans red kidney beans, ½ cup chili sauce, 1 cup bourbon, and 1 cup strong coffee. Let stand 3 hours. Thicken with 1 tablespoon cornstarch, if necessary. Top with brown sugar and cook at 375° for 1 hour, 30 minutes.*

# Tomato Bread Pudding

*...a stewed tomato of sorts, brings summer color to a winter table when tomatoes are inedible*

Combine tomato purée, water, butter, salt, and sugar in a 1-quart saucepan. Bring to a boil. Cook and stir about 5 minutes, being careful not to scorch. Spread bread in a buttered 8X10 inch pan. Pour tomato mixture over bread and toss until liquid is absorbed. Bake at 375° for 35 minutes.

1 (10-ounce) can tomato purée
¾ cup water
½ tablespoon butter
½ teaspoon salt
1 cup packed brown sugar
2 cups bread pieces

**Yield: 4 servings**

# Spoon Bread

*...if time allows, separate eggs, beating yolks with white wine and folding egg whites into the mixture before baking*

Scald milk in a heavy kettle. Slowly stir in cornmeal and salt. Cook and stir over low heat for 3 to 4 minutes or until mixture is thick. Remove from heat and stir in butter. In a bowl, beat eggs and wine. Slowly stir into cornmeal mixture. Pour into a well-buttered 1½-quart baking dish. Bake at 375°, in lower half of oven, for 60 minutes or until bread is puffed and lightly browned on top. Serve immediately.

3¼ cups milk
1 cup yellow cornmeal
1½ teaspoons salt
2 tablespoons butter
4 eggs
¾ cup California white wine

**Yield: 6 to 8 servings**

# Raw Cranberry Salad

*...a tradition on many holiday tables*

1 (3-ounce) package
   lemon-flavored
   gelatin
1 cup boiling water
1 cup cold water
8 ounces raw
   cranberries, ground
¼ cup sugar
¾ cup chopped celery
¾ cup pecan pieces
2 oranges, peeled and
   diced

Dissolve gelatin in boiling water. Add cold water and let stand until mixture begins to thicken. Combine cranberries and sugar and let stand several minutes. Mix in celery, pecans, and orange. Stir into gelatin. Pour into a 4-cup mold and chill until set.

**Yield: 8 to 10 servings**

# Orange Mousse Mold

*...a very delicate molded "salad" that would go nicely with cold grilled chicken breasts for a luncheon - unmold on a bed of butter lettuce*

2 (¼-ounce) packages
   unflavored gelatin
2 cups sugar
dash of salt
4 egg yolks
2½ cups fresh orange
   juice, divided
zest of 1 orange
zest of ½ lemon
3 tablespoons fresh
   lemon juice
1½ cups mandarin orange
   sections
2 cups heavy cream,
   whipped

Combine gelatin, sugar, and salt in a saucepan. Beat together egg yolks and 1 cup orange juice. Stir into gelatin mixture. Bring to a boil over medium heat, stirring constantly. Remove from heat. Add remaining 1½ cups orange juice, orange and lemon zests, and lemon juice. Chill, stirring occasionally, until mixture forms a mound on a spoon. Stir in orange sections. Fold in cream. Pour into a 2-quart mold and chill until set. Unmold before serving.

**Yield: 8 servings**

# Gelatin Beet Salad

*...the tangy bold flavors of this salad would complement a grilled pork loin for a summer buffet*

Combine gelatin and boiling water in a bowl. Stir until completely dissolved. Mix in beet juice, salt, and vinegar. Chill to thicken slightly. Add remaining ingredients. Pour into a 4-cup mold. Chill until set. Unmold and serve.

1 (3-ounce) package lemon-flavored gelatin
1 cup boiling water
1 cup beet juice
½ teaspoon salt
2 tablespoons vinegar
1 tablespoon horseradish
1 cup julienned beets, or one (16-ounce) can, drained and julienned
1 cup diced celery
1½ tablespoons grated onion

**Yield: 6 servings**

# Raspberry "Salad"

*...this "salad" was popular long before the spicier tomato sauces came to the market*

Dissolve gelatin in boiling water. Stir in tomatoes and Tabasco sauce. Pour into an oiled 1½-quart mold. Chill until set. Unmold and serve.

1 (6-ounce) package raspberry-flavored gelatin
⅔ cup boiling water
2 (16-ounce) cans stewed tomatoes
dash of Tabasco sauce

**Yield: 6 to 8 servings**

# St. Louis Gooey Butter Cake

*...St. Louisans claim they invented the hot dog and the ice cream cone, but a lesser known treat that originated here is even more popular. According to the legend of the gooey butter cake, in the 1930's, a baker making a butter cake assembled the wrong proportion of ingredients. The result was a coffee cake with a thin, rich, doughy layer on the bottom and a sweet filling, topped with powdered sugar. Since it was the Depression, the baker sold the cake anyway, and customers loved it!*

**crust**
- 1 cup all-purpose flour
- 3 tablespoons granulated sugar
- 5 tablespoons butter

**filling**
- 1¼ cups granulated sugar
- 1½ sticks butter
- ¼ cup light corn syrup
- 1 egg
- 1 cup all-purpose flour
- ⅔ cup evaporated milk
- sifted powdered sugar (optional)

**Yield: 9 servings**

Prepare crust by combining flour and sugar. Cut in butter until mixture resembles fine crumbs and starts to cling. Pat into bottom of a 9X9X2 inch baking pan. To make filling, cream granulated sugar and butter in a bowl. Beat in syrup and egg. Alternately add flour and milk, mixing just until combined. Batter will appear slightly curdled. Pour over crust. Bake at 350° for 35 minutes or until cake is nearly firm. Cool in pan on a rack. Sprinkle with powdered sugar.

# Grandma Taylor's Chocolate Cake With Chocolate Frosting

*...the traditional birthday cake for several generations*

Combine boiling water, cocoa, and baking soda. Set aside and allow to cool. Cream sugar and butter. In a separate bowl, beat egg yolks until light and fluffy. Blend into sugar mixture. Sift together flour and baking powder. Alternately add dry ingredients and milk to sugar mixture. Beat egg whites until stiff. Mix egg whites and cocoa mixture into batter. Divide batter evenly among 3 (8-inch) round cake pans lined with wax paper. Bake at 350° for 25 minutes. Cool on a rack and remove from pans. To prepare frosting, combine chocolate, cream, and butter in a medium saucepan. Stir over medium heat until smooth. Remove from heat and beat in sugar. Transfer to a bowl set in ice. Beat frosting until it holds its shape. Spread frosting over each cake layer. Stack layers and frost sides and top in a decorative swirling pattern. Refrigerate at least 60 minutes before serving.

½ cup boiling water
½ cup cocoa powder
½ teaspoon baking soda
2 cups sugar
1 stick butter
3 eggs, separated
2 cups all-purpose flour
1 teaspoon baking powder
¾ cup milk

### chocolate frosting

2 (6-ounce) packages semi-sweet chocolate chips
1 cup light cream
4 sticks butter
5 cups powdered sugar

**Yield: 12 servings**

# Old-fashioned Chocolate Pudding With Coffee Sauce

*...a lower fat variation on an old favorite*

1 cup all-purpose flour
⅓ cup granulated sugar
¼ cup cocoa powder
2 teaspoons baking powder
½ teaspoon salt
½ cup skim milk
1 egg, lightly beaten
2 tablespoons walnut or canola oil
2 teaspoons vanilla
1⅓ cups brewed or instant coffee, hot
¾ cup packed brown sugar
2 tablespoons chopped pecans or walnuts, toasted
powdered sugar for topping

**Yield: 6 servings**

In a large bowl, combine flour, sugar, cocoa powder, baking powder, and salt. In a separate bowl, mix together milk, egg, oil, and vanilla. Pour into dry ingredients and mix until just combined. Divide batter among 6 (1¼-cup) buttered ramekins or custard cups. Place on a baking sheet. Combine coffee and brown sugar. Pour an equal amount into each cup. Sprinkle pecans on top. Bake at 375° for 15 to 20 minutes or until top springs back when touched. Cool 5 minutes. Sprinkle with powdered sugar. Serve hot or cold.

# Hot Chocolate

*...topped with marshmallows or a cinnamon stick, all you need is a cozy sofa and a good book*

2 cups nonfat dry milk
¾ cup sugar
½ cup cocoa powder
½ cup powdered nondairy creamer
dash of salt

**Yield: 4 servings**

Combine all ingredients and store in an airtight container. To serve, combine ¼ cup of mixture with ¾ cup boiling water in a mug. Stir well.

# Snow Pudding/Oeufs À La Neige Grand Marnier

*...this is removed from the old-fashioned nursery snow pudding by virtue of the liqueur*

To prepare lemon snow, combine gelatin and sugar in a large mixing bowl. Add boiling water and stir until dissolved. Add lemon zest and juice. Chill in an ice bath for 30 minutes or until thickened to a syrupy consistency. Transfer to a refrigerator and chill 60 minutes longer. Beat egg whites until stiff. Add whites to lemon mixture and beat 5 minutes or until slightly thickened. Pour into a serving dish and chill 2 hours or until set. To make topping, chill cream in a small bowl in an ice bath. Beat until thick and glossy, but not stiff. Refrigerate. Using the same beaters, beat egg yolks until thick and lemon colored. Gradually beat in sugar. Slowly add butter, lemon juice, and Grand Marnier. Fold in zest and whipped cream. Chill thoroughly. Serve topping over each portion of lemon snow.

## lemon snow
- 1 (¼-ounce) package unflavored gelatin
- ⅔ cup sugar
- 1½ cups boiling water
- ¼ teaspoon lemon zest
- ⅓ cup fresh lemon juice
- 3 egg whites

## topping
- ½ cup heavy cream
- 3 egg yolks
- ¼ cup sugar
- 5 tablespoons butter, melted
- 3 tablespoons fresh lemon juice
- 1 tablespoon Grand Marnier
- 1 teaspoon lemon zest

**Yield: 6 servings**

# Haddie's Rum Pie

*...not a pie, but a mousse, encased in lady fingers - but it's just Haddie's Rum Pie!*

6 egg yolks
1 cup sugar
1 (¼-ounce) package
  unflavored gelatin
½ cup cold water
2 cups heavy cream,
  whipped
½ cup dark rum
ladyfingers
bitter chocolate shavings
  for garnish

**Yield: 6 servings**

Beat egg yolks until light. Slowly beat in sugar. Soak gelatin in cold water in a saucepan. Bring to a boil over low heat. Briskly stir gelatin into egg mixture. Fold into whipped cream. Stir in rum and cool until mixture starts to set. Line a glass dish with ladyfingers. Pour gelatin mixture over ladyfingers. Sprinkle with chocolate shavings and cool until completely set.

# Peach Pie

*...a summer favorite, when peaches are in season, this pie has a sour cream/ brown sugar topping that is broiled, giving it a crunchy top*

4-5 peaches, peeled and
  sliced
1 pie crust, unbaked
⅓ cup all-purpose flour
½ cup granulated sugar
1 cup sour cream
¼ cup packed brown
  sugar

**Yield: 8 servings**

Arrange peach slices in crust. Beat together flour, granulated sugar, and sour cream. Spoon mixture over peaches. Bake at 450° for 15 minutes. Reduce heat to 350° and bake 30 minutes longer. Cool. Sprinkle with brown sugar and broil 2 to 3 minutes.

# Molasses Cookies

*...Santa's favorite*

**B**eat together butter, sugar, and molasses. Mix in remaining ingredients. Chill. Form into balls and roll in sugar. Place on a buttered baking sheet. Bake at 375° for 8 to 10 minutes.

1½ sticks butter, melted
1 cup sugar, plus extra for rolling balls
¼ cup molasses
1 egg
2 cups all-purpose flour
2 teaspoons baking soda
2 teaspoons cinnamon
1½ teaspoons ginger
pinch of salt
pinch of ground cloves

**Yield: 1 to 2 dozen...depends on size of balls**

# Thumbprint Cookies

*...mint jelly or strawberry preserves make these festive holiday cookies*

**C**ream shortening and sugar. Stir in egg yolk and vanilla. In a separate bowl, combine flour and salt. Blend dry ingredients into shortening mixture. Roll teaspoonfuls of dough into balls. Lightly beat egg white. Dip dough balls into egg white, then roll in nuts. Place balls 1 inch apart on a baking sheet. Press thumb into center of each ball. Bake at 350° for 10 to 12 minutes or until set. Cool. Fill cookie centers with pie filling, jelly, or fruits.

½ cup shortening
¼ cup packed brown sugar
1 egg, separated
½ teaspoon vanilla
1 cup all-purpose flour
¼ teaspoon salt
¾ cup finely chopped nuts
pie filling, jelly, or fruits for topping

**Yield: 3 dozen cookies**

# English Butter Toffee

*...if your English Butter Toffee utterly fails to behave, don't throw it out. Add milk, cream, or half and half to create the world's best caramel sauce*

1 stick butter, softened
1 stick margarine, softened
1 cup sugar
½ cup shaved almonds
4 ounces milk chocolate, chopped
⅓-½ cup chopped walnuts or pecans

Combine butter, margarine, sugar, and almonds in a pan over high heat. Cook and stir constantly with a wooden spoon for 15 minutes or until mixture turns light caramel-colored and begins to smoke. Remove immediately from heat and pour into a buttered 8X8 inch pan. Tap pan with wooden spoon to evenly distribute mixture. Sprinkle chocolate over top. Spread chocolate, when melted, with a spatula. Sprinkle nuts over top. Cool and cut into pieces.

# Peanut Brittle

*...a Christmas gift favorite for both giver and receiver!*

1 cup light corn syrup
2 cups sugar
2 cups raw peanuts
1 heaping teaspoon baking soda
1 teaspoon butter

Combine syrup, sugar, and peanuts in a large skillet. Cook and stir over medium heat until golden brown. Remove from heat and mix in baking soda and butter. Pour into 7 or 8 buttered pie pans. When cooled, pop brittle from pans and break into pieces.

# Cookbook Contributors and Recipe Testers

The Cookbook Committee expresses its appreciation to Auxilians and friends who contributed so much to this book. We regret that many recipes could not be included due to similarity or lack of space.

Elliot Abbey

Patty Aitken

John S. Alberici

Anny Allan

Eileen Allman

Donna Altepeter

Marilynn Anderson

Shirley Anton

Charles Armbruster

Debbie Armor

Jerome Aronberg, M.D.

Hermon Atkinson

Susan Atkinson

Suzanne Baetz

Rosemary Baty

Jane Bauer

Jim Becker

Tancy Becker

Bernie Belz

Henry Belz

Susan Berdy, M.D.

Mary Lou Biggs

Thomas Birch

Laura Boyd

Geraldine Brink

Dodie Brodhead

Fred L. Brown

Linda Bruns

Kelley Bryan

Betsy Buddy

Sandy Buetow

Alice Burst

Don Burst, M.D.

Julie Bush

Robin Bushur

Gene Byrd

Barb Casey

Stacey Cassmeyer

Roberto Civitelli, M.D.

Fifi Lugo Chalfant

Sue Chalfant

T. P. Chandrika

Nini Chapin

Betty Cheatham

Barb Clark

Steve Clark

Thelma Clark

Bonnie Coder

Cathy Coleman

Libby Coleman

Parker Condie

Anne H. Cross

Timmie Cullen

Torry Cullen

Joan Culver

Madelyn Curry

Leane Darnold

Peggy Davenport

Sandy Davidson

Fran Davis

Mable Deluca

Carolyn Devilbiss

Beth Dinkela

Sheryl Dobbin

Eliabeth Fritschle Duffy

Virginia Duffy

Sue Eddens

Joan Edwards

Carol Eisenbraun

Gloria Elliott

Loba Emam

Nancy Engler

Maria Estelle

Judy Evans

Ronald Evens, M.D.

Martha Eyermann

Mildred Feldman

Nancy Fell

Pansy Fell

Brigid Fernandez

Patty Finan

Lynne Finnerty

Eileen Fleer

Nancy Forcier

Gene Foeller

Pat Foeller

Bob Frank

Catchy Frank

Lanita Freeman

Mary Ann Fritschle

Marge Gable

Joan Gallagher

Gary L. Gambill, M.D.

Susan Garrett

Helen Gavril

Dana Gelfeld

Kate Gibbs

Jane Gilbert

Bill Gilmore

Claire Goosev

Larry Graden

Susan Graham

May Grant

Zelda Greenberg

Dorene Grim

Ann Montalvo Guillerman

Pyllis Gulbranson

Maureen Habel

William K. Hall, M.D.

Pat Hamilton

Clay Hancock

John Hart

Robert Hartley, M.D.

Jo Hatton

Mary Hazlett

Fern Heider

Gloria Heinemann

Mary Lee Hermann

Godofredo M. Herzog, M.D.

Sissy Hicks

Brenda Higgins

Merle Hoffman

Barbara Hogue

Karen Hoops

William E. Houck, M.D.

Marie Howard

Susan Pike Hughes

Nina L. Hutchinson

Fran Jacques

Patricia Janovsky

Laney Johnson

Judy Kamper

Lorna Kahn

Gisela Kasselt

Mary Katzenberger

Mildred Kaufman

Mary Kennedy

Tina Kennedy, M.D.

Jane E. Keuss

Lana G. King

Margaret Kinnaman

Joan Koepke

# Cookbook Contributors and Testers

Norma Jean Kolb
Doris Kostecki
Raema Kraus
Philomena Kreutz
Corinne Kurlandski
Ann Lauer
Sheryl Lauter
Mildred Lee
Darcy Leimbach
Sallie S. Lindsey
Penelope Loeb
Margaret Loering
Betty Lupher
Nancy Lutz
Marilyn MacDonald
Rebecca MacDonald
Lisa Mahiger
Jennifer Major
Susan Mallory, M.D.
Cindy Marrs
Philip Martin, M.D.
Dawn Mason
Mary Jane Maxwell
Ann McCandless
Nancy McClane
Mary McDonald, M.D.
Bonnie Meltzer
Peter Menke, M.D.
Paul A. Mennes, M.D.
Mary Jane Meyer
Robin Meyer
Molly Middendorf
Keithly Miller
Marilyn Miller
Sharon Minogue
Don Morgan

Mary Morgan, M.D.
Margie Moscowitz
Robert G. Moussa
Lydia Mower
Matt Moynihan
Henry Muldowney
Alice Murphy
George Murphy
Mary Ellen Murray
Jeanne Myers
Jennifer Nagel
Jean Neal
Magda Nemes
Billie Newcomb
Pam Odgers
Fran Olszewski
Cathie Osborne
Ann Owens
Patricia Owens
Benedict Painter, M.D.
Elly Painter
Judy Parham
Teresa Parisi
Clarice Parsons
Brian Pehr
Anita Penlesky
Joel Perlmutter
Lynne Piening
Phyllis Plaster
Eleanor Potter
Margaret Poulos, M.D.
Carol Powers
Joseph M. Primrose, M.D.
Vicki Primrose
Peter Rafferty
Mary Rassieur
Stephanie Regan

Laura Reinders
Sally Reynolds
Carolyn Richardson
Pat Richter
Vera Riley
Kris Rinne
Michael Rosso
Sally Russell
Ginny Ruzicka
Nancy Ruzicka
Ray Ruzicka
Sudha R. Saha
Linda Saltman
Robert Saltman, M.D.
Christine Saracino
Jennifer Sargent
Rena Schechter
Gretchen Schmidt
Lorraine Schmidt
Teri Schoenlaub
Mary R. Schulte
Edith R. Schwartz
Rachel Scott
Stella Scott
Marian Seabaugh
Maureen Shah
Jean Shahan
Dolores Shepard
Valerie Siemer
Sylvia Silver
Sue Simon
Peggy Simpson
Rebecca Sinclair
Mitzi Sisson
Kim Skrainka
Helen Skoczylas
Betty D. Smith
Debbie Sommers
Mildred Spitzer

Karen St. Amour
Jane Sterling
Pat Stickdale
Marleah Strominger
Lori A. Sullivan
Betty Sutter
Florida Sykes
Joan Teaford
Elaine Thorne
Jean Thurston, M.D.
George Tichacek
Clara Tremayne
Karen Trone
Betty Tucker
Hubert van Gent
Anne Vaughan
Ross Verbisky
Steven Vickery
Jim Vouga
Victor Vouga
Bruce J. Walz, M.D.
Susan Webb
Jennifer Wehrle
Jennifer Wendt
Margie Werner
Timmie Wiant
Ginny Wharton
Anne Whiteside
Bob Whiteside
Sue Williams
Annabelle Williamson
Ellen Wilsdon
Christine Wolf
Christopher Wolf
Cynthia Woolsey
Audrey Wortham
Katie Beyer Ziebell

# Index

## SAVOUR ST. LOUIS

Barnes Hospital Auxiliary – Cookbook
One Barnes Hospital Plaza
St. Louis, Missouri 63110

Please send _____ copies of *Savour St. Louis*          @ $19.95 each _____
                                    Postage and handling          @    4.50 each _____
                                                                                      TOTAL _____

Make checks payable to *Barnes Hospital Auxiliary – Cookbook*.
Mail cookbook(s) to:

Name _____

Address _____

City _____ State _____ Zip _____

*Proceeds from the sale of Savour St. Louis will benefit the many projects*
*of the Barnes Hospital Auxiliary.*

- - - - - - - - - - - - - - - - - - - - - - - - - - - - - - -

## SAVOUR ST. LOUIS

Barnes Hospital Auxiliary – Cookbook
One Barnes Hospital Plaza
St. Louis, Missouri 63110

Please send _____ copies of *Savour St. Louis*          @ $19.95 each _____
                                    Postage and handling          @    4.50 each _____
                                                                                      TOTAL _____

Make checks payable to *Barnes Hospital Auxiliary – Cookbook*.
Mail cookbook(s) to:

Name _____

Address _____

City _____ State _____ Zip _____

*Proceeds from the sale of Savour St. Louis will benefit the many projects*
*of the Barnes Hospital Auxiliary.*

- - - - - - - - - - - - - - - - - - - - - - - - - - - - - - -

## SAVOUR ST. LOUIS

Barnes Hospital Auxiliary – Cookbook
One Barnes Hospital Plaza
St. Louis, Missouri 63110

Please send _____ copies of *Savour St. Louis*          @ $19.95 each _____
                                    Postage and handling          @    4.50 each _____
                                                                                      TOTAL _____

Make checks payable to *Barnes Hospital Auxiliary – Cookbook*.
Mail cookbook(s) to:

Name _____

Address _____

City _____ State _____ Zip _____

*Proceeds from the sale of Savour St. Louis will benefit the many projects*
*of the Barnes Hospital Auxiliary.*